STANDARD ENCYCLOPEDIA OF

Opalescent Glass

SEVENTH EDITION

*IDENTIFICATION
&
VALUES*

MIKE CARWILE

COLLECTOR BOOKS
A Division of Schroeder Publishing

Front Cover: Queen's Crown Epergne, vaseline, $3,500.00.
Back Cover: Double Marmalade, lemonescent, $450.00.

Cover and book design: *Terri Hunter*

COLLECTOR BOOKS

P.O. Box 3009
Paducah, Kentucky 42002-3009

www.collectorbooks.com

Mike Carwile
180 Cheyenne Dr.
Lynchburg, VA 24502
mcarwile@jetbroadband.com
SASE required for written reply.

Copyright © 2011 Mike Carwile

The current values in this book should be used only as a guide. They are not intended to set prices, which vary from one section of the country to another. Auction prices as well as dealer prices vary greatly and are affected by condition as well as demand. Neither the author nor the publisher assumes responsibility for any losses that might be incurred as a result of consulting this guide.

Proudly printed and bound in the
United States of America

Contents

Part I:
Opalescent Glass,
1880 – 1930
Page 13

Part II:
Whimsey Pieces
Page 159

Part III:
Opalescent Glass,
1930 – 1970
Page 169

Dedication

To Dave and Vickie Peterson for the nice cover photos as well as additional photos and information within this edition.

Acknowledgments

A special thanks to the following people for their contributions to this book: Bill Walter and Laurel Walton, Rich and Debbie Graham, Frank and Melissa Keathley, John and Candice Shertz, Bob Lamoureux, Gary and Sharon Vandevander, Steve and Radka Sandeman, John and Mary Petrasich, Rachel Spinella, Bob Harry, Roberto Leal, Lou Ann Novak, Chuck and Dianna Hollenbach, Erin N. Cole, Madolyn Courter, Dale Meese Jr., Kathy Gresko, Joan and Wayne Jolliffe, John Loggie III, Phil Barber, Richard and Mary Houghton, Cindy Mackley, Tom Foozer, Len Galloway, Susan Parker, John Scherz, Amy Sexton, Donna Stout, Sharron Lancaster, Samantha Prince, King Hoopel, Kris and Debra Remmen, Judy Parker, Marty Vogel, Tim Cantrell, Don and Jane Henson, Janine Patterson, Valerie Caudill, Donna Drohan, Neila and Tom Bredehoft, John and Monica Vanspall, Winfred Huff, and The West Virginia Museum of American Glass, Ltd.; to Thom; and a special thanks to the membership of the Vaseline Group for the "Name That Pattern" segment sponsored by the club; as well as anyone I may have overlooked.

Also a big thanks to jetbroadband.com for keeping me in touch with the world.

Special Note to Readers

Please don't hesitate to contact me should you have any comments, suggestions, corrections, or additions to this book. They will all be considered and certainly appreciated.

Although there are new patterns and a good number of replacement photos in this new edition, you will notice that some patterns have been dropped from previous editions.

Some patterns were discovered to be newer production items that just didn't fit, even into the after 1930s section (for which I've set a cut off date of 1970, when Fenton began to use their logo on pieces). Some of the whimsies have also been dropped because they were not true whimsies, but rather production pieces.

This decision was made primarily to provide needed room for the continued growth of this publication.

I hope you will enjoy this edition and I do look forward to hearing of new and exciting finds from the many collectors of this beautiful glass.

Introduction

From its inception in the 1880s, opalescent glass has enjoyed a receptive audience, both in England where it was introduced and here in America where a young but growing market was ready for any touch of brightness and beauty for the hearth and home.

Early American makers, such as Hobbs, Brockunier and Company (1863 – 1888), Buckeye Glass (1878 – 1896), La Belle Glass (1872 – 1888), American Glass (1889 – 1891), Nickel Plate Glass (1888 – 1893), and of course, the Northwood Glass Company in its various locations (1888 until its demise in 1924), were the primary producers, especially in early blown opalescent glass production. They were not by themselves, of course. Other companies, such as Model Flint (1893 – 1899), Fostoria Shade & Lamp Co. (1890 – 1894), Consolidated Lamp & Glass (1894 – 1897), Elson Glass (1882 – 1893), West Virginia Glass (1893 – 1896), National Glass (1899 – 1903), Beaumont Glass (1895 – 1906), Dugan Glass (1904 – 1913, which became Diamond Glass, 1914 – 1931), Coudersport Glass (1900 – 1904), and finally the Jefferson Glass Company (1900 – 1933), added their talents to all sorts of opalescent items in both blown and pressed glass.

The major production covered 40 years (1880 – 1920); however, beginning shortly after the turn of the century, the Fenton Glass Company of Williamstown, West Virginia, joined the ranks of opalescent manufacturers, and has continued production off and on until the present time. Its production from 1907 to 1940 is an important part of the opalescent field and has been covered to some extent in this book. The Fenton factory, along with Dugan Glass and Jefferson Glass, produced quality opalescent glass items, primarily pressed items in patterns they had used for other types of glassware, long after the rest of the companies had ceased operations.

In 1899 A. H. Heisey & Company began a very limited production of some opalescent glass in white and blue by adding a milky formula to the glass while it was still in the mould. Patterns known are #1255 Pineapple and Fan in white and vaseline (1898), #2 Plaid Chrysanthemum in vaseline (1904), #1220 Punty Band in white and blue (1904 – 1910), #1280 Winged Scroll in white (1910), #357 Prison Stripe in white (1905), #300 Peerless in blue, and a Pluto candlestick in experimental gold opalescent. Most of these were made in very small amounts for very short periods of time, and by 1915 they were no longer in production.

To understand just what opalescent glass is has always been easy; to explain the process of making this glass is quite another matter. If the novice will think of two layers of glass, one colored and one clear, that have been fused so that the clear areas become milky when fired a second or third time, the picture of the process becomes easier to see, although keep in mind that not all opalescent glass is layered. It is, of course, much more complicated than that, but for the sake of clarity, imagine the clear layer being pressed so that the second firing gives this opal milkiness to the outer edges, either to the designs or to the edges themselves, and the process becomes clearer. It is, of course, the skill of the glassmaker to control this opalescence so that it does what he wants. It is a fascinating process and anyone who has had the privilege of watching a glassmaker at work can testify to it being a near miracle.

Today, thousands of collectors seek opalescent glass, and each has his or her own favorites. Current markets place blown opalescent glass as more desirable, with cranberry leading the color field, but there are many ways to collect, and groupings of one shape or one pattern or even one manufacturer are not uncommon. When you purchase this glass, the same rules apply as for any other glass collectible: (1) look for any damage and do not pay normal prices for damage, (2) choose good color as well as good milky opalescence, (3) buy what pleases you. You have to live with it, so buy what you like. To care for your glass, wash it carefully in lukewarm water with a mild soap; never put old glass in a dishwasher. Display your glass in an area that is well lit and enjoy it.

Opalescent Producers & Factory Sites

I believe there is a need for a brief history of the early makers of opalescent glass and their various factory locations. Often, a glass producer moved frequently to replace a lost factory site (factories burned because of the very nature of the heat used to produce glass) or to join other makers in new ventures. Gas supplies diminished, combines were formed, and workers moved on. Glassworkers, by nature, were a gypsy lot, moving after a winter season, camping out in good weather in some instances, and generally going where the jobs led them. It was not unusual for a worker to have been employed by every plant in their area at one time or another.

For these reasons, I've tried to put together a brief factory history that tells where the makers of opalescent glass were located in the years of major production. I include a brief history of England's best-known producers as well as those in America, and hope this is a helpful addition for beginning as well as seasoned collectors.

A.J. Beatty & Sons *Steubenville, Ohio (1845 – 1890), Tiffin, Ohio (1890 – 1891), joined USG.*

The Steubenville factory was also absorbed by U.S. Glass but never operated. Mr. A.J. Beatty also involved in the Brilliant and Federal Glass factories, among others. Patterns: Beatty Rib, D&B with V-Ornament, Beatty Waffle, Over-all Hobnail, Orinoco. A July 1888 journal lists their No. 87 new opalescent line, as well as No. 79 crystal set, plain or engraved.

American Glass Company (1889 – 1890) *Anderson, Indiana*

American Glass Company was opened in mid-1889 by John Miller and Andrew Gottschalk (former managers of the Buckeye Glass Company). It produced fancy colored tableware, opalescent glass, and marblescent lamps, as well as other wares. Opalescent glass probably included its version of Reverse Swirl and a line of Chrysanthemum Swirl pieces. In early 1890 Mr. Gottschalk returned to Buckeye, and only months later, the plant closed and the factory site was sold in 1891, becomming the Hoosier Glass Company where prescription ware was made. John Miller went to the Eagle Glass Company, then to Riverside, and in 1901 became the manager of Model Flint Glass in Albany, Indiana, where opalescent glass was made.

Beaumont Glass Company *Martins Ferry, Ohio (1895 – 1902), Grafton, West Virginia (1902 – 1906)*

Percy Beaumont was the brother-in-law of Harry Northwood. He worked at the Northwood factory and left his position of shipping clerk there to begin a job at Hobbs, Brockunier & Company as a glass decorator. In 1893 he moved to West Virginia Glass (Elson's plant), where he was employed as a metalworker and chemist. He is credited with designing the Polka Dot pattern and the Fern moulds as well as the Daisy in Criss-Cross pattern. Opalescent glass seems to have been made before 1901, but not after the factory moved to the new site in Grafton, West Virginia. Beaumont sold his interests in this company in 1906, and the factory name was changed to Tygert Valley Glass. Beaumont later managed Union Stopper at Morgantown, and when this firm closed, he began a new firm that was first a decorating plant and later a lighting wares factory. Percy Beaumont died in the 1940s.

Buckeye Glass Company (1878 – 1896) *Martins Ferry, Ohio*

Founded by wealthy entrepreneur, Henry Helling (a later investor in the Northwood Company), the Buckeye Glass Company opened in 1878 as a tableware company that introduced color into its glass line very early. The manager was John F. Miller (later associated with the Model Flint Glass Company). Buckeye produced opalescent glass and cased art glass in tableware, night lamps, cruets, syrups, and more. Patterns included Buckeye, Lattice, Reverse Swirl, Coinspot (cylinder lamps), Stripe, Big Windows, and possibly Chrysanthemum Swirl. The factory began to fail as early as 1891 and returned to tableware and opaque glass and oil lamps. Labor problems, a number of fires blamed on arson, and a large, consuming fire led to the closing of the factory in February 1896.

George Davidson & Company (1867 – 1987) *Gateshead, England*

In 1888, eleven years after Sowerby produced its opal ware, the Davidson Company registered its Pearline opal ware in pale yellow (canary), soft blue, light green, and clear (white opalescent). Davidson's had been founded in 1867 by George Davidson, but his son, Thomas, became the firm's driving force in 1891. Davidson's Pearline patterns are numerous and include Brideshead (1889), Cane Rings, Lady Chippendale (1887), Daisy and Greek Key (unconfirmed at this time), Pearline Epergne, Davidson's Shell (1889), Lady Caroline (1891), Linking Rings (1894), Lords and Ladies (1896), Princess Diana (1890), Prince William (1893), Queen's Spill (1891), Queen Victoria (plate #254027, 1895), Quilted Daisy Fairy Lamp, Quilted Pillow Sham (1893), Richelieu, Sea Scroll, Somerset (1895), Victoria and Albert (1897), War of Roses (1893), Whitechapel (not confirmed as Davidson), and William and Mary (1903).

Dugan Glass Company (1904 – 1913)   *Indiana, Pennsylvania*

Thomas E. Dugan, Harry Northwood's cousin, began his career at Hobbs, Brockunier, then moved to Buckeye Glass, to the Northwood Ellwood City plant, and then managed the Indiana, Pennsylvania, plant for National after Northwood's joining. In 1904, he gathered a group of financial backers to purchase the Indiana, Pennsylvania, plant from National, and the Dugan Glass Company was begun. Early production contained opalescent, but after 1910 iridescent glass became the mainstay. Opalescent patterns included Swastika, Diamond and Clubs, Daisy and Fern, Swirl, Coinspot (1903), Diamond Spearhead (1901), Victor or Jeweled Heart (1905), Circled Scroll (1904), New York (Beaded Shell), and many novelty items including Waterlily, Corn Vase, and Palisades.

In 1913 Thomas Dugan resigned from the firm, and the company was renamed the Diamond Glass Company, with a trademarked "diamond with a D in the center." The Diamond Company remained in business until the plant burned in 1931. Thomas Dugan went on to be associated with a new Dugan company at Lonaconing and eventually became a minor player with Anchor Hocking.

Elson Glass Company (1882 – 1893), West Virginia Glass Company (1893 – 1896),
West Virginia Glass Mfg. Company (1897 – 1899),
National Glass Company (operating West Virginia Glass Works from 1899 to 1903)   *Martins Ferry, Ohio*

Readers may find this factory site a bit puzzling since no less than five companies operated here. First it was Elson, which is known to have made a castor set from Beaumont moulds in opalescent glass. The Elson Dewdrop pattern bears its name despite being made in 1893 as a design from West Virginia Glass Company. The owners of the West Virginia Glass Company had reorganized Elson and then produced blown opalescent glass. Some patterns known are Polka Dot and Fern (in #203 optic moulds). The company made both blown and pressed glass until late 1895 when the plant was closed for nearly a year during a depression. The factory was then sold in 1896 and reorganized as the West Virginia Glass Mfg. Company, operating for nearly two years before joining National Glass in 1899. In 1901 the plant was operated by Crystal Glass Company (their second branch factory), but after Ed Muhleman offered his resignation in 1901 to begin building the Imperial plant in Bellaire, the factory declined and finally closed in 1903.

Fenton Art Glass Company (1907 – present)   *Williamstown, West Virginia*

In 1905 in Martins Ferry, Ohio, brothers Frank L. and John W. Fenton opened the Fenton Art Glass Company as a decorating shop using blanks from other glassmakers. Both had worked for other glassmakers. Soon another brother, Charles H. Fenton joined them. Two years later, they purchased a site in Williamstown, West Virginia, and not long afterwards produced their first glass. John was president, Frank, general manager, and Charles headed the decorating shop. Another brother, James E. Fenton, became maintenance supervisor in late 1908. Soon afterwards, John left Williamstown to form the famous Millersburg Glass Company in Millersburg, Ohio.

Early glassware included opalescent glass in topaz, blue, green, and in 1908, amethyst. By 1910, iridized glass had become the rage and the Fenton factory produced the first of this product, which is today called carnival glass. Over the years, the Fenton company has continued to produce opalescent wares both for itself and for other companies, including the L.G. Wright Company in the 1930s, 1940s, and 1950s. The Fenton Art Glass Company remains the only major glass plant that still makes hand-worked glass and has outlasted all its competitors in the field.

Fostoria Shade & Lamp Company (1890 – 1894),
Consolidated Lamp and Glass Company (1894 – 1896)   *Fostoria, Ohio*

This firm was first known as the Fostoria Shade & Lamp Company and managed by Nicholas Kopp and Charles Etz. The name was changed in 1894 to the Consolidated Lamp and Glass Company. A line of tableware was released in 1893 and the opalescent ware included Consolidated's Criss-Cross pattern. A new factory was built in 1896 in Coraopolis, Pennsylvania, after the firm merged with the Wallace & McAfee Company, with headquarters in Pittsburgh. The company then specialized in Kopp-cased colors and produced tableware, lamps, and shades. The factory produced Martele tableware in the 1920s, shut down in depression times, reopened in 1936, and closed for good in 1964.

Greener & Company (1871 – 1885), controlled by James A. Jobling (1886 – present)   *Sunderland, England*

Henry Greener worked at the Sowerby firm until 1857 when he began working in Sunderland. In 1871 he became head of the business and bought the land where James A. Jobling & Company stood. (Jobling was a chemical merchant who supplied Greener with chemicals for glassmaking and is later remembered for making Pyrex ware.) Greener renewed his Lion trademark in 1890, but Jobling was then the manager, I believe. Patterns were made in malachite (slag), jet (obviously copying Sowerby's technique), and commemorative glass items. When Jobling took over the plant in 1910, he began to copy Rene Lalique's opal glass art and produced a product the company called "Jobling's Opalique." Examples of opalescent glass made at the Greener firm include Royal Jubilee, Contessa, and several small plate designs that resemble Lalique ware. Some of Greener's opal ware is found in strange colors like amber.

A.H. Heisey Glass Co. *Newark, Ohio (1895 – 1957)*

Augustus H. Heisey founded the company after his family immigrated to the United States in the mid 1800s, with construction beginning in 1895. The famous "H" in a diamond logo was copyrighted in 1901. Heisey produced various types of glassware of high quality throughout its years of operation including, but not limited to, the following patterns: Ring Band, Winged Scroll, Locket on Chain, Greek Key, Punty Band, Plain Band, Fandango, Fancy Loop, Pineapple with Fan, Continental, Kalonyal, and Touraine.

Hobbs, Brockunier & Company (1863 – 1888), Hobbs Glass Company (1888 – 1891)
U.S. Glass Company (Factory H 1891 – 1893) *Wheeling, West Virginia*

An earlier glass plant controlled by James Barnes and John L. Hobbs operated at this site until it closed during the Civil War. In 1863 the firm of Hobbs, Brockunier & Company was begun at the plant. In 1887, the firm was reorganized and in 1888 it became the Hobbs Glass Company. William Leighton Jr. left to join Dalzell, Gilmore & Leighton at Finlay, Ohio, and sales manager L.B. Martin departed to help forge the new Fostoria plant. Nicholas Kopp took charge and during this period, blown opalescent glass was produced. Absorbed by the U.S. Glass merger in 1891, the factory closed in 1893 during a strike and was finally purchased by Harry Northwood in 1903 (he had worked for Hobbs briefly as a glass engraver in 1882). The factory was refurbished and became the H. Northwood & Company Glass Works that year.

Jefferson Glass Company *Steubenville, Ohio (1900 – 1907), Follansbee, West Virginia (1907 – 1933)*

In an abandoned factory in Steubenville, Ohio, in 1900, the Jefferson Glass Company began its first production of glassware. The president, Harry Bastow, had earlier worked for Harry Northwood in Indiana, Pennsylvania, and the sales manager, George Mortimer, had also been associated with Northwood (oddly, both Frank and John Fenton were also associated with Jefferson for a time). Opalescent patterns from Jefferson were made from 1901 to 1907 and after that, the factory seemed to specialize in crystal. In 1908 Jefferson bought several patterns from the Ohio Flint Glass Company, including the Chippendale pattern, and put the company's energies into the production of items with the "Krys-tol" trademark they had also purchased from Ohio Flint. In 1910 the firm was sold again and the factory turned to lighting wares. In the opalescent years, patterns at Jefferson were abundant and included Coinspot, Swirl, Buttons and Braids, and Swirling Maze, as well as several novelty bowl and vase patterns.

La Belle Glass Company (1872 – 1888) *Bridgeport, Ohio*

La Belle Glass Company was established in 1872 as a tableware company. In 1884 Harry Northwood arrived, fresh from his position at the Hobbs, Brockunier factory, only to face a strike that closed La Belle. Two years later with the factory back up and running, Northwood returned (after working at Phoenix) and opalescent production began with a copycat version of Hobbs's Hobnail pattern. The La Belle factory burned in 1887 but the company leased new facilities in Brilliant, Ohio, while a new plant was built. The financial drain was too much, however, and brought on bankruptcy in 1888. The new plant was sold and then became the Crystal Glass Works where no opalescent glass was made to the best of my knowledge.

Millersburg Glass Company (1909 – 1912), Radium Glass Company (1912 – 1913) *Millersburg, Ohio*

Founded by John W. Fenton upon leaving the Fenton Art Glass Company in 1909, this glass factory concentrated on crystal and carnival glass but did produce one pattern in an opalescent treatment: small bowls in two sizes (6" or 7½") in a pattern called Country Kitchen by carnival collectors and Milky Way by opalescent collectors. These were products of the last days of the Millersburg plant before it became the Radium Glass Company and few of these bowls exist today. They are desirable and very much collectors' prizes in either size. The Radium factory closed in 1913 and was purchased by Jefferson Glass. For a few years, they made lantern glass and glass parts for railroad lanterns but the plant closed permanently in 1916.

Model Flint Glass Company (1893 – 1899),
National Glass Company (operating Model Flint — 1900 – 1902) *Albany, Indiana*

The company was first formed in 1888 in Findlay, Ohio, and moved to Albany, Indiana, in July 1893. Findlay production had been primarily tableware and this continued for the most part in Albany until the plant became part of the emerging

National Company in 1900. In 1901 blown opalescent glass was produced. Patterns include Wreath and Shell (Manila), Ribbed Spiral, Reverse Swirl, Stripe, Fern, Dolphin & Herons, Broken Pillar & Reed (Kismet), Ala-Bock, Calyx, Corolla, Diamond Stem, and Lotus. The factory was closed in 1902.

Nickel Plate Glass Company (1888 – 1893)
Fostoria, Ohio

Staffed with several men who had previously worked for other companies that made opalescent glass, Nickel Plate boasted such names as A.J. Smith, formerly with La Belle, and J.B. Russell who had worked for Hobbs. Nickel Plate opened in 1888 and part of their production seems to have been in blown opalescent glass in Wide Stripe, Swirl, and other patterns that may include Double Greek Key items. Opalescent colors ran the gamut and included blue, white, cranberry, and canary. The company joined U.S. Glass in 1891 as part of the giant merger, and then closed abruptly in 1893.

Northwood Company (1888 – 1892) *Martins Ferry, Ohio*
The Northwood Glass Company (1892 – 1896) *Ellwood City, Pennsylvania*
The Northwood Company (1896 – 1899) *Indiana, Pennsylvania, as part of National Glass Company (1900 – 1904)*
H. Northwood & Company (1902 – 1924) *Wheeling, West Virginia*

Harry Northwood's career was full of twists and turns, opening one factory and a few years later, moving to another location. He never actually owned any of the factories that bore his name but either managed or controlled them.

The first Northwood Company was opened at an abandoned factory that had once been the Union Glass Company. Despite Northwood's production there, the venture was considered a failure. In 1892, the name of the company was changed slightly, and the Northwood Glass Company moved to Ellwood City, Pennsylvania, where production included opalescent, coralene, cranberry, and onyx treatments. The move in 1896 to Indiana, Pennsylvania, was partially financed by relatives and opalescent glass was again a featured item, primarily mould blown.

In 1902 and 1903 there were two factories with the Northwood name and Harry had established his last plant at Wheeling, West Virginia. Here, pressed opalescent became the norm along with all the other famous treatments including carnival glass (after 1907).

Phoenix Glass Company (1880 – 1940s)
Monaco, Pennsylvania

Founded in 1880 by Andrew Howard (president) and William I. Miller (secretary-treasurer) to make lamp chimneys and reflectors, the company made lamp shades from 1882 until the plant burned in 1884. The company then bought an abandoned chimney works that had been Doyle & Sons at Phillipsburg (and when a new plant was built, this became the Phoenix #3 plant). When the rebuilt plant opened in 1885 a second furnace was added. This plant eventually burned in 1893. In 1883 the factories had begun to produce art glass when Joseph Webb, nephew of the famous English glassmaker, came aboard as plant superintendent. Mr. Webb had a great influence on the direction of Phoenix and was aided by Harry Northwood who came to Phoenix in 1885. Art glass and opalescent glass were made until 1892 when the firm tried to make cut glass. Then in 1900, they again added lighting wares, moulds from Co-operative Flint and Consolidated in the 1930s, and a line of sculptured artware in the 1940s. Today, Phoenix is part of the Anchor-Hocking Company.

Sowerby's Ellison Glass Works (1811 – 1957)
Gateshead-on-Tyne, England

Long one of England's three great glass firms from the country's northeast area, the Sowerby name is well known in the glass world. Richard Sowerby had been a partner in the firm of Robertson & Company. He died in 1811 and George Sowerby took his place, and in 1816 the firm became Sowerby and Lowry Glass. In 1824, George became the owner of the New Stourbridge Works and in 1857 the factory became Sowerby's Ellison Glass Works with John Sowerby in charge. Later, J.G. Sowerby, John's son, became the manager and the peacock head trademark was established. The company made slag or marble glass, jet (black) glass, and various types of Vitroporcelain. In 1879 the company began a limited production of opalescent glass. Patterns such as Diamond Pyramid, English Duck, Sowerby Swan, Victorian Hamper, and Paneled Cornflower are examples of their products.

United States Glass Co., (1891 – 1963)
Pittsburgh, Pennsylvania

This was a consolidation of factories. Although most were closed by the time the Great Depression ended, the Glassport and Tiffin factories remained in operation until 1963. The Glassport factory was destroyed by a tornado and the Tiffin factory became Tiffin Art Glass Co., which was dismantled in 1985.

Member factories:
A.   Adams & Co., Pittsburgh, Pennsylvania

B.   Bryce Bros., Pittsburgh, Pennsylvania
C.   Challinor, Taylor & Co., Ltd., Tarentum, Pennsylvania
D.   George Duncan & Sons, Pittsburgh, Pennsylvania
E.   Richards & Hartley, Tarentum, Pennsylvania
F.   Ripley & Co., Pittsburgh, Pennsylvania
G.   Gillinder & Sons, Greensburgh, Pennsylvania
H.   Hobbs Glass Co., Wheeling, West Virginia
J.   Columbia Glass Co., Findlay, Ohio
K.   King Glass Co., Pittsburgh, Pennsylvania
L.   O'Hara Glass Co., Pittsburgh, Pennsylvania
M.   Bellaire Goblet Co., Findlay, Ohio
N.   Nickel Plate Glass Co., Fostoria, Ohio
O.   Central Glass Co., Wheeling, West Virginia
P.   Doyle & Co., Pittsburgh, Pennsylvania
R.   A.J. Beatty & Sons, Tiffin, Ohio
S.   A.J. Beatty & Sons, Steubenville, Ohio (non-operating)
T.   Novelty Glass Co., Fostoria, Ohio
*New factories built: Glassport, Pennsylvania, and Gas City, Indiana

In addition to the forementioned companies, others made smaller contributions to both pressed and blown opalescent glass. Here is a brief list of those I believe are in that group:
Dalzell, Gilmore & Leighton Company, Findlay, Ohio
King Glass Company, Pittsburgh, Pennsylvania
Central Glass Works, Wheeling, West Virginia
Belmont Glass Company, Bellaire, Ohio
Mount Washington Glass Works, New Bedford, Massachusetts
Burtles, Tate & Company, Manchester, England
Molineaux, Webb & Company, Manchester, England
Richardsons of Wordsley, Stourbridge, England
Stevens and Williams, Stourbridge, England
Thomas Webb & Sons, Stourbridge, England
George Baccus & Sons, Birmingham, England
A. Jobling & Company, Sunderland, England
John Walsh Walsh, Birmingham, England
Tygart Valley Glass Company, Grafton, West Virginia

Who Made It?

Confusion abounds over the Northwood/National/Dugan connection, as well as the Jefferson/Northwood connection. In 1896 Harry Northwood, Samuel Dugan Sr., and his sons Thomas, Alfred, and Samuel Dugan Jr. came to Indiana, Pennsylvania, operating the Northwood Glass Company until 1899, when Harry Northwood joined the newly formed National Glass Company combine. In 1903, he moved his operation to Wheeling at the old Hobbs, Brockunier plant, and Thomas Dugan remained at the Indiana plant operating it as the Dugan Glass Company.

From 1896 on, several patterns were produced as first Northwood, then National, and finally as Dugan, patterns such as Argonaut Shell/Nautilus, for example. There were many others that have previously been classified as either Northwood or Dugan that are actually Northwood/National/Dugan or even National/Dugan.

In addition, certain patterns were duplicated by both Jefferson and Northwood, with little explanation as to why moulds that were once Jefferson's became Northwood's. These companies were competitors, but examples of some patterns can be traced to both companies. It is also evident most patterns with a cranberry edging are really Jefferson, not Northwood as once believed.

Every answer raises new questions. Answers come in their own time and at their own pace. One day collectors will know most of what is questioned today and that is what drives us all. I learn every day, mostly by contact with other collectors and so, I'm sure, do all of you.

What Collecting Is All About

Sometimes I run across collections that are just too good to show piecemeal and I long for a way to display the entire collection so that other collectors may see just what one can do with a single pattern or a single shape. You will see pieces from various makers in a host of shapes: pitchers, barber bottles, Diamond Stem vases, Ribbed Spiral toothpicks as well as vases made from those toothpicks, from the Rick and Debbie Graham collection. You will also see many rare and collectible pitchers as well as wall-to-wall display cabinets from the Bill Walter and Laurel Walton collection.

I hope readers will enjoy seeing what a wonder this glass can be when arranged in such a fashionable display, and again I thank these collectors for sharing their wonderful opalescent glass collections.

Abalone

Found only in bowls with small handles, the Abalone pattern is believed to be from the Jefferson Glass Company and dates from the 1902 – 1905 period. Colors are blue, white, green, and rarely canary opalescent glass. The design, a series of graduated arcs in columns separated by a line of bubble-like dots, is nice, but nothing special.

Acorn Burrs

Here is one of the well-known Northwood patterns that was made in the 1907 – 1909 era. In opalescent glass this pattern is limited to the small berry bowl. Opalescent colors are very rare, so consider yourself fortunate if you find an example of this rare pattern.

Acorns

This lidded jar sports a banded group of acorns circling the lower half of the bottom with a bark like pattern continuing nearly to the top. The top is covered with acorn caps around the outer edge and smaller acorns inside. This is one of the earlier Jobling "Opalique" pieces, with an Rd. #796182, which places it in 1934. Colors are white and blue opalescent. Photo courtesy of the Petrasichs.

Acorn with Bee

This flint glass sugar with lid has a bottom that shows heavy opalescence; however, the top is just average. I feel it is English in origin, but this is speculation. Additional information is welcomed. Photo courtesy of the Sandemans.

Adonis Pineapple

Shown is a claret bottle (missing its stopper) from the Aetna Glass & Manufacturing Co., circa 1888. It can be found in either amber or blue with the opalescent design on the bottom portion. Thanks to the Petrasichs for sharing it.

Ala-Bock

This Model Flint Glass pattern was made around 1900. This pattern seems to be more available in the rose bowl shape. It was only made in a few shapes and two colors. I've never seen pieces of the reported water set. It is also known as Galaxy.

Alaska

One of the early Northwood patterns, Alaska dates from 1897 and can be found in a wide range of shapes. The tumblers and shakers are interchangeable with plain Fluted Scrolls and Jackson pieces. Various colors are known.

Albany Reverse Swirl

This was made in Albany, Indiana, in 1901 and 1902, and can be found in a host of shapes and several colors. Albany was made by Model Flint Glass Company. It is known as Albany glass and Model Flint glass by collectors.

Albany Stripe

This beautiful, quite scarce water set was made about 1900 with the same moulds as the Albany Fern set. The pattern is also found in three other shapes and in various colors.

Alfred and James

This pale vaseline rose bowl has the Rd. #9807, which indicates it was made by Alfred and James Davies, Stourbridge, England, July 15, 1884. Photo courtesy of the Petrasichs.

Alhambra

Often confused with the Spanish Lace pattern, Alhambra is really an Albany Glass pattern. It is found in only a few shapes and colors. The confirmation of a tumbler suggests the possibility of a pitcher, but none has been reported. Photo courtesy of Rachel Spinella.

Alva

This very impressive oil lamp is found in several variations including a blue opal stripe with frosted base and a vaseline stripe with the same base treatment. Dating from the 1890s, this lamp is quality all the way.

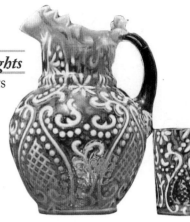

Arabian Nights

Dating from 1895 or 1896, this Northwood pattern is confined to water sets and a syrup, and can be found in four colors. The design (swirls, blossoms, and dots) combines the best of both Spanish Lace and Daisy and Fern and is a very striking pattern.

Arched Panel

When I first showed this 9" bowl, I speculated about the maker, but now I know it was made by Jefferson Glass in both large and small berry bowls. There are 12 wide panels around the bowl, the top is scalloped, and there is a many rayed star in the base. Heisey made a similar opalescent set called their #300 Peerless pattern.

Argonaut Shell (Nautilus)

Originally a Northwood pattern, the opalescent examples were made by National or by Dugan after Northwood left National. This pattern is found in three colors and in a variety of shapes.

Arrowhead

This John Walsh Walsh pattern is similar in design to the Sharks Tooth pattern. It is found in a vase shape and a jar with lid and spoon (shown without the lid and spoon). The only color reported is vaseline. Thanks to Ruth Harvey for sharing it.

Ascot

This pattern was made by the Greener Company of England as #262018 in 1895 and can be found in blue or canary opalescent glass. A complete table set and a biscuit jar with lid are the shapes I've heard about. The design is one of arcs around a circle of file.

Astro

Astro was made by the Jefferson Glass Company about 1905 as primarily a bowl pattern. It is a simple design of six circular comet-like rings on a threaded background above three rings of beads that are grouped from the lower center of the bowl upward.

Aurora Borealis

This Jefferson Glass Company vase pattern, dating from 1903, is very typical of stemmed vases in the opalescent glass era. Rising from a notched base, the stem widens with a series of bubbles and scored lines that end in a flame-shaped top. From the sides are three handle-like projections, giving a very nautical feeling.

Autumn Leaves

I am very drawn to this beautiful bowl pattern, attributed to the Northwood Company from 1905. The design is quite good with large, well-veined leaves around the bowl, connected by twisting branches and a single leaf in the bowl's center.

Azzuro Verde

This pretty vase has a vaseline base and an azure blue top, hence the name from the owner Ruth Harvey. I do not know the maker but the treatment is similar to Hobbs's formulas. I welcome any information about this treatment as well as the vase, which has an interior wide panel design.

Baby Coinspot

Shown is a 7" tall vase in a white opalescent color. I believe it is English and it has a polished pontil on the base. Baby Coinspot dates from the early 1900s and was previously shown in a syrup from Belmont Glass and an American vase shape. In addition, Fenton reproduced this pattern.

Ball Foot Hobnail

So very little is really known about this pattern. It may have been a product of New Brighton Glass Company of New Brighton, Pennsylvania, but this hasn't been confirmed. The date of production seems to be around 1889, and most items are crystal while only a few have opalescence. The distinguishing points of identification seem to be the scallops on the edges and while some pieces do indeed have ball feet, others are collar based.

Banded Hobnail

The owner of this strange dresser bottle believes it may be either English or from Europe (I believe the latter). It stands 5" tall and has a strange three-hobnail finial on the stopper. Bands of threading are found around the bottle in three places and at its neck and the hobnails go all the way under the base. The age is unknown to me.

Banded Lily Epergne

Similar to the Serpent Threaded epergne shown elsewhere, this is likely a European piece but I have no information as to the maker at this time. This ruffled base epergne has one large ruffled center lily with a pinch banded application around the neck area. Vaseline is the only color reported. Thanks to Ruth Harvey for sharing this nice piece.

Banded Neck and Scale Optic

This very attractive small vase (5½" tall) is mould blown and has a pontil mark on the base. The scale optic pattern is on the inside and only the banding around the neck elevates this vase above the ordinary. It has been reported only in white to date.

Banded Star and Fan

This Model Flint Glass bowl in blue opalescent is found in 9" and 11" sizes and they are the only reported shapes to date. Additional information is appreciated. Photo courtesy of the Petrasichs.

Barbells

Barbells is found only on the bowl shape in opalescent glass and is credited to the Jefferson Glass Company in 1905. This design is identical to a Hobbs, Brockunier one called Mario (their #341). It is even possible Jefferson used the same 8" bowl mould. Other shapes are known.

Beaded Base Vase

This pattern is very similar to a design by the Northwood Company and is shown in an old Butler Brothers ad. This attractive jack-in-the-pulpit vase is enameled with sprigs of flowers and has dots painted on the stem and around the base. If anyone has more information about this piece I'd appreciate hearing from them.

Beaded Basket

There seems to be some dispute over whether this pattern was made by Dugan Glass or after Diamond took over the plant. It is found mostly in carnival glass and since pink examples exist I know it was made very late into the 1920s (Dugan became Diamond in 1913). But here is the first reported example in opalescent glass putting it firmly in the Dugan time period, also.

Beaded Block

Beaded Block was made in 1913 by the Imperial Glass Company in limited amounts of opalescent glass, and can also be found in crystal or carnival glass (called Frosted Block by carnival glass collectors). This pattern was made in various shapes and colors.

Beaded Button Arches

The nice compote shown, 4½" high and 5½" across the top, comes from Greener and Company in Sunderland, England. The Rd. #304505 puts production in 1897. Shapes known are a compote, creamer, and sugar, but other shapes may well exist. Thanks to the Petrasichs for sharing.

Beaded Cable

This well-known Northwood pattern can be found in several treatments including opalescent, carnival, and custard. Rose bowls and open bowls from the same mould are known. The design is simple yet effective and dates from 1904.

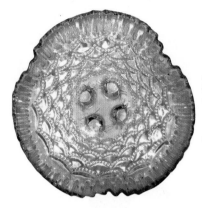

Beaded Drapes

This very attractive pattern is thought to be from the Northwood Company although examples with cranberry edging like some Jefferson items can be found. The 1905 pattern can be found in a variety of shapes and colors.

Beaded Fans

This pattern is found mostly on footed rose bowls from the same mould as the bowl shown. It is like Shell and Dots minus the dotted base. The pattern dates from 1905. It has been credited to Northwood, but it is shown in Jefferson Glass ads as #211, so I know it is a Jefferson pattern.

Beaded Fleur de Lis

Attributed to Jefferson Glass, this stemmed compote can be found with the top opened out or turned in like a rose bowl. It was made in the 1906 era. The design is quite good, and the base is very distinctive with three wide feet and beaded rings on the stems.

Beaded Moon and Stars

This pattern is nearly the same as the Beaded Stars and Swag pattern shown elsewhere (both were made by the Fenton Art Glass Company) and is often called just Beaded Stars by carnival glass collectors. It was made in several shapes and colors.

Beaded Ovals in Sand

Originally called Erie, this Dugan/Diamond pattern is very closely related to two other designs from this company. It can be found in a good number of shapes and colors. Opalescent pieces are rather scarce.

Beaded Ovals with Holly

I am pleased to be able to show this Dugan/Diamond pattern, which has to be quite rare. This is the only example reported. It is a 4¼" spooner shape in white opalescent. If you look at the Beaded Ovals In Sand pattern you notice that it lacks the added holly berry and leaf design shown here. I'd like to hear about other shapes and colors in this interesting pattern. Thanks to the Petrasichs for sharing this beauty.

Beaded Shell

While this Dugan pattern is known as Shell in opalescent glass, collectors of carnival and other types of glass recognize it as the Beaded Shell pattern. It was made in 1905, in a host of shapes and colors. It has been reproduced by Mosser.

Beaded Star Medallion

Although often credited to the Imperial Glass Company in carnival glass, a recent find of marked marigold carnival pieces confirms this to be a Northwood pattern. In opalescent glass, it can be found in three standard colors. The pattern dates from the 1909 era and was made for both gas and electric shades.

Beaded Stars

The opalescent version of this pattern was made by the Fenton Glass Company in 1907. Shapes are various. The bowl and the plate are known with advertising: SOUVENIR LION STORE HAMMOND (shown) and are quite rare. Photo courtesy of Rick and Debbie Graham.

Beaded V's and Buttons

I have taken the liberty of naming this pattern and would appreciate hearing from anyone with solid information concerning it. This creamer is reported in blue only, but I would certainly think it came in other shapes and possibly other colors as well. It has a Rd. # which is illegible but possibly indicates a Greener and Company product. Thanks again to John and Mary Petrasich for sharing this nice piece.

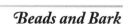

Beads and Bark

Shown as early as 1903, this Northwood pattern was made in their Mosaic or purple slag treatment, as well as appearing in opalescent colors of white, blue, canary, and limited amounts of green. Like on so many vases of the time, the theme was rustic with tree limbs forming the supports to the base. In the case of Beads and Bark, these supports generate into a bowl that is a series of inverted loops with beaded edging forming three rows of design.

Beads and Curlycues

This scarce short-stemmed Northwood piece was advertised in Butler Brothers in 1906. It has an open-edged top, much like Shell and Wild Rose pieces. In the example shown, the top is fanned out evenly all around, but other pieces show a variety of tops.

Beatty Honeycomb

The Honeycomb pattern, made by Beatty & Sons in Tiffin, Ohio, dates to 1888, and is also known as Beatty Waffle. It can be found in a host of shapes but only two colors. Be aware the pattern was reproduced in the 1960s by the Fenton Glass Company in blue and emerald green in vases, baskets, rose bowls, and a covered sugar.

Beatty Rib

The A.J. Beatty & Sons Company originally made glass in Steubenville, Ohio, until they merged with U.S. Glass and moved their operation to Tiffin, Ohio, in 1891. Beatty Rib dates from 1889 and was made in both blue and white in a vast array of shapes.

Beatty Swirl

Like its sister pattern Beatty Rib, this popular design was produced in 1889 in blue, white, and occasionally canary opalescent glass. It is found in a wide variety of shapes, with other shapes possible.

Beaumont Coinspot

Beaumont Coinspot dates from 1900 and is found in the usual colors. The pitcher can be recognized by the squared top and slightly deeper coloring, especially on blue pieces. Thanks to Mary and John Petrasich for sharing this piece with me.

Beaumont Stripe

While one writer thought this was a Northwood pattern, the water pitcher shown has the same shape as that of the Stars and Stripes water set, first made by Hobbs and then by Beaumont in 1899. I believe it was actually made by Beaumont and have so named it, and I'll hear from collectors if I'm wrong. The set sits on a tray in the Beatty Swirl pattern.

Beaumont Swirl

I believe this pitcher in Swirl is from the Beaumont Glass Company but have no proof. It is speculated about in Heacock's Book 9, *Cranberry Opalescent from A to Z*, but that's the only reference I've found.

Bell Flower Centerpiece Vase

This 16" vase is cousin to the Thorn Vase and has applications of green leaves and feet, pinkish flowers, and the thorns are certainly noticeable with their white opal tips. Thanks to Ruth Harvey for the nice photo.

Berry Patch

This design, made by the Jefferson Glass Company in 1905 as their #261 pattern, seems to be limited to small bowls and plates with a dome base. The design is a simple one, a trailing of vine, leaves, and small berry clusters that ramble around the inside bowl. The example shown, a flattened piece with the edges rolled up, is called a plate by some collectors. The pattern is accented in a goofus treatment of soft coloring, unlike most examples seen. Thanks to Judy Parker for the photo.

Big Diamond

This amberish or apricot colored vase with enameling is either from Phoenix Glass or possibly a Bohemian product of Harrach Glass. I'd like to know more if anyone has concrete information. Photo courtesy of Bill Walter and Laurel Walton.

Big Dot

This average size bowl has a simple pattern of raised dots on the exterior and vaseline is the only color reported to date. I welcome additional information. Thanks to the Petersons for sharing it.

Big Windows Swirled

This Buckeye Glass Co. pattern, also called Big Windows Reverse Swirl, is made in a variety of shapes and colors. Notice the difference in pattern design to the Windows pattern shown later in this book. Fenton later produced their Coin Dot pattern which is not to be confused with this pattern. Thanks to the Petrasichs for sharing it.

Bird in a Tree

This very unusual novelty piece was made by Burtles, Tate & Company in 1885 (Rd 34196) and is found on the rose opalescent color shown. It is shown here through the courtesy of Mary and John Petrasich and I certainly thank them for sharing it with me.

Blackberry

While the pattern is sometimes called Northwood's Blackberry, I have no doubt it was produced by the Fenton Glass Company. It has been seen mostly in small sauce shapes but occasionally one of these is pulled into a whimsey shape. It is found in a variety of colors.

Blackberry Spray

Although very similar to the Blackberry pattern above, this Fenton design has less detail and more sprays. This same pattern and shape was made in carnival glass during the same time span and 1911 ads are known.

Block

Formerly called Northwood Block, this pattern is from Jefferson and was shown in their ads. It is found in a variety of shapes and colors. Photo courtesy of Bill Walter and Laurel Walton.

Block (English)

This Greener and Company pattern from 1891 has the Rd. #182002 and can be found in a pitcher, two sizes of tumblers, and a platter. Many thanks to the Petrasichs for sharing it.

Blocked Thumbprint and Beads

While the history of this pattern tends to be confusing, mainly because it is only one in a series of patterns done by the Dugan/Diamond Glass Company over a period of time, the study of two closely designed patterns sets the picture in order. Blocked Thumbprint and Beads and Leaf Rosette and Beads (shown elsewhere in this book) are very much alike. When you add a Dugan carnival glass item called Fishscale and Beads (shown elsewhere in this book) to the picture, you can see that all three patterns came from the same maker. The latter is simply the original Blocked Thumbprint and Beads with an interior pattern of scaling. It is found in the standard opalescent colors. Thanks to Roger Lane for the photo.

Blooms and Blossoms

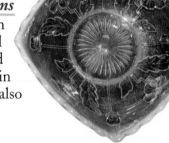

Blooms and Blossoms is also known as Mikado, and if you look further in this edition at Northwood's Mikado you'll see why. It is known in several glass treatments. In opalescent glass the usual shape is this square-shaped nappy with one handle. It has been called an olive nappy and can be found in three primary colors. If two names aren't enough, it can also be found as Flower and Bud in some books.

Blossoms and Palms

Blossoms and Palms was first made by the Northwood Company in carnival glass and opalescent glass in 1905, and some pieces like the one shown have a goofus treatment. Some pieces have the Northwood trademark. The design consists of three acanthus-like leaves with a stem of flowers and leaves separating each of them.

Blossoms and Web

Advertised in 1906 as part of Northwood's Egyptian Art Decorated offering, this was one name for the goofus treatment over opalescent items. Blossoms and Web is a difficult pattern to find and is a collector's favorite. The design of six blossoms connected by a webbing of stems with one center blossom is simple but effective. Photo courtesy of Rick and Debbie Graham.

Blossom Top Caster Set

Shown is a four-piece set with metal stand that I believe is European. The owner says there are traces of gilt on the bottoms of the bottles and the soft opalescence covers most of the pieces. I chose the name because of the glass stoppers on the bottles. Anyone with more information is asked to contact me.

Blown Diamonds

I now have evidence this pattern may be from the Coudersport Glass Company (1900 – 1904) and may have a companion pitcher in the same shape with interior draping. This latter pitcher is in the Potter County, Pennsylvania, Historical Society Museum and is white opalescent glass. Only time will tell if I can link these two water pitchers but for now I am convinced there will be such a link found.

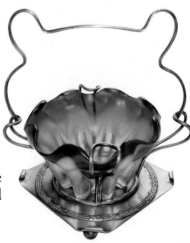

Blown Drapery

This very beautiful tankard water set and companion sugar shaker, made by Northwood as part of the National Glass combine in 1903, are mould blown and can be found in several colors. Please compare this set with the later Fenton Drapery set (shown elsewhere in this book) for a complete understanding of just how this pattern varies from blown to pressed ware. Also, be aware that Blown Drapery has been reproduced in a cruet by L.G. Wright.

Blown Rope

This vase is similar to the Twisted Rope vase shown elsewhere in this edition. It is blown and not pressed. Blown Rope may well be from England but I have no proof and I'd certainly like any information readers may have about this piece.

Blown Twist

This pattern and its sister pattern (Blown Drapery) were made at the Northwood plant when it was part of National Glass, date from 1903, and are shown in a Butler Brothers ad from that year. Besides the rare water set, a celery vase is known in canary or blue opalescent glass, and the water sets are found in several colors.

Bluerescent Webb

I'll go ahead and say that this is probably the rarest marmalade in all of opalescent glass, and possibly in any other type of glass. It was made by Thomas Webb, circa 1885. This color was likely an experimental one, since Webb was not supposed to have made it in any color other than Lemonescent (vaseline base color). I am thrilled to show this extremely rare item. Photo courtesy of John and Candice Shertz.

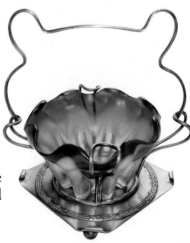

Boat with Wheels

This very interesting four-wheel boat has a rather plain design of vertical ribbing on the side and is a characteristic "v" bottom boat. The color is vaseline and I can only assume it was used as a pickle or relish dish. Other than to say this is English, I have no other information to offer at this time. Thanks to Steve and Radka Sandeman for sharing this interesting novelty.

Boggy Bayou

Boggy Bayou is often confused with another Fenton pattern called Reverse Drapery. It is found only on vase shapes in sizes from 6" to 13" tall. Production dates from 1907 in both opalescent glass and carnival glass. A comparison of the bases will help distinguish one pattern from the other. A Reverse Drapery whimsey vase is shown in the whimsey section.

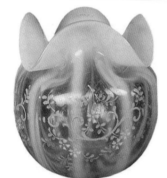

Bohemian Stripe

I'm told that this nice enameled piece is Bohemian (possibly Harrach), but I have no concrete proof. Nonetheless, it is a nicely done item and the enameled work is always pleasing to the eye. Blue is the only color reported, but I'm sure other shapes and colors exist. Thanks to Donna Drohan for the nice photo.

Bohemian Tulip Epergne

Almost certainly a Kralik piece from 1880 – 1905, this towering 21½" single lily epergne is a sight to behold. The color is a pale cranberry and vaseline. Any additional information on this piece would be appreciated. Photo courtesy of the Keathleys.

Bough and Blossom

I believe this beautiful lavender rose bowl with squared top, gilded flowers, and an opal edging is English, but I have no evidence. It was shared by the Petrasichs and would grace any fine collection.

Brass Nailhead

This strange mug stands 1¾" tall and can be found in white opalescent glass. Some pieces are marked France, so I know the origin and the date (1890s). I certainly welcome any additional information. The example shown is from Mary and John Petrasich.

Brick

What a joy this little castle shape is. It was produced by Molineaux, Webb, and Company in 1885 and is marked Rd 29780. The only color reported is white. The Petrasichs report there are other shapes with the brick design.

Brideshead

As I said before, this pattern was made by the Davidson Glass Works in England and bears their registration number, 130643, dated 1889. Shapes are numerous; however, it is only found in two colors.

Bridesmaid

I am really taken by this exquisite pattern, shown here in the amber pitcher and tumblers. Often mistaken for Davidson's Brideshead, this is actually a Greener and Company pattern. It has no Rd. number, while the Davidson pieces do. Reported shapes are bowls in various sizes, large oval bowl, pitcher, tumbler, and tray. All pieces are hard to come by. Thanks to the Petrasichs for the information and photo.

Brilynacee Lace

Brilynacee Lace was made by Model Flint Glass of Albany, Indiana, and is very similar to Spanish Lace, Alhambra, and Ala-Bock. The blown pitcher is the first to be reported (surely there were matching tumblers). The pattern was named by the owner, Kelvin Russell.

British Flute

I believe this pattern is from England, possibly by Davidson. It has a base pontil mark, 16 inside flute or wide panels, and is somewhat square in shape. The top has an interesting three-and-one ruffling much like that done by the Dugan/Diamond Company on some of their glass. This beautiful vaseline opalescent piece is 8" tall and probably came in other colors.

Broken Pillar

This pattern, called Kismet (#909) by some collectors, was made in the 1895 – 1900 era by Model Flint Glass and advertised in many shapes in crystal, decorated colors, and the one stemmed tray piece in opalescent glass. The design is all exterior with a very heavily patterned stem.

Bubble Lattice

This pattern was called Plaid by Marion Hartung but is more commonly known as Bubble Lattice or simply Lattice. It was made in Wheeling by Hobbs, Brockunier & Company in 1889, and can be found in many shapes in the standard four opalescent colors. The finish was occasionally satinized. Photo courtesy of Rick and Debbie Graham.

Bubble Lattice Lamp (Northwood's Paneled Mould)

The owner of this 4" tall lamp believes it was from Markham, but the shaping of the glass is like Northwood's Paneled mould found on cruets and shakers, so I believe it is probably theirs. I'd certainly like any information about this lamp from readers.

Buckeye Bubble Lattice

The shape of this pitcher tells that it was a product of the Buckeye Glass Company of Martins Ferry, Ohio. This same shape is found in other opalescent patterns like Reverse Swirl and Big Windows. Other shapes are known.

Buckeye Coinspot

Often collectors have difficulty telling one maker's Coinspot pieces from another so I am showing several examples to help. Here is the Buckeye Glass pitcher, made in 1889, in the usual colors. Note that the top is round and the neck is short.

Bull's Eye

This seldom seen pattern (attributed to Hobbs by some writers) is found in the water bottle shown as well as light shades and a bride's bowl. In addition, there seems to be some speculation that this pattern was also made by La Belle as well as Phoenix in other shapes than the ones listed in the included price guide in this edition.

Bull's Eye and Fan Variant

U.S. Glass must have done a lot of fiddling with this pattern. This was the second variation. The first is called Daisies in Oval Panels (see my *Collector's Encyclopedia of Carnival Glass*). Here is the first piece of opalescent glass reported. It has no bottom fan and no daisy motif in the bullseye. Thanks to the Petrasichs for sharing it.

Bull's Eye and Leaves

At first glance this looks like the normal Netted Roses pattern from Northwood, but here I show a prototype bowl that was later retooled into the latter. Notice the area that became roses is only circles or bull's eyes in this version. Thanks to Joan and Wayne Joliffe for sharing this rarity.

Bushel Basket (Northwood)

This Northwood pattern was first made in 1905 in opalescent glass in three standard colors, and later in custard glass and carnival glass. Some pieces have the trademark while others do not and a few items were gilded or decorated. This is a very popular pattern with most glass collectors.

Butterfly (Fenton)

This neat little Fenton compote is shown in the 1917 and 1918 Butler Brothers catalogs. The only opalescent color reported is white and the only shape reported is the small compote found in a round shape, Jack-in-the-Pulpit (shown with gold butterflies), or a square shape. Thanks to Mitchell Stewart for sharing this nice piece.

Button Panels

This pattern was advertised as early as 1899 at the Northwood factory, was still shown in Dugan ads later, and was also produced at the Coudersport Tile & Ornamental Glass Company sometime between 1900 and 1904. There it was called Shadow and it was made in three shapes and several colors. Just who made what pieces is a real puzzle as is how three companies ended up with this pattern.

Buttons and Braids

Although questions have come up as to the maker of this pattern, it was first credited to Jefferson in 1905 and was shown in old Fenton catalog ads from 1910. This pattern comes in water sets and bowls in most of the standard colors. Tumblers can be either blown or pressed and some can be found in a strange greenish vaseline that is like some Northwood pieces. It is suspected that this pattern was also made by Northwood for National and may have even been a product of Dugan, once Northwood left the Indiana, Pennsylvania, plant.

Cabbage Leaf

Cabbage Leaf is exactly like Winter Cabbage shown elsewhere in this book, except Cabbage Leaf has three large leaf patterns over the twig-like feet. This piece is usually turned up to form a very neat vase. Both patterns are from the Northwood Company and date from 1906 – 1907.

Cactus (Northwood)

This circa 1893 Northwood item is reasonably hard to find. The colors found in this shaker are blue, vaseline, and cranberry opalescent. Again, thanks to Ruth Harvey for sharing the photo.

Calyx

This pattern was made by the Model Flint Glass Company during their association with National and dates from 1899 or a bit later. This scarce vase can be found in a wide variety of color treatments on various types of glass.

Canary/Blue JIP Vase

Like the rubina verde vase, this vase is from Hobbs, Brockunier in the 1880s, but is even rarer. The bottom is canary opalescent glass while the top is blue opalescent glass. It is a blown item, 6½" tall, and a really beautiful piece of true art glass. Thanks to Connie Wilson for sharing this with me.

Cane Rings

This pattern can be found in several books that feature glass from England as a product of the Davidson Company, but has never been named as far as I can ascertain, so I've corrected that oversight. I know of bowls, a celery vase, a creamer, and an open sugar in this pattern, but more shapes were probably made.

Carousel

This was made by the Jefferson Glass Company in 1905 as their #264 pattern. The only shape I've seen is the standard novelty bowl shape, often with varied edge treatments. The design is a simple one with little imagination. All colors are difficult to locate. Thanks to Bill Walter and Laurel Walton for the photo.

Casbah

This pattern, now known to be a product of the Fenne Glassworks of Saarland, Germany, is found in the compote shape as well as a 10" bowl with candy-ribbon edge. I thank Siegmar Geiselberger of Germany for his glass research on this pattern.

Cashews

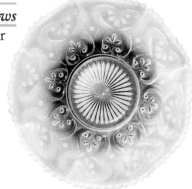

Cashews is attributed to the Northwood Glass Company and I suspect it was later continued by Dugan/Diamond. Shapes are bowls, plates, and a nice rose bowl, all from the same mould. Colors are white, blue, and green opalescent with some white examples found with a goofus treatment.

Cathedral

This 8" Greener and Co. pitcher (or jug) has Rd. #241930 from 1894. There are other known shapes but this blue piece is the only reported opalescent piece. Photo courtesy of the Petrasichs.

Centipede

This very unusual bowl gets its name from the strange feet that support it. The glass is delicate and has a cased edging. I believe this is another English pattern but have no proof. I welcome any information from readers about this pattern. Photo courtesy of Bill Walter and Laurel Walton.

Cherry

The Cherry pattern was made by Bakewell, Pears, and Company about 1870, and can be found in crystal as well as opalescent glass in many shapes. The cherry design is very realistic and the leaves form arcs.

Cherry Panel (Dugan Cherry)

This Dugan pattern is better known in carnival glass, but can also seen in three of the four standard opalescent colors. The example shown has a goofus treatment with the cherries done in red and the leaves in gold. Production dates from 1907. The only shape reported in opalescent glass is the three-footed bowl, often shaped in a variety of ways, including a vase whimsey.

Christmas Pearls

Occasionally called Beaded Panel (it isn't the same as the Beaded Panels pattern often called Opal Open), this quite rare and beautiful pattern is most likely a Jefferson Glass design that dates from 1901 – 1903. The only shapes reported are the cruet shown and a salt shaker.

Christmas Snowflake

This pattern was produced by the Northwood Company in 1888, and later continued by Dugan Glass after Northwood left the Indiana, Pennsylvania, factory. It was made in both plain and ribbed pieces in water sets (at least two distinct pitcher shapes are known), as well as a few other shapes. In 1980 several reproduction shapes were sold by L.G. Wright including a plain water set, and new shapes that include a sugar shaker, barber bottle, syrup, basket, cruet, bride's bowl, milk pitcher, creamer, and rose bowls in two sizes. The original lamps were made in three sizes. Colors for old pieces are the standard ones, with the old cruet known only in white.

Chrysanthemum Base Swirl

This was first from Buckeye Glass, then Northwood (speckled finish). Production dates from 1890 in white, blue, or cranberry (shown), sometimes in a satin finish. It was made in a host of shapes. Northwood's speckled pieces are in the same shapes. Photo courtesy of Rick and Debbie Graham.

Chrysanthemum Swirl Variant

Here is a very scarce variant pattern that is credited to the Northwood Company by some. It has even been called a mystery variant. In size and make-up, the tankard pitcher is much like Ribbed Opal Lattice, also credited to Northwood from 1888; however, if you examine the color of the pitcher here, you will find it anything but typical of that company. It isn't blue or even green, but a very strong teal. It can also be found in white and cranberry. It is possible the design was first made elsewhere and Northwood produced later versions.

Circled Scroll

This pattern was made in 1904 by the Dugan Glass Company and continued when the factory became Diamond. It is found in carnival glass, apple green glass, and opalescent glass. It can be found in a variety of shapes in three standard colors.

Cirrus Feather Lamp

This 16" oil lamp is reported to be from Czechoslovakia and is the first I've seen. Vaseline is the only reported color on this rather large lamp. Photo courtesy of the Sandemans.

Cleopatra's Fan

After a series of names, the latest seems to be Cleopatra's Fan. This pattern is actually a product of Dugan and was never a part of the Northwood line. It is known in white, blue, and green opalescent glass and is quite scarce and collectible.

Coin Dot Lamps

There are three very distinctive oil lamps known in the Coin Dot pattern. The largest lamp is called Inverted Thumbprint and Fan base and dates from 1890. It can be found in white and blue opal. The other table lamp is called Chevron Base and is shown in an 1893 U.S. Glass ad, made by King Glass of Pittsburgh. I strongly suspect the small hand lamp was from the same company since they have the same font shape.

Coinspot (Dugan)

Coinspot was made from 1906 to 1909 and shown in a Dugan/Diamond company catalog in 1907 as their #900 lemonade set. This very nicely shaped pitcher was made in decorated glass as well as opalescent glass. The almost melon ribbing of the lower portion of the pitcher is the distinctive characteristic. The ad shows pitchers and tumblers on a tray that probably didn't match. Photo courtesy of the Petrasichs.

Coinspot (Jefferson)

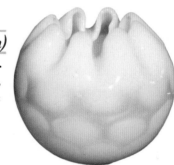

I believe this rose bowl was made by Jefferson from their salad bowl (Jefferson's #83). This company also made the water set (#180) in white, blue, green, and cranberry, which was later copied by the Fenton Company. Please note the base which has been ground.

Coinspot (Northwood)

Shown is the Northwood water pitcher with a ruffled top in a different shape than was shown in the fifth edition. These water sets were made at the Indiana, Pennsylvania, plant and production was continued when Dugan took over the plant. Butler Brothers catalog ads show this pattern in 1903 – 1904 from the Northwood/National production.

Coinspot and Swirl

Coinspot and Swirl was first thought to be from Hobbs and now is believed to be from Northwood. It was probably continued after the National Glass merger; production dates seem to be about 1898 – 1902. Several colors are known in this pattern. Shapes include a syrup (rare in cranberry) and a cruet (in the Parian Swirl mould). In addition, a rare amber has been reported but not confirmed by me.

Coin Spot (Phoenix)

This nice enameled bulbous vase is suspected to be a product of Phoenix Glass. Actually, some of the coin spots seem to be distorted into diamond shapes. The coloring is a light amber or apricot hue. Photo courtesy of Bill Walter and Laurel Walton.

Coinspot Syrup

While it is, at best, difficult to distinguish some moulds of one company from those of another, I truly believe the syrup shown is from the West Virginia Glass Company since the same shape can be found in their Polka Dot items where the dots are colored rather than opalescent.

Colonial Stairsteps

Although mostly found on this toothpick holder shape, a breakfast set consisting of a creamer and sugar is also known. Colors are crystal and blue opalescent only. Although the breakfast set has been reported with the Northwood trademark, none has been seen to date so the attribution is a bit shaky at this time.

Commonwealth

Shown is a standard tumbler, 3½" tall, with no pattern whatsoever. I believe this piece was used like the Universal tumbler and could be put with various pitchers to form a water set. Colors are blue or white opalescent, but certainly other treatments were made from this same mould. Opalescent pieces are known to have been enameled also.

Compass

This pattern was made by the Dugan/Diamond factory primarily as an exterior pattern on their Heavy Grape carnival glass pieces. It comes into its own in opalescent glass. It can be found on both 9" and 5½" bowls, as well as on 10" and 6½" plates. Some of these pieces are marked with the Diamond-D mark. The pattern is a good one with eight overlapping arcs and a marie (base) design of oversecting stars.

Concave Columns (#617)

As stated elsewhere (see Pressed Coinspot), this pattern was originally called #617 in a 1901 National Glass catalog and was later continued by Dugan/Diamond Glass in an ad assortment in the compote shape. For some strange reason, the vase has become known as Concave Columns. The compote in opalescent glass is known as Pressed Coinspot and in carnival glass it is simply called Coinspot. Shapes from the same mould are vases, compotes, goblets, and a stemmed banana boat. It is found in most of the standard colors.

Conch and Twig

This is another of those marvelous wall pocket vases the British made in opalescent glass. It was made by Burtles, Tate, and Company of England in 1885 with Rd. #39807. This one has the very natural look of a sea-shell with a twig-like holder or hanger. Most standard colors are known.

Consolidated Criss-Cross

Consolidated Criss Cross was produced by Consolidated Lamp & Glass Company of Fostoria, Ohio, from 1893 to 1894. This pattern is found in a host of shapes and most of the standard colors. This is a very collectible and scarce pattern.

Consolidated Shell

This beautiful 5" tall rose bowl was made by Consolidated Lamp & Shade Company in 1894. It is often found in opaque glass or crystal, but here is a beautiful vaseline glass example with rubina verde treatment and opalescent edges. The applied enameling of flowers and vines is very nice. It is also known as Shell and Seaweed. Thanks to the Petrasichs for sharing it.

Constellation

This very scarce compote was shown in a 1914 Butler Brothers ad for Dugan/Diamond Glass Company and was reported to be available in both white and blue opalescent. Originally the mould for this piece was the S-Repeat goblet (the pattern was originally called National and was a product of Northwood/National Glass from 1903). When Dugan obtained the National moulds, the exterior pattern became S-Repeat and the goblet was turned into a compote with a pattern on the interior called Constellation. In addition to the few opalescent items, many shapes were made in colored crystal with gilding, as well as a few shapes in carnival glass including the compote where the S-Repeat exterior is known as Seafoam.

Contessa

This hobnailed pattern, made by Greener & Company in England in 1890 and bearing Rd. #160244, can be found in several shapes including a pitcher, a two-piece footed breakfast set consisting of creamer and open sugar (shown), stemmed cake plate, and a handled basket. (All other shapes are considered much rarer.) Opalescent colors include blue, canary, and a rare amber.

Convex Rib

This pattern was made by Jefferson Glass around 1905. The vase has 24 convex ribs running from the indented base to near the top. It was also made in green, white, and vaseline opalescent as well as the blue shown.

Coral

The Coral pattern, found only on bowls with odd open work around the edging, may well be a product of the Jefferson Company. Colors are the usual: white, blue, green, and vaseline. While it has the same name as a Fenton carnival glass pattern, the design is far different.

Coral and Shell

This large, 9½" bowl is a standout in any collection. Designed and made by W. H. Heppell, the molds for this pattern were acquired by George Davidson & Co. when Heppell went out of business in the mid 1880s. Any opalescent pieces found should be considered to have been made by Davidson, with other types of glass being by Heppell. The bowl shown is listed in an 1885 catalog as pattern #134. Although other shapes were made in crystal and slag, the bowl is the only reported shape in opalescent glass to date. Thanks to the Petrasichs for the information and photo.

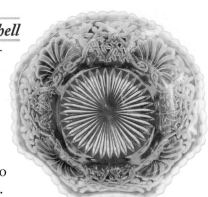

Coral Reef

While most collectors have lumped this pattern with Seaweed, it truly is a different pattern. It took a letter from a collector and an article by John D. Sewell to set the record straight. Seaweed has branches and distinct round dots while Coral Reef (Mr. Sewell's name) has a rambling line pattern with square-type extensions rather than dots. Coral Reef can be found in bitters bottles, barber bottles (round or square), finger bowls, rose bowls, lamps in four sizes including a mini night lamp, a stemmed oil lamp, a finger lamp, and a stemmed finger lamp. Photo courtesy of Rick and Debbie Graham.

Cornucopia

This 1905 Northwood novelty vase with handles can be found in white, blue, or green opalescent glass. Production continued for at least two years and despite there being rumors of this piece in carnival glass, none has ever surfaced. The design is almost like a wicker basketweave that rolls at the bottom to rest on a decorative base.

Cornucopia Vase

These little 4½" vases, 8" with the stand, are often attributed to Davidson but they don't actually match any known Davidson pattern. The closest resemblance would be to the Queen's Crown pattern, but still no match. They are fairly hard to come by, especially with the stand. Any new information about this piece would be appreciated. Photo courtesy of the Petrasichs.

Curtain Tie-Backs

Curtain Tie-Backs can be found in many shapes and with various designs. This particular set shows a daisy like flower pattern. White is the only reported color to date. Photo courtesy of Bill Walter and Laurel Walton.

Curvy

I have very little information concerning this nice epergne center lily except that it is almost certainly English. Vaseline is the only color reported and this is the only shape epergne I've seen. Thanks to the Sandemans for sharing it.

Cyclone

In previous editions I've shown this very scarce Northwood vase in vaseline (three reported) and blue (three reported), and here is the first white example I've seen. Cyclone measures about 7½" tall, has a base that matches the Beads and Bark vase, and a body like the Ocean Shell pattern.

Daffodils

Daffodils has been credited to Northwood and continued by Dugan at the Indiana, Pennsylvania, factory. This pattern is found in water sets (various shaped pitchers), two shapes of vases, lamps, and a bowl whimsey in white, canary, green, and blue. The example I show here is canary and has an enameled spider between the lower leaves, adding a real artist's touch to the piece.

Daffodils Oil Lamp

While both Northwood and Dugan/Diamond made this pattern in water sets, I believe this oil lamp shape was made by only Northwood about 1904 or 1905. Correspondence from their factory indicates they were making opalescent glass lamps, some with goofus base decorations and others with ruby staining on the base. Shown is a white opalescent glass table lamp with goofus on the base.

Daffodils Shade

I have no positive proof of the maker of this shade but highly suspect it to be English rather than from Northwood or Dugan like most Daffodil pieces. Richardson's, John Walsh Walsh, it's simply guesswork at this time. I'd like to thank the Sandemans for sharing it and encourage anyone with information on this pattern to contact me.

Dahlia

While I have questions about this piece shown (it sure looks like old glass), I know at least some of the opalescent pieces in this pattern (originally from Dugan in other treatments) are supposed to be new. L.G. Wright began marketing new Dahlia pieces in 1978. After their demise, production has been continued by others. Shapes known are water sets (with a new tumbler mould) and table sets, but others may exist. Buy with caution.

Dahlia Twist

Dahlia Twist was made by the Jefferson Glass Company around 1905 as their #207 pattern. It is a typical cone-shaped vase on a circular base with a flared and ruffled top. The real interest comes in the ribbing that is twisted against an interior optic that runs in the opposite direction.

Dahlia Twist Epergne

I am thrilled to show this very beautiful epergne as it was originally sold. Most collectors believe this Jefferson Glass lily had a glass dome-based bowl as a holder, but the lily was made expressly for decorative metal holders as shown in ads of the day. Most were silvered but a few were gilded as the one shown. The lily came in the usual opalescent colors and a similar lily and metal holder in the Fishnet pattern was sold by the Dugan/Diamond Company.

Daisies Lamp

This nicely done English oil lamp sports a well suited marbled stem and platform just above the base and has a very complementary design on the metalwork as well. The only color reported is vaseline. Photo courtesy of Steve and Radka Sandeman.

Daisies in Pentagon

This lamp, although somewhat similar to the Daisies Lamp, is a bit more sophisticated in appearance. With double green marble platforms separated by a band of fleur-de-lis in metalwork, this bracket footed lamp is a true piece of beauty. I feel certain it is English and thank the Sandemans for sharing this nice vaseline opalescent item with me.

Daisy and Button

Believed to be from Edward Bolton (Oxford Lane Glass Works) in England, this pattern and shape were later copied by Hobbs in non-opalescent colors and even later made by the Fenton Company for L.G. Wright. Both English and Hobbs productions date from the 1880s and the reproductions for Wright began in the late 1930s. Vintage and reproduction pieces are both found in the same colors.

Daisy and Button With Diamonds

This small 4½" bowl in vaseline is the only shape reported at this time and the only information I can give at this time is to say it is likely English. Any information would be appreciated. Photo courtesy of the Petrasichs.

Daisy and Drape

Daisy and Drape was produced by the Northwood Company primarily as a carnival glass pattern. This rare piece is one of three known in vaseline opalescent. It stands 6½" tall and has three rolled feet that carry the drape design from the vase on down. The pattern very much resembles a U.S. Glass pattern called Vermont, except for the ring of daisies that borders the top of the vase.

Daisy and Fern

This pattern was made at several factories including West Virginia Glass, Northwood (alone and as part of National), and the Dugan Company. It was reproduced and sold by L.G. Wright as early as 1939. New pieces are found in vaseline but not vintage pieces. Rose bowls, barber bottles, and cruets have been reproduced. Note: This same pattern is used on the three following molds from Northwood. Photo is courtesy of Sharron Lancaster.

Daisy and Fern (Apple Blossom Mould)

Northwood's Apple Blossom Mould line was never reproduced like many other Daisy and Fern items. It can be found in several shapes including a spooner (shown), creamer, sugar, and night lamp. The spooner shape also doubled as a pickle caster insert. (This is the same pattern as Daisy and Fern, using a different mould.)

Daisy and Fern (Parian Swirl Mould)

This pattern is on Northwood's Parian Swirl mould just like the Christmas Snowflake cruet. A close examination reveals the swirl design in the mould, shown just below the handle on the cruet shown. (This is the same pattern as Daisy and Fern, using a different mould.)

Daisy and Fern (Swirl Mould)

This Northwood mould has a wide swirl in the glass. It can be found in several shapes including a water pitcher, tumbler, cruet, salt shaker, syrup, berry bowl, sauce, toothpick holder, spooner (caster insert), sugar shaker, covered sugar, covered creamer, and a covered butter dish. (This is the same pattern as Daisy and Fern, using a different mould.) Photo courtesy of Rick and Debbie Graham.

Daisy and Greek Key

Recent evidence now confirms this pattern isn't from Davidson but was a product of Gerbruder von Streit of Germany in 1900. It was made in many shapes in crystal as well as opalescent glass according to Seigmar Geiselberger, a glass researcher in Germany.

Daisy and Plume

While this famous design was made for years under the Northwood/National banner, the example shown comes from the Dugan Company, despite having no holes in the legs. The mould work is excellent and there is no Northwood marking. Dugan ads date from 1907 on this footed rose bowl.

Daisy Block Row Boat

This novelty piece was from Sowerby in England as early as 1886. It is found in opalescent glass and other types of glass. The pieces originally had a stand. Sizes of 10", 12", and 15" are known (the largest size is shown). Colors in opalescent glass are limited to this very pale vaseline or green coloring.

Daisy Dear

This unimaginative exterior pattern was made by the Dugan/Diamond Company and is well known to carnival glass collectors. It is found in white, green, or blue opalescent glass bowls of all shapes and plates like the ruffled example shown. Production began in 1907. The pattern shows four blossom-and-leaf sprigs around the bowl and a daisy design on the marie.

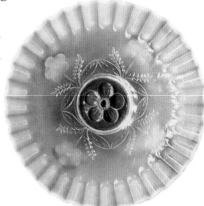

Daisy Drape

This well done creamer in vaseline opalescent is the only shape and color reported at this time and I'm certain it is of English origin. Any information on this pattern would be appreciated. Thanks to Kent with the Vaseline Glass Collectors Group for the name.

Daisy in Criss-Cross

Daisy in Criss-Cross is believed to be from Beaumont Glass Company, dating from about 1895. It can be found in water sets and a scarce syrup. Both the pitcher and the syrup have a ringed neck. Colors are mostly blue, white, cranberry, sapphire blue, and a strange pastel sapphire, but there is also a scarce green set, which I am happy to finally show.

Daisy May

This design was made by the Dugan Glass Company, primarily as a carnival glass novelty called Leaf Rays. It is also found in opalescent glass on the spade-shaped nappy. While the carnival design is interior, the opalescent pieces have the pattern on the exterior.

Daisy Swirl

I suspect the bowl and plate shown is English, probably from Davidson, but have no proof. It is fairly deep and has great vaseline color with strong opalescence. It is also found on a whimsey in a metal stand. I'd certainly appreciate hearing from anyone who has additional information about this pattern. Photo courtesy of the Petersons.

Daisy With Panels

This interesting little bowl has 12 panels with daisy-like medallions jutting out and downwards at a slight angle with additional daisies around the footed area. Blue is the only color reported and this piece is the only shape reported to date. Thanks to the Petrasichs for sharing it.

Daisy Wreath

I am extremely pleased to show this very rare item from the Westmoreland Company. It is usually found in carnival glass on a milk glass base, but here is a rich blue glass with opalescent edges. The bowl is 9" in diameter and is the only example in opalescent glass I've seen without iridescence.

Dandelion Mug

This mug is found mostly in carnival glass in a host of colors. It is rarer than even the Singing Birds mugs, also by the Northwood Company. Here I show one of the ultra-rare blue opalescent versions (three or four known) and its beauty is obvious. The carnival version dates from early 1912, so I believe the Dandelion opalescent ones were made at the same time. Thanks to the late Jack Beckwith for sharing this rarity.

Davidson Drape

I feel safe in calling this another piece from the Davidson & Company Glass Works of England. I'm surprised I haven't seen more of these. This one is vaseline and I'm sure blue was made. Thanks to the Petrasichs for sharing it.

Davidson Germany Souvenir

What a nice little piece this is. The 5½" plate is labeled Strandschloss Kohlberg, which is a resort town on the German/Belgium border. This George Davidson pattern has the Rd. #340825 which places it in 1899. This is actually the same pattern as Double Rib & Block shown later in this edition. I've shown both examples of labels, although there are other labels found on this same piece. This is not a transfer, but rather an example of where the usual star pattern on the base is replaced with a smooth disk, then the cardboard souvenir is placed in the center. Thanks to Dave Peterson for the photo and information.

Davidson Open Salts

I'm happy to be able to show several open salt dips from George Davidson, all of which are different in shape and size to some degree. The color on each is vaseline opalescent although other colors may exist. Most of these can also be found in metal holders.
Thanks again to the Petersons for sharing glass from their nice collection.

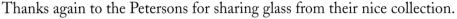

Davidson Pearline Epergne

This dramatic 14" four-lily epergne sits on a very deep well bowl with the same feet Davidson used on other items (see Lady Caroline pattern). I believe this epergne was made in blue pearline also and possibly white which Davidson called Moonshine Pearline. The glass is thin and of very fine quality.

Davidson Shell

Here is the spill vase shape in this Davidson pattern advertised in 1889. It is found in canary or blue opalescent glass. Thanks to Ruth Harvey for sharing this piece with me.

Davidson's #269

This English marmalade set is encircled with daisy or dotted medallions and sits in a fitted metal holder. The Rd. #533040 indicates a date of 1908. It is found in a larger bowl shape and was one of Davidson's more popular patterns. Photo courtesy of Ruth Harvey.

Davidson Swan

This 6" swan is reported to be from Davidson. There is also a 3½" version. It has only been reported in two opalescent colors to date. Photo courtesy of the Petrasichs.

Deco Lily

I have no information about this nice 7¾" vase. The Petrasichs who own it believe it is American and it certainly doesn't have the look of English or European glass. It is green opalescent but has a strong vaseline look. I welcome any information about it.

Decorated English Swirl

The Swirl pattern was made in England as well as America. Here is one in a beautiful rose bowl that shades from white to cranberry and has an enameled decoration of flowers and leaves. This piece has a pontil mark and is, of course, blown. Photo courtesy of Kathy Gresko.

Desert Garden

This novelty dome-base bowl pattern can be found in three opalescent colors. The design of three sets of leaves bracketing a stylized blossom with a stippled background isn't very imaginative but does fill most of the available space. The example shown, like most, has a ribbon-candy edging that adds to the appearance. The maker hasn't been determined, but I lean toward Dugan/Diamond.

Diagonal Swirl

The maker of this piece in its nice metal holder has not been determined. It has a gold foil sticker on the side with "22 Carat Gold Plate" around the edge with a script "L" with a flower to the right of it. Any information is appreciated on this piece. Photo courtesy of Bill Walter and Laurel Walton.

Diagonal Wave

Like the Waves pattern and the Diamond Wave pattern, this piece is very thin glass that has been mould blown. I suspect this piece may be British and probably came in blue as well as the vaseline shown.

Diamond

This pattern of simple diamonds is likely English but it is not confirmed as such to date. This is the only color and shape reported. Photo courtesy of the Petrasichs.

Diamond and Daisy (Caroline)

Ads in a 1909 Butler Brothers catalog identify this pattern as part of the Intaglio line from the Dugan Company. It is clearly shown in a handled basket shape, so I know at least two shapes were made. Dugan first advertised the Intaglio line in 1905 in blue, green, and white opalescent. The pattern of Diamond and Daisy is very similar to the Wheel and Block pattern. It is known as Caroline in carnival glass. Photo courtesy of Rick and Debbie Graham.

Diamond and Oval Thumbprint

This very attractive design, found only on the vase shape, is from the Jefferson Glass Company, circa 1904. It can be found in white, blue, and green opalescent glass and may vary in size from 6" tall to 14".

Diamond Band

This diamond pattern vanity jar (lid missing) is possibly English but I have no proof. This is the only shape and color reported in this pattern at this time. Photo courtesy of the Petrasichs.

Diamond Dot

This nicely done pattern appears to be a product of John Walsh Walsh, although I have no solid proof. Shapes are the compote shown and a shade. The only color reported at this time is vaseline opalescent. Anyone with information is urged to contact me. Thanks to the Keathleys for sharing this nice item.

Diamond-in-Diamond

What a beautiful pattern this is! It consists of smaller diamonds that are blocked into larger shapes. The opalescence is outstanding. It has the look of British glass but I haven't been able to pin the maker down yet. The blue glass has a slight aqua tint.

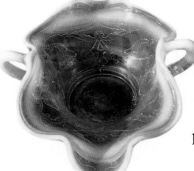

Diamond Maple Leaf

This hard-to-find two-handled bonbon attributed to the Dugan Glass Company (Dugan/Diamond) can be found three opalescent colors. The design shows rather realistic maple leaves flanked by very flowing scroll designs that give the piece a real artistic look. Diamond Maple Leaf dates from 1909.

Diamond Optic

I know very little about this attractive piece except it is from England. I base this on the finish and shaping. It may be known by another name also, but I felt this name summed up the configuration as well as any. The diamond pattern is all on the inside and runs from the outer rim to a middle diameter above the stem. It has been reported only in white opalescent to date.

Diamond Point

This Northwood pattern dates from 1907. It is found only on the vase shape in white, blue, and green opalescent glass, and many carnival glass colors. Sizes range from 8" to a lofty 14" that has been swung to reach that size.

Diamond Point and Fleur-de-Lis

This pattern was made by the Northwood Company and illustrated in their 1906 ads. Most pieces can be found with the Northwood trademark. Novelty bowls with a collar base can be found, some shapes have been whimsied, and a nut bowl shape is known. It is reported in white, blue, and green opalescent. Thanks to Samantha Prince for the photo.

Diamond Point Columns

While many carnival glass collectors are familiar with this pattern and associate it with the Imperial Glass Company of Bellaire, Ohio, it was a product of the Fenton Company, shown in Butler Brothers ads with other Fenton patterns. In opalescent glass, only the vase has been reported, and I am very happy to show an example of this. This opalescent piece stands 12" tall and was made in 1907.

Diamond Pyramid

Here is a better shot of the four-footed bowl shown previously. The pattern is unlisted as far as I know, but certainly looks English and probably came from Sowerby. I've taken the liberty of naming it. The color is strong vaseline and other colors and shapes are possible. Anyone with information on this pattern is urged to contact me.

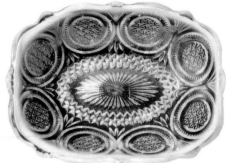

Diamond Rings

I have little information on this nice rectangular bowl other than to say it is English. This is the only shape reported at this time and vaseline is the only color I've seen. Many thanks again to the Vaseline Glass Collectors Group for naming this pattern and thanks to the Sandemans for the nice photo.

Diamonds

Once thought to be from Hobbs, Brockunier, or Northwood, and possibly later from Czechoslovakia (unconfirmed), this is now known to be a product of Phoenix Glass Co. of Monaco, PA, circa 1888. Shapes include a water set (4 pitcher sizes are known), cruet, a sugar shaker, various bowls as well as a handgrip bowl. Colors are white, blue, cranberry, and rubina opalescent glass. Pieces may be crackled or not. Thanks to Bill Walter and Laurel Walton.

Diamonds and Swags

This 8⅝" bowl shows characteristics from Greener and Co. but I have no proof that it was made at that concern. The name given by its owner certainly seems appropriate. This is the only shape I've seen to date, and vaseline is the only reported color so far. Additional information is appreciated. Thanks to the Petrasichs for sharing it.

Diamonds and Wedges

This square bowl of fine crystal is the only reported shape in this pattern and white is the only color I've seen. Additional information is requested. Photo courtesy of the Petrasichs.

Diamond Spearhead

This is Northwood's #22 pattern made when they were part of National in 1901. It can be found in crystal as well as opalescent glass. It is found in a host of shapes and several colors. The water pitcher and the creamer are found in more than one size.

Diamond Stem

This very scarce vase from Model Flint dates from about 1900. It's now known to be made in three sizes, 6½", 8½", and 10½". It is found in a variety of colors. Vases are found in straight, ruffled, flared, and the familiar turned-in top. Some of these shapes can be seen in "What Collecting Is All About" in this edition. The name comes from the knob on the stem that has diamond facets.

Diamond Tree

This beautiful vaseline opalescent bowl is a real mystery. I haven't been able to locate it anywhere, but strongly suspect it to be English. At any rate I've given it a name and welcome any information readers may offer. A tumbler is also known.

Diamond Wave

Diamond Weave was first found in amethyst opalescent or cranberry opalescent, and here I show a pitcher with lid in vaseline. A child's or demitasse cup and saucer are also known in canary. It was made in the Czech Republic, about 1880 – 1890. All items reported are mould blown. No new information has surfaced on this pattern since the previous edition, but I would certainly like to know more. Photo courtesy of Kelvin Russell.

Diamond Wide Stripe

This mystery pattern is credited to Nickel Plate, Hobbs, and others, but here is a pitcher that has the Northwood Swirl mould. Whoever made it, the pattern is stunning with a diamond crosshatching added. Some call this Diamond Quilted Wide Stripe as well. The color is cranberry.

Dimple

Similar to the British Flute shaping but without the interior fluting, this British piece can be found with squared dimpling on each side or plain like the example shown. I suspect this piece is from Greener & Company, but have no proof. The shape shown is called a spill and was used to hold matches (some refer to it as a toothpick holder). Thanks to the Sandemans for sharing it.

Dogwood Drape

I want to thank all those who pointed out the pattern I called Palm Rosette was really Dogwood Drape. The plate and the compote are still the only shapes I've heard about and I still suspect the design is English although I have no proof. Only white opalescent has been reported to date.

Dolly Madison

This Jefferson Glass Company pattern, originally called #271, was first produced in 1907. Several shapes and colors are known. The design uses flowers, stems, and leaves in every other panel.

Dolphin

Originally made by the Northwood Company as early as 1902, this beautiful compote has been widely reproduced in all colors, so buy only what you are confident with. The older compotes have a stronger color and better glass clarity but those are about the only differences.

Dolphin and Herons

This rare and desirable pattern, made in Albany, Indiana, by Model Flint Glass, is found mostly in opalescent glass in a stemmed compote or the card tray shown. (A very rare crystal vase from the same mould is known and shown in my pressed glass book.) Colors vary, with cranberry being rare. The design has a dolphin for a stem with the bowl in its mouth with a herons design on the bowl. It is approximately 6½" tall.

Dolphin and Shell

The owner of this very nice spill tells me that the seller thought it was possibly a Sowerby piece but that it also looked somewhat like Westmoreland's Dolphin and Shell, although no opalescent pieces have surfaced in that pattern from Westmoreland. So, at this time it will remain as maker unknown. White opalescent is the only color reported at this time. Thanks to the Petrasichs for sharing it.

Dolphin Petticoat

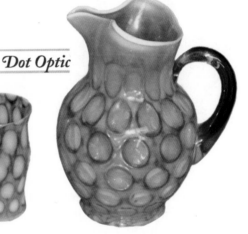

Shards of these lovely candlesticks have been found at the Indiana, Pennsylvania, factory dump site and the pattern is shown in a National Glass ad, so I know the Northwood Company made these while a part of the National combine. The mould work is outstanding, as is the design.

Dorset

According to recent information this pattern is a product of Greener & Company. Various sizes of oval and round bowls, a creamer, and sugar are the only pieces reported to date. Colors reported are blue and vaseline. There was a bit of confusion as to whether the bowl shown was the same pattern as the creamer shown on the back cover of the fifth edition but I am most certain they are the same pattern. Thanks to the Petrasichs and the Sandemans for photos sent to me in this pattern as well as providing the additional shapes to add to the list.

Dot Optic

Dot Optic was made by the Fenton Glass Company as early as 1910 in amethyst opalescent items. The pitcher shown dates from 1921. It is a tankard shape but the same design can be found in bulbous styles as well. Dot Optic is characterized by dots that recede into the glass and differ from the similar Coin Dot pattern in this respect. It can be found in four shapes and most of the standard colors.

Dotted Spiral

This English pattern can be found in a variety of vase shapes as well as a bowl in metal holder with a handle. The only color reported at this time is vaseline opalescent. The maker is uncertain.

Double Diamonds

This bowl has a pattern consisting of a series of diamonds within diamonds and it has a heavy opalescent treatment on the edge. The color is a nice vaseline opal and I'm certain it is English, although the maker has yet to be established. Thanks to the Sandemans for sharing it.

Double Dolphin

The opalescent production of Fenton's #1533 pattern, dating from the 1920s, was very limited. Colors I've verified are blue and white (Fenton calls this French opalescent). This dolphin design was, of course, one of the company's favorites and has been used in many shapes and sizes for 75 years.

Double Greek Key

Double Greek Key was first a product of the Nickel Plate Glass Company of Fostoria, Ohio, and after 1892 it was a product of U.S. Glass. Shapes include a table set, berry set, water set, a celery vase, toothpick holder, mustard pot, syrup, pickle dish, and shakers. Colors in opalescent glass are white and blue.

Double Marmalade

This Thomas Webb pattern is shown in a color known as Lemonescent, which uses a combination of cranberry and vaseline glass. The holder is an aftermarket piece modeled from an original that was made for a single marmalade holder. Photo and information courtesy of the Petersons.

Double Panel

I know very little about this English bowl except to say it has an exterior paneling that is in two parts, hence the name. In addition it has a very attractive etched blossom and vine running around the upper bowl. I'd certainly appreciate any information about this bowl and am indebted to the Petrasichs for sharing it with me.

Double Rib and Block

The same process is used on this bowl as on the Davidson Germany Souvenir piece shown earlier in this book, and in fact they are both the same pattern with different labels. (There are other labels found on these pieces as well.) This particular George Davidson & Co. 5½" bowl has the Rd. #340825 made in 1899. The only color reported is vaseline. Thanks to the Petrasichs for sharing it.

Double Salt with Ring Handle

This ribbed double salt is likely a European product but there is no reported maker to date. Notice the ring handle, which is a nice touch. Any information is welcomed. Photo courtesy of the Petrasichs.

English Mystery Shade

This interesting shade has been a puzzle to me for quite some time. No collector I conferred with seems to know it by name or could speculate on any possibility of a maker other than maybe John Walsh Walsh. I finally assigned this name and do hope someone will shed some light on this piece. To add to the interest of this shade, one only needs to look at the ruffled top on the two examples shown; the patterns are upside down from one another. Photo courtesy goes to the Keathleys and to Bill Walter and Laurel Walton.

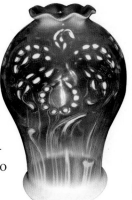

English Oak Leaf

English Oak Leaf is found in this strange tri-colored bowl, a boat shape, and rectangular posy. It is from Bartles, Tate, and Company and has the Rd. #29106, dating it to 1885. It is patterned on the exterior with oak leaves. The exterior base is wedge-shaped. I've seen this piece in both the canary shown and blue opalescent glass.

English Optic Epergne

Standing 17" tall, this four-lily epergne with rigoree decoration, cranberry-throated lilies, and applied edging is about as decorative a piece of opalescent art glass as you are apt to see. It is English and probably dates to the 1880s or 1890s.

English Ripple

This is very similar to the Herringbone pattern, but has a softer rolling of the opalescent lines. I strongly suspect this is an English pattern. Please note that the base ends in panels that run from the top of the tumbler and extend down and over the bottom. It was probably made in blue also but I haven't seen one. Thanks to the Petrasichs for sharing it.

English Salt Dip

What a fancy piece of table service this is! The vaseline opalescent salt dip, measuring 2¼" wide and 1⅜" tall, sits atop a silver tray that bears the marking: JH EPNS. The coloring of the dip (or fill) is typically English but I'm confident these came in other colors too. It was made by Davidson, circa 1911, and has Rd. #577153.

English Shell

This nice little shell piece is only 2" tall and 3" wide. I assume it was used as a salt dip. Note the applied feet with a fan design stamped in between each foot. Surely English in origin, this is the only example I've had reported to date. Photo courtesy of Ruth Harvey.

English Swan

This beautiful swan is the smaller (and the rarer) of two sizes made by Burtles, Tate & Company of England. These were made in 1885. The example shown is 3½" long and 3½" tall. The larger size measures 4½" long and has Rd. #20086. These are mostly found in canary opalescent glass with a soft coloring but can also be found in white and blue opalescent.

English Swirl (Cased)

Reported to be from England, this water set is an opalescent reverse swirl design with an inner casing of cranberry glass. The pitcher is a squat ball-shaped one with an applied reeded handle. The owner describes this set as being like striped candy.

English Wide Stripe

This pitcher is a bit of a mystery. I believe it may well be an English version of the Wide Stripe pattern but I can't rule out other makers like Phoenix or La Belle. As you can see, the coloring is cranberry with a distinctive amber reed handle. I'd appreciate any information readers may have about this piece.

Entangled Branches

The owner of this interesting oil lamp thought the design looked like branches so I incorporated her observation into the name and I hope she approves. This is the only example I've seen to date of this nice vaseline opalescent lamp. Thanks to Ruth Harvey for sharing this interesting item.

Estate

This pattern, also called Stippled Estate, is known to have been made by the Dugan/Diamond Company in 1906 and by Model Flint in 1900 – 1902. In opalescent glass, colors are white, blue, and green, but it is also found in carnival glass and in green, amber, and speckled glass. Vases come in 2½", 3½", 4½", and 5½" and Model Flint also made a cruet shape.

European Lily Epergnes

These two epergnes with single lilies are from Sweden. They differ in size but both have similar lilies that are blown with a top twist and have interior ridges. The holders appear to be silver plate and are identical.

Everglades

This 1903 Northwood pattern was originally called Carnelian. It was made in several glass treatments with opalescent glass being found in several shapes and colors.

Everglades (Cambridge)

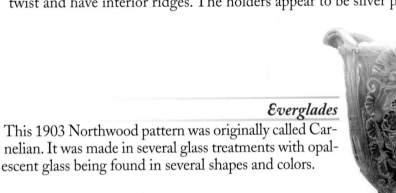

Everglades is a production name used by the Cambridge Company covering a line of items made from 1920 to the 1930s. The compote shown in white opalescent glass is simply one design from this line. It measures 7½" in diameter. In 1933, the Cambridge catalog listed 43 items in this line, including vases with flower patterns and a bowl with an Indian on horseback hunting buffalo. The line was made in many treatments and colors from 1924 to 1958.

Exterior Thumbprint Vase

I've learned very little about this beautiful vaseline opalescent vase since I first saw it. It measures 13¾" tall and has a 13-pointed star base and six large thumbprints on the exterior, just above the base. In addition there is a series of six vertical ribs that separate the thumbprints. I'd appreciate any input readers may have about this pattern.

Fan

Although long considered a Northwood pattern, Fan is actually from the Dugan/Diamond plant. Water sets, berry sets, and table sets are shown in green, white, and blue opalescent glass in a 1907 company ad. In a whimsey plate that was shaped from the spooner, the glass almost glows with opalescence.

Fan and Shell

I am told by the owner of this beautiful vase that it may be from Greener & Company and I believe this may well be true. The base is shaped like a shell and another shell design extends up to the middle of the vase. I'd appreciate any information about this pattern. Thanks to Ruth Harvey for sharing it.

Fancy Fantails

While others credit this pattern to the Northwood Company, I'm convinced it is from Jefferson. As I've said before, research has convinced me most, if not all, of the cranberry decorated items came from Jefferson Glass. Fancy Fantails dates from 1905 and can be found in both rose bowls and candy dishes from the same mould.

Feathered Hearts

No maker has been confirmed for this lovely English shade, shown in cranberry opalescent, but nonetheless it is a really nice item and I like the design. I've heard it called Peacock Eye but have elected to go with another name to avoid confusing it with other items of that name. I would think other shapes exist but haven't seen them to date. Thanks to John and Monica Vanspall for sharing this fine piece of glass.

Feathers

There's no question about the maker of this vase since most are marked with the Northwood trademark. Vases are the only shape, and the colors are white, blue, and green opalescent. Sizes range from 7" to a pulled 13". I've seen a blue opalescent and a white opalescent vase with gold edging.

Fenton's #100 Ringed Bowl

This small bowl on stubby feet was made first in 1929 and measures 7½" across and the plate from the same mould is ½" wider. The only pattern is the exterior rings that extend from the feet up the sides of the piece. This pattern is called Hoops in carnival glass.

Fenton's #220 Stripe

This popular Fenton pattern, produced in 1929, is found in iced tea sets (there are two shapes and sizes in pitchers), creamer, sugar, and tumble ups (guest sets). Colors are blue, green, white, and vaseline, and both pitcher and tumblers have contrasting colored handles. Note that the pitcher shown has a matching lid but not all shapes do.

Fenton's #260

This regal 7" tall compote was made by the Fenton Art Glass Company in all sorts of glass treatments including ebony opaque, stretch glass, Grecian gold carnival, and opalescent glass as shown, where the colors are white, topaz, and blue. Production of the compote dates from 1915 to the 1930s in ruby glass.

Fenton's #370

This beauty dates from the 1924 – 1927 period of Fenton production. The cameo opalescent coloring is a real treat and I'm happy to be able to show this example. This same coloring can be found in many patterns and shapes in the Fenton line including bowls, vases, nappies, and bonbons. The vase color is a strong amber and the opalescence is a rich creamy tint.

Fenton's Plain Jane

Usually seen on white opalescent glass, this completely plain design from the Fenton Art Glass Company is rarely seen in amethyst opalescent glass. A water set with tankard pitcher and a hat shape are known.

Fern

This pattern was made by several companies including West Virginia Glass, Beaumont, Model Flint, and probably Northwood. It is found in a wide variety of shapes and in several colors. Production of Fern dates from 1898 to 1906 and the Fenton Company reproduced this pattern beginning in the 1950s. Thanks to Kelvin Russell for the photo.

Fern Panels (Fenton)

Occasionally found in carnival glass, this is the very first piece in opalescent glass I've heard about and as you can see, it is a beautiful amethyst opalescent color. The shape is a hat that has been pulled in a JIP shape.

Festive Flowers

This very nicely done spill vase from England is decorated in coralene (frit) which gives the vase a very interesting look. I'm also told that it has a patent mark on the bottom. White is the only color reported to date and this is the only shape I've been made aware of. Thanks to Ruth Harvey for sharing it.

Field Flowers

In addition to the compotes in 7½" and 9" sizes, I am happy to report the opalescent bowl that measures 7¼" in diameter in this pattern. Many shapes are shown in the Inwald Glass Works of Czechoslovakia 1900 catalog in crystal so I may well expect other shapes to turn up in opalescent glass.

Field of Flowers

I'm showing the interior of this nice compote in order to give readers a better look at the pattern for identification purposes. Ten flowers circle the outer edge of the compote (which has a totally stippled background) with many entangled stems going into the center and also you'll see the presence of two buds in the design. Blue is the only reported color at this time and the compote is the only shape known to me presently, although I feel other shapes and colors may exist. Any information on this nice pattern would be appreciated. Thanks to the Sandemans for sharing it.

File and Fan

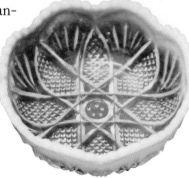

Despite not locating this pattern in any reference sources, I feel this bowl may be foreign, possibly German or Czechoslovakian. I've given it a name but if any reader knows it by something else, I welcome your information. Thanks to the Petrasichs for sharing it.

Finecut and Roses

Early opalescent production of this pattern was at Jefferson's Steubenville plant and Northwood later produced it in their lines of custard and carnival glass. Shapes (all from the same mould) are footed candy dishes, rose bowls, and a spooner that is slightly ruffled.

Fine Rib (Fenton)

I'm very happy to show this very rare Fenton vase pattern in opalescent glass. As you can see, the pattern was made in a beautiful vaseline opalescent treatment. This vase stands 11¼" tall with a 2⅞" base and a 3⅝" top opening. The opalescence runs well down the ribs and is just stunning. I believe this vase was made in the 1908 – 1910 era and there may well be other opalescent colors in this pattern.

Fine Rib (Northwood)

Opalescent glass collectors often refer to this as Many Ribs. Although not rare when found in opalescent glass, it is mostly found in carnival glass. Unlike the Model Flint Glass example with this name, the base of the Northwood pattern is not columnated, and the design just rolls to an even finish above the straight base. Colors and sizes vary.

Fine Rib Epergne

I know very little about this attractive epergne except the Fine Rib design is very close to the Northwood and Fenton vase patterns found mostly in carnival glass (the Fenton design is also shown in a rare opalescent vase). The metal work on this epergne isn't brass as on most shown but is a pot metal called speltzer, here with a silvered finish. Any additional information on this epergne would be helpful.

Fish-in-the-Sea

The speculation is now over concerning the maker of this well done piece of glass. Thanks to a monograph from the West Virginia Museum of American Glass, Ltd. (edited by Neila & Tom Bredehoft), it is confirmed that this wonderful pattern was made by the Tygart Valley Glass Co. of Grafton, West Virginia. This vase is a very scarce item, much sought by collectors. Photo courtesy of Rick and Debbie Graham.

Fishnet Epergne

This four-lily epergne with a dome base is a puzzle. It has the fishnet lilies normally associated with the Dugan Company but it also has cranberry frit that suggests a Jefferson origin. In addition, the center lily is the same one found on the Strawberry Epergne I see in carnival glass that was made by Dugan, so maybe I have to consider this company as a frit user too. Thanks to Bill Walter and Laurel Walton for the photo.

Fishscale and Beads

This pattern was actually misnamed by Heacock some years ago; it was originally named Scales by Marion Hartung in the 1950s (there is another carnival pattern she named Fishscale and Beads). The opalescent bowls were made by Dugan and predate the carnival items. The beads are on the exterior while the scales are interior.

Fleur-de-lis

This 7¾" pitcher is unknown to me but the pattern has a look similar to some Northwood pieces, although I haven't found it in any catalog reprints to date and haven't seen this shape pitcher from Northwood. The interesting feature on this pitcher is the circle of teardrops on the base. This is the only shape I've seen and white is the only color reported to date. Thanks to the Petrasichs for sharing it and I do welcome any information readers might have concerning this pattern.

Fleur-de-lis in Panels

I suspect this piece is a marmalade dish which was once in a metal holder, but have no proof of such. The design and color is very similar to items made in the Stourbridge region of England. (Note the similarities to the Striped Lemonescent set by Thomas Webb shown later in this edition.) The color is a combination of cranberry and vaseline. This is the only piece reported in this pattern at the current time. Thanks to the Petrasichs for sharing.

Flora

Dating from 1898, this Beaumont pattern can be found in a variety of colors and shapes, and several novelty bowl shapes exist.

Floradine

If you will compare this piece with the Onyx one in this book, you will see they are the same pattern (both made in 1889 by Finley Glass) but have different treatments. The Floradine pieces are found in a satin treatment in ruby or autumn and shapes are various.

Floral and Vines

This pattern consists of flowers and entangled vines. This English shade, possibly Richardson's or John Walsh Walsh, is reported only in vaseline to date and the shade is the only shape I've seen so far. This pattern is simple but very nicely done and would grace any collection. Photo courtesy of the Sandemans.

Floral Eyelet

Little is known about this very scarce pattern. It is believed to be a product of Northwood/ National or even Dugan at the Indiana, Pennsylvania, plant. The time of production has been speculated from 1896 to 1905. The only shapes are a water pitcher and tumbler in white, blue, and cranberry opalescent. The tumbler is shown here. The reproduced pitcher, made by the L.G. Wright Company, is shown in the second edition of this book. The new pitchers have reeded handles while the old do not.

Floral Freeze

Although unmarked, this is a Davidson pattern shown in publications from that concern. The only pieces brought to my attention are the creamer and open sugar in blue, although other shapes and colors possibly exist. Photo courtesy of the Petrasichs.

Flower and Leaf

This very nice piece has Rd. #30704 which places it from Henry Johnson, Holbon Glass Maker, August 1, 1885. No other shapes or color are reported. Photo courtesy of the Petrasichs.

Flower Form

I have no idea what type of flower is represented on this English pattern but nonetheless it's nicely done and well worth owning. The shapes reported are a toothpick and a bulbous single lily epergne in a metal holder. Vaseline is the only color I've seen to date. Any information would be appreciated. Thanks to Ruth Harvey and the Petrasichs for the photo submissions.

Flowering Vine

I'm using what I'm told is the more commonly known name for this pattern in opalescent glass, although in non-opalescent glass it is referred to as Daisy Swag. It is not an easy pattern to find. It is found in several shapes but only in one opalescent color. Speculation puts this as a Davidson pattern although no examples have been found in Davidson catalog reprints or other publications. Thanks to the Petrasichs and the Sandemans for the photo submissions.

Flower Starburst

The rather large flowers on this lamp font seem to provide total coverage, leaving little room for any other addition to the pattern. The ornate base and overall look of this lamp would make it a welcomed edition to any collector's group of lamps or opalescent glass. The only color reported so far is vaseline. The maker in unknown. Thanks to Steve and Radka Sandeman for the photo.

Fluted and Box Pleated Epergne

This 23" tall Stevens and Williams epergne has two lilies on the side, one center lily, and two side hanging baskets. This wonderful epergne is reported in vaseline only. Photo courtesy of the Keathleys.

Fluted Bars and Beads

Once thought to be from Northwood, Fluted Bars and Beads is now known to be from Jefferson Glass, first made in 1904. Shapes are compotes and novelty whimsies from the same mould. It is found in the standard opalescent colors. Many pieces have frit trim.

Fluted Scrolls (Jackson)

Made by Northwood in 1898 under the name Klondike, this pattern is known today as Fluted Scrolls or Jackson. It can be found in several opalescent colors and a host of shapes. It has been reproduced for Rosso.

Fluted Scroll with Vine

This Northwood pattern is shown as early as 1899 in a Butler Brothers ad. The design of flowers, stems, and leaves winding around a fluted, cone-shaped vase is very pretty; when you add the base of spread leaves and the top rim of scalloped blossoms, the whole piece becomes a real work of art. Photo courtesy of Samantha Prince.

Footed Stripe

With feet resembling roots as well as the overall look of this piece it most certainly has to be English, although no maker is confirmed at this time. The only noticeable pattern is the rather wide stripes, hence the name. This is the only shape reported and vaseline opalescent is the color. Thanks to Ruth Harvey for the photo.

Forked Stripe

If you look at the base of this barber bottle, you'll se the stripes end in points, so I've given it this name. This piece is white opalescent, measures 7" tall, and has a base diameter of 3½". It is marked on the base "PAT-PENGING." The maker isn't known at this time, but a pitcher from a very limited Imperial Glass production in 1930 has this same pointed finish to its stripe except it is reversed and faces upwards.

Fountain With Bows

In previous editions this was listed as Jack-in-the-Pulpit. Being as the JIP name primarily describes a shape, I decided to change the name to better suit this particular pattern design. The pattern has a distinct bow at the bottom of what looks like a fountain spraying up into the air. Shapes are lamp shades and various vases. Colors are vaseline opalescent and a cranberry opalescent. It is likely made in England although no specific maker is reported at this time. Thanks to Ruth Harvey for sharing it.

Four-Footed Hobnail

This pattern is now confirmed to be a product of La Belle Glass of Bridgeport, Ohio, in 1886. The only shapes are the butter, creamer, sugar, and spooner. Colors are white, dark blue, and canary. Thanks to the Petrasichs for sharing it.

Four Pillars

Four Pillars was made in opalescent glass by Northwood and later in carnival glass by both Northwood and Dugan/Diamond. This vase is also found with advertising on some Northwood carnival pieces. The four columns or pillars run from top to bottom and end in four rounded feet. Sizes range from 9" to 14" tall, and some pieces from Dugan/Diamond have gilding.

Frosted Leaf and Basketweave

This pattern was a product of the Chicago Flint Glass Company of Chesterton, Indiana (it was long thought to be from Northwood). It is found in table set pieces and the spooner can be found whimsied into a vase shape.

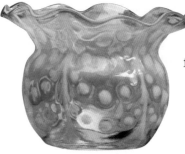

Fruit Tree

The design of this interesting ruffled vase appears to have berries hanging from tree branches. I suspect this is an English product, possibly from John Walsh Walsh. Additional information is appreciated. Photo and name are courtesy of Ruth Harvey.

Garland of Roses

Garland of Roses is found primarily in crystal or vaseline glass. This is a small cake stand or card tray, flattened from a jelly compote shape. This is the only shape reported at this time. I'd like to hear from anyone having other shapes or colors of this pattern in an opalescent treatment. The piece shown measures 6⅝" across and stands 2" tall.

Giant Clam Shell

This 8" shell bowl is almost certainly an English product but the maker is unconfirmed to date. This is the only shape and size I've seen on this vaseline piece. Thanks to Frank and Melissa Keathley for sharing it.

Gonterman (Adonis) Hob

Like the Swirl pattern with the same titles, this is an Aetna Glass pattern dating from 1886 (despite bearing "Pat'd Aug 4, 1876" on the base). Unlike the Swirl pattern, there doesn't seem to be a blue version, only the amber. Only the cruet shown has been reported, and it is extremely hard to find and has to be considered rare.

Gonterman (Adonis) Swirl

This pattern is also known as Adonis Swirl. It can be found on both frosted and opalescent pieces and is attributed to Aetna Glass by most collectors (the patent was issued to Hobbs, Brockunier & Company for the joining process). One writer believes Hobbs may have licensed Aetna to do the pattern. Pieces are known in either blue or amber with opalescence in a variety of shapes. Pieces are marked "Patented August 5, 1876," but this refers to the joining process and is not a production date, which is a decade later. Photo courtesy of Rick and Debbie Graham.

Grace Darling

Grace Darling was a heroine during the early nineteenth century in England who helped rescue a group of people who had been shipwrecked. Books have been written about her. She was about 12 or 13 years old when she helped her father rescue the stranded boaters. Grace Darling is actually embossed inside this boat, both in the bottom and the stern. The Rd. number is 39414. A second number is just for the inscription of Grace Darling Boat: Rd. #23527. The piece was made by Edward Bolton and the design was registered on December 11, 1885. The version shown is 11¼" in length. There is also a 13" version. It is uncertain if other sizes exist. Vaseline is the only reported color. Many thanks to Dave and Vickie Peterson for the photo and information.

Grape and Cable (Northwood and Fenton)

Very little production of this pattern in opalescent glass is found besides the very rare bonbon (shown) and several shapes of the large footed fruit bowl (some are turned like a centerpiece bowl). The bonbon has been reported in vaseline only, while the footed bowl has been seen in white and vaseline. Bonbons carry the famous Northwood basketweave as the exterior pattern. The Fenton Company made a white opalescent Grape and Cable large fruit bowl nearly identical to Northwood's. Photo courtesy of the Petrasichs.

Grape and Cable with Thumbprint (Northwood)

This well-known Northwood pattern differs from the regular Grape and Cable pattern only in the thumbprint design around the bottom. It is only found in this bowl shape to date. The blue example shown has the circle in the bottom but not the "N" underlined. Please note that Fenton reproduced this pattern in several iridized colors in the late 70s and early 80s. All should have the late Fenton logo on the bottom. Photo courtesy of the Petrasichs.

Grape and Cherry

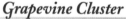

Grape and Cherry is known in both carnival glass and opalescent glass. The first production was by Sowerby of England, but blue opalescent has been reproduced by L.G. Wright in 1978 as simply Cherry. Old opalescent pieces are found in three colors, and these came from Sowerby. Several shapes can be found, all from the same mould.

Grape Cluster

This interesting little square bowl (5⅜" by 2" tall) is most likely a Fenton product, although I haven't located it yet. The pattern design as well as the candy ribbon edge treatment all point to Fenton. This is the only piece I've seen in this pattern to date. The color is a light blue opalescent. Any information is appreciated. Many thanks to the Hollenbachs for sharing it.

Grapevine Cluster

Made by the Northwood Glass Company in 1905, this very realistic vase pattern is found in several opalescent colors. The design features heavy grape and leaf patterns, grapevine supporting branches, and a grape leaf base. The pattern is a collector's favorite and always brings a high price when sold. Some of the blue examples tend toward a soft aqua color.

Grecian Urn

The owner of this small pretty vase (4¼" tall with a 2" base diameter) named this piece and it seems to fit. I believe this piece may be English, but I could be wrong. The opalescence is outstanding. I'd be interested in hearing from anyone who knows more about this pattern or of other colors.

Greek Key and Ribs

This Northwood bowl pattern from 1907 is similar to the Greek Key and Scales bowl shown below. The dome-based bowl can be found in several opalescent colors. Just why one company would create two moulds so similar is a mystery, but it seemed to happen frequently, especially in opalescent and carnival glass. Perhaps competition forced so many variations, but I can't be sure. At any rate, it makes collecting more interesting for all of us.

Greek Key and Scales

This often-marked pattern, made by the Northwood Company in 1905, is well known in both opalescent and carnival glass. The bowl shape has a dome base and is usually ruffled.

Greener Boat

This nice 7" boat shape piece (a 5" boat is also known) is reported in blue only. The interior transom bears the Greener & Co. logo (lion holding an axe) which was used from 1885 to 1890. Other sizes and colors may exist but haven't been brought to my attention. Thanks again to the Petrasichs for sharing this piece from their collection.

Greener Dewdrop

I've now seen two pieces of this pattern from Greener and both have been in amber opalescent glass typical of that company. The first was a stemmed cake plate and the second is the 5" bowl shown. Other shapes and colors wouldn't surprise me and I welcome any information. Thanks to the Petrasichs.

Greener Diamond Column Epergne

Made by the Greener Company, this beautiful 13" tall epergne is a standout in pressed glass. It is amber opalescent with a glass bowl and matching lily and metal base and fittings. Again, I have to thank the Petrasichs for sharing this fine item with me.

Half Lattice

With the top turned in closely, this 6" piece is mostly referred to as a rose bowl (or an Ivy bowl when not ruffled). The interesting pattern is one of an opposing lattice design and between there is no pattern at all. This is the only shape and color reported in this interesting pattern to date. Photo and name are courtesy of the Petrasichs.

Harlequin

This regular Harlequin pattern is found in cranberry with vaseline, blue with vaseline, plain vaseline as well as other treatments and occasionally decorated with enamel work. Shapes are a rose bowl, ewer, shade, and many different vase sizes and shapes, in both flat and footed. The pattern is Bohemian and also known as Quadruple Diamonds.

Harlequin Decorated

Although a part of the regular Harlequin pattern line, I decided to show this nice decorated version. It is probably Bohemian or English in origin. The color is cranberry with applied rigoree. Photo courtesy of Bill Walter and Laurel Walton.

Harlequin Striped

Yet another Harlequin pattern, this vaseline shade has wide stripes or bars surrounding it. It is likely English in origin. This is the only shape and color reported. Photo and name courtesy of Ruth Harvey.

Harlequin Variant

This Bohemian piece was shown in the last edition with the regular Harlequin pattern but it is actually a variant, I'm told. With its wavy design I can agree that the variant name should apply. Thanks to Marty Vogel for the nice photo.

Harrow

This English pattern has been unnamed to the best of my knowledge so I've taken the liberty of calling it Harrow. It stands 6" tall and bears an Rd #217749. A stemmed wine or cordial has been seen, and the possibility exists that a table set could have been made. Blue is the only reported color to date.

Heart Handled Open O's

While this is primarily the same pattern as the Open O's I show elsewhere, the handled ring basket has always been shown on its own and I will keep it that way. It is a Northwood pattern, 1905 – 1906.

Heart In Diamond Lamp

The font of this lamp has three rows of hearts inside of diamonds circling it. This is the only example of this pattern I've seen to date. The maker is unknown to me at this time. Additional information is appreciated. Photo courtesy of the Keathleys.

Heart Posey

This heart-shaped piece has the Rd. #70422, indicating Molineaux Webb & Co. of Manchester and a date of March 23, 1887. This is the only shape and color I've had reported in this pattern to date. Photo courtesy of the Petrasichs.

Hearts and Clubs

This Jefferson Glass Company pattern was originally their #274 and was produced about 1905. As you can see, the footed bowl shown here has a goofus treatment, but it can be found on blue and green opalescent glass as well. The three feet of the bowl are shaped like those on the Daisy and Plume pieces made by Northwood and later Dugan, but are solid without any portholes.

Hearts and Flowers

This well-known Northwood pattern can be found in carnival, custard, and opalescent glass. In the latter, it is seen on compotes and bowls in white, blue, and very rarely, vaseline. Production dates from 1908, when the maker added several well-known patterns to their opalescent production on a limited basis, including Singing Birds, Peacock on the Fence, Rose Show, Grape and Cable, Three Fruits, Bushel Basket, Acorn Burrs, Beaded Cable, Finecut and Roses, and Daisy and Plume. All were made mainly in white and blue, with a few vaseline items.

Heatherbloom

This seldom-discussed pattern, Jefferson Glass's #268, circa 1905, is found only on vases. Colors in opalescent glass are the usual white, blue, and green with the latter hardest to find. The design has a tendency to blur as the vase is swung to taller sizes, and only the shorter ones really show the pattern at its best.

Heavenly Stars

I am told this bowl is from England. As you can see, it is rather large and has three brass legs. The pattern consists of a series of double bands that form areas for the stars. I believe this is a Sowerby product. Photo courtesy of the Petrasichs.

Helen Louise

This is a creamer from Davidson that is reported to have been made in 1885. It is 3⅞" tall. John Petrasich reports an open sugar to match. Although similar, this is not to be confused with the Bridesmaid pattern.

Heron and Peacock

While I have very little information about this child's mug known as Heron and Peacock, I believe it is an old example. I've been told it has been made in many glass treatments over the years and is listed in one book on children's collectibles as having once been made in crystal and cobalt blue, but this is the first I've actually seen. It may well have been made in other opalescent colors, and a blue or canary one would be outstanding. The design has a peacock on one side and a heron on the other, with floral sprays dividing them. It is currently being reproduced by Boyd Crystal Art Glass, Cambridge, Ohio.

Herringbone (Plain)

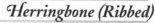

Since shards of this pattern were found at the Indiana, Pennsylvania, plant, I can be confident one of the makers of Herringbone (both plain and ribbed) was the Northwood Glass Company. Shard colors were white, vaseline, and blue, but cranberry items are also known. Shapes known are water sets, cruets, syrups, and crimped salad bowls. Some treatments are cased mother-of-pearl in a satin finish. The plain Herringbone dates from 1885, when Harry Northwood was at Phoenix Glass.

Herringbone (Ribbed)

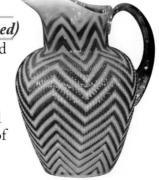

As I said in the narrative about Plain Herringbone, this is most likely a Northwood pattern. While the Plain Herringbone came first and dates from Northwood's days at Phoenix, the Ribbed Herringbone is believed to date from about 1902, at the Indiana plant. Since I felt the two treatments were so different, I chose to discuss them as separate items. It was made in several shapes and most of the standard colors. Photo courtesy of Bill Walter and Laurel Walton.

Herringbone and Crocus

This interesting 4½" herringbone vase with applied crocus has a rough pontil on the bottom suggesting an English origin, although the Phoenix Art Glass Co. has also been known to have made various pieces using the herringbone pattern. Green is the only color reported. Thanks again to the Petrasichs for sharing the photo and information.

Hidden Hearts

Only the piece shown and a hat shape in a metal holder have been reported in this pattern. If you'll look closely you can see the Heart designs throughout the pattern. The only colors reported are cranberry and vaseline opalescent. Maker is unknown to date. Many thanks to Rachel Spinella for sharing the photo.

Hilltop Vines

This unusual 5" tall compote is shown in Northwood ads as early as 1906, so I know who made it. It is found in three standard colors. Outstanding features are the leaves that overlap making up the bowl of the compote, the branch-like legs that form the stem, and the domed base covered with tiny bubble-like circles.

Hilltop Vines Variant

This example is like the regular Hilltop Vines pattern from Northwood except the leaves are veined and stippled. I believe this variant was a later mould recutting and is somewhat harder to find than the regular one. Thanks to John Loggie for sharing it with me.

Hobbs Polka Dot

This Hobbs pattern was made in many exotic colors (shown is a green to sapphire bowl) and dates from 1884. It is found in a wide variety of shapes. Photo courtesy of Bill Walter and Laurel Walton.

Hobbs Swirl

This 1888 Hobbs, Brockunier & Co. pattern is found in a wide variety of shapes and colors. Shown is a nice barber bottle in blue opalescent. Photo courtesy of Bill Walter and Laurel Walton.

Hobnail (Hobbs)

Here is Hobnail from Hobbs, Brockunier. A host of shapes are known. Production of the Hobbs Hobnail design began in 1885 and lasted until 1892. Colors reported are white, blue, rubina, vaseline, and cranberry. It is also known as Hobbs Dew Drop.

Hobnail and Paneled Thumbprint

Most collectors credit this pattern to Northwood but I know of no proof it was made at that concern. The pattern dates from 1905 or 1906 and can be found in berry sets, table sets, water sets, and vases that have been pulled from the spooner shape.

Hobnail-in-Square
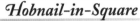

This Aetna Glass and Manufacturing Company of Bellaire, Ohio, pattern dates from 1887 and is often confused with a recent pattern called Vesta made by the Fenton Company since the 1950s. Colors of the original pattern are primarily white opalescent. A variety of shapes are known.

Hobnail Smoke Bell

Most of the smoke bells, or deflectors as some call them, are flattened out more than the one shown here. They were commonly hung over floor or table candles and lamps to keep the flame from heating up and smoking up the ceiling, or anything that may be above the flame. The maker and date of this piece are not known at this time. Photo courtesy of Ruth Harvey.

Hobnail Toy Mug

I have no idea who made this tiny 2" mug in vaseline and can only guess that it might have been used either as a child's mug or a toothpick holder. Either way, it has to be the smallest piece of opalescent glass I've seen and it is really a conversation piece for sure. Thanks to the Sandemans for sharing this cute miniature piece.

Hobnail Twist

This very nice vase, or lily if you will, comes in a metal holder which has a design of grapes and leaves circling about the metal stand. The vase consists of rows of hobnails and is twisted in a diagonal spiral with a ruffled top. This is the only shape reported to date and the color is rubina verde. Thanks to the Sandemans for sharing this nice item.

Hobnail with Bars

Hobnail with Bars was made by U.S. Glass, mostly in crystal. But here is the cruet in a white opalescent treatment, which I believe is on the scarce side. Thanks to Mary and John Petrasich for sharing it.

Holly and Berry

Primarily a carnival glass pattern from Dugan/Diamond, the nappy shape has surfaced in opalescent glass in white only. The design is a good one with a center cluster of holly berries and leaves and the same design in a wreath shape around the rim with three strings of leaves and berries. The nappy is a large one, measuring 7" across the top from handle to pouring lip.

Holly Berry Lamp

In past editions this wonderful lamp was shown with a rubina verde shade, but here is an example with the correct shade. The pattern is one of holly berries, hence the name. Of English origin, this oil lamp (drilled for electric use later on) was made between 1880 and 1890. Thanks to Steve and Radka Sandeman for sharing this beauty.

Honeycomb

This pattern is called Hobbs Honeycomb or Opal Honeycomb by some collectors. Actually there is no evidence this was a pattern from Hobbs, Brockunier, and the more I see of this pattern, the more I am convinced it was made by someone else. All the shapes reported are from the same mould and consist of a vase or a bowl that has been pulled from the vase. Besides the honeycombing, the only other design is the ribbed-skirt base.

Honeycomb and Clover

Honeycomb and Clover was made by the Fenton Company in several types of glass including carnival, opalescent, and gilt decorated. Production in opalescent glass dates from 1910. It is found in several shapes and the standard colors. The pattern is exterior and consists of an allover honeycombing with clover and leaves twining over it.

Honeycomb Open Edge

There are many reticulated edge bowls made in various types of glass from American makers. I believe this one to be English, but have no proof. The color is a very nice deep blue and it is the only piece reported in this pattern. Photo courtesy of the Petrasichs.

Horse Chestnut

This pattern had only been reported in a compote shape, but here is a nice ruffled vase shape in vaseline opalescent, courtesy of Frank and Melissa Keathley. This pattern was first credited to Richardson's of England in 1916 and then to Thomas Webb in 1936.

Ice Castles

This generous size shade is a real beauty. The owners believe it may be Sabino or Jobling, and I have nothing to prove otherwise. White, or French opalescent, is the only color reported to date. Photo courtesy of Bill Walter and Laurel Walton.

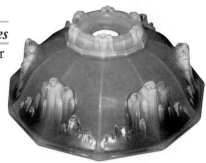

Idyll

Jefferson Glass Company's Idyll is found in a water set, table set, berry set, toothpick holder, cruet, shakers, a bowl, and a tray. Idyll was first made in 1907. It is a well-done pattern, pleasing to the eye for collectors. In addition, sometimes the opalescent pieces are decorated with gilding. Photo courtesy of Rick and Debbie Graham.

Imitation Cut #1

This basket from Greener & Co. bears three different Rd numbers, which is somewhat unusual. The first number is 96775, which I'm told is for the handle. The second and third numbers are 95935 and 98551, all three from 1888. I believe one of the second numbers would be for the pattern design but I'm not sure what the other is pertaining to. The only color reported is blue opalescent. Thanks to the Petrasichs for the photo and information.

Imitation Cut #2

Here again we see the same situation as in the previous pattern, Imitation Cut #1. This also has three different Rd. numbers and they are the exact same numbers seen on the first piece, although the handle and design show obvious differences. This particular piece is in white opalescent and the pattern design shows some what of a Japanese art look. Thanks again to the Petrasichs for the photo and information.

Infinity

The owner of this 8" by 5½" bowl gave it this name. I think the figure eight elongated loops which resemble the infinity symbol can be noticed with little trouble and I do like the name. Although this blue opalescent piece has some characteristics of Davidson, it isn't found in any of their catalogs, thus leading the owner to believe it may be a Greener product and I won't argue with that observation. Photo courtesy of the Petrasichs.

Inside Ribbing

Beaumont Glass of Martins Ferry, Ohio, made this very pretty glass in the early 1900s, and while it isn't plentiful, many times it is overlooked. It is found in three colors and a host of shapes. Some pieces have enameled decoration adding to the interest.

Intaglio

Intaglio was one of Northwood's earlier patterns dating from 1897 in custard production. It was made in a host of shapes in most of the standard colors and is quite popular with collectors.

Intaglio Holly (Dugan's)

Like the other Intaglio patterns from the Dugan Company, this one had a goofus treatment when it was sold. The pattern is very similar to Dugan's Holly and Berry design. Intaglio Holly is found in large and small bowls in white opalescent.

Intaglio Lattice

The Petrasichs named this bowl and I believe the name is fitting. I've been able to learn nothing about the pattern and certainly hope readers can offer something more. I believe the piece may be either English or European, but can't be sure.

Intaglio Morning Glory

Morning Glory, another of Dugan's 1907 patterns in their vast Intaglio line, is a standout. It is found on both large and small bowls. The white opalescent glass is decorated in a goofus treatment of red and gold.

Intaglio Panels

This pattern, which was named by the owner, can be found in a small 4¾" bowl and a tumbler. The only color reported so far is white opalescent. Thanks to the Petrasichs for sharing it.

Interior Flute

Interior Flute has wide panels that are about twice as far apart as Fenton's Interior Panel pattern. Shown is a 5½" vase in lavender opalescent glass with a jack-in-the-pulpit top. I believe this is a Dugan/Diamond pattern but can't be sure at this time.

Interior Panel

This very nice Fenton vase dates from the early to late 1920s. Besides the fine example in amber opalescent, it is known in the standard opalescent colors. The same mould was used to make several different whimsey shaped vases also. The example shown is 8" tall and has a fan spread of 5".

Interior Poinsettia (Pressed)

Unlike the blown Poinsettia pattern, this one is pressed and seems to be found only on the tumbler shape. It is found in most of the standard opalescent colors. The pattern is credited to the Northwood Company, and a trademark can be seen on the inside of the tumbler.

Interior Swirl

Interior Swirl is much like the Inside Ribbing pattern but with a twist. This very pretty rose bowl is perfectly plain on the outside and has a ribbing that has been twisted on the interior. Notice the cranberry frit along the top indicating this pattern is most likely from Jefferson Glass. One writer dates this pattern from the 1890s, but I'd place it closer to 1904 or 1905. The canary coloring is quite good and the base prominent.

Interior Wide Stripe

If you look closely at this tumbler, you will see the exterior is flat and the opalescent wide stripe is on the inside. I believe this water set may have been made by La Belle Glass but I could be wrong (one writer says it may be from Phoenix Glass).

Inverted Chevron

This very attractive vase is sometimes confused with Fenton's Plume Panels vase, a pattern well known to carnival glass collectors. But on close examination, it is very different. I suspect it may be from Jefferson Glass and I've named it Inverted Chevron. While blue and green are the only colors I've seen to date.

Inverted Fan and Feather

This well-known pattern was made first by Northwood in custard glass and then by Dugan in opalescent glass. It is found in a wide variety of shapes and in several colors. Shown is a blue gilded footed sauce.

Iris (English)

I apologize for lumping this pattern with Daffodils in previous books, but they are so very much alike I overlooked the differences. Iris is found in a water set (lidded pitcher is shown), a hand lamp, and a vase (there may be additional shapes I haven't heard about). Photo courtesy of Frank and Melissa Keathley.

Iris (Northwood)

This Iris design is similar to the Daffodils pattern that was made by both Northwood and Dugan, but it shows a different flower. I believe it is from Northwood, but I could be wrong. Shapes reported so far are a water set, a vase (shown), and a lamp, but there are surely more.

Iris with Meander

Iris with Meander is also known as Fleur-de-Lis Scrolled and is a product of Jefferson Glass, dating from 1902 or 1903. It was made in a host of shapes and colors.

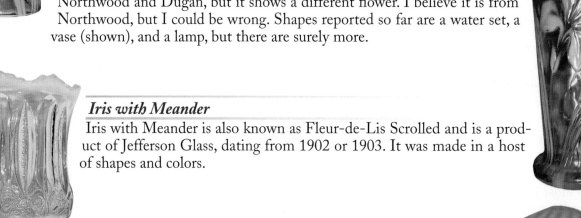

Ivy Ball

I have little information to offer on this swirl pattern piece other than to say the color is white opalescent, the stand doesn't look old to me, and it may in fact be a late Fenton piece. Any information would be appreciated. Thanks to Judy Parker for the photo.

Jazz

While I can't find this pattern pictured in any Dugan/Diamond ad, I feel sure it came from that company. The base has two levels and the unusual treatment of the top is sassy and bold, so I've named it Jazz. Date of production should be in the 1906 – 1909 time frame, I'd bet. It is 6" tall.

Jefferson #270 (Jefferson Colonial)

At first glance this looks like another Jefferson pattern called Iris with Meander. Indeed, the moulds may have been the same, but this design is missing the fleur-de-lis at the base and the beading in the slots. Shown is the master berry bowl in blue. Colors are the usual Jefferson ones of white, blue, green, and canary.

Jefferson Shield

This elusive pattern was Jefferson Glass Company's #262 pattern. It is a dome-based bowl, found in green, white, and blue opalescent. It has a series of 13 shields around the center of the bowl. If you are the owner of one of these bowls, consider yourself very lucky, for they are very scarce. Photo courtesy of Rick and Debbie Graham.

Jefferson Spatter Vase

This vase was made on the same mould shape as the Convex Rib vase from Jefferson. It has a spatter decoration and the ribs can actually be felt on the inside, Ruth Harvey tells me. It has been reported only in vaseline to date.

Jefferson Spool

This very unusual hyacinth vase from the Jefferson Glass Company looks as if it were turned on a lathe. It stands approximately 8" tall and was made in 1905. Colors are the standard opalescent ones. No other shapes have been reported to date.

Jefferson Stripe

This is Jefferson's #33 Lily vase, shown in a 1902 ad. This nice vase (shown in amber) can be found with a variety of top shapes and is 7½" tall. Pieces may be found with or without the cranberry glass frit on the top edge. The green tends to be a bit dark, almost an emerald green shade. Thanks to Janine Patterson for the nice photo.

Jefferson Wheel

This very attractive bowl dating from 1905 is, as the name implies, another pattern from Jefferson Glass. It was originally Jefferson's #260 pattern and can be found in white, blue, and green opalescent glass.

Jewel and Fan

Jefferson made a lot of opalescent glass and this pattern was originally identified as their #125. It is found on bowls and an elongated banana bowl in white, blue, green, and rarely, canary. The design is simple but very effective.

Jewel and Flower

This very attractive pattern was made by the Northwood Company in 1904, and originally called Encore. It can can be found in several shapes and colors, often decorated with gilding. Incidentally, there is a variant with the design going all the way to the base and eliminating the beading and threading band.

Jeweled Heart

Although long credited to Northwood, Jeweled Heart (or Victor, as it was originally called) was first made by Dugan in 1905. A wide variety of shapes and colors are known, but only three in opalescent glass. Some items have the Diamond-D marking.

Jewels and Drapery

This very pretty Northwood vase dates from 1907 and can be found in ads from that year, labeled the Fairmont opal assortment. As you can see, the drapery is very well done with a tiny tassel ending between the folds. Around the base is a series of jewels or raised dots. Strangely, in a Northwood ad in a 1906 Lyons Brothers catalog, there is a similar vase shown that has an additional row of pendants below the jewels.

Jewels and Drapery Variant

As I said earlier, this pattern is exactly like the Jewels and Drapery pattern except for the row of pendants that hang like fringe below the row of jewels. This pattern was shown in a 1906 glass ad called the Fairmont opal assortment.

Jolly Bear

Jolly Bear was made by the Jefferson Glass Company in 1906 or 1907. The white pieces (and occasionally blue) sometimes have gilding on them, leading to the possibility they were also used with a goofus treatment. The bear is very much like that on the U.S. Glass pattern called Frolicking Bears and would be an excellent companion piece. Various shaped bowls are found in three colors. Photo courtesy of Rick and Debbie Graham.

Jubilee (Hickman)

Jubilee was originally made by McKee & Brothers in crystal, so this blue opalescent bowl is a bit of a mystery. It has fewer fans than the original pattern and is opalescent glass. I do question its age, but will show it here and hope readers can shed some light on it. Thanks to the Petrasichs for sharing it with me.

Keyhole

The keyhole pattern is shown in 1905 Dugan Glass Company ads. It can be found in opalescent glass on bowls that have a dome base in white, blue, and green, and painted or goofus treatment on the white. A few years later, it was adapted for use as the exterior of carnival glass bowls with the Raindrop pattern as an interior and on a very rare marigold bowl where the exterior is plain and Keyhole became the interior pattern.

King Melon

This nice oil lamp is from the King Glass Co. and although other colors are possible I haven't seen them to date. Photo courtesy of Bill Walter and Laurel Walton.

King Richard

More recent information now places this pattern, which is also known as Waffle and Vine, as a product of the short-lived Coudersport Glass concern (1900 – 1904). All pieces are considered rare. The scroll-supported stem and the interior design of vines and a scroll filled with waffle or file are very well done.

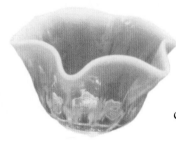

King's Panel

Besides the bowl I showed in the previous edition, I now know of a creamer and open sugar. The pattern is all interior ribs or panels. Colors are both canary and blue opalescent. It was made by Davidson.

King's X

This 3¼" spill is from Greener & Co. and is quite rare. It bears the Greener logo which dates it between 1875 and 1885. Blue is the only reported color at this time. I'd appreciate hearing of additional shapes or colors. Thanks to the Petrasichs for sharing it.

Kittens

Kittens is from the Fenton Company (their #299) and is primarily found in carnival glass. This very rare cup and saucer set in amethyst opalescent are the only examples reported in opalescent glass to date. The saucer is really a 4" plate since all Kittens pieces were toy items, intended for children. Probably other pieces in this opalescent treatment were made but none have been reported.

Knobby Seaweed

The pattern on this seaweed design piece protrudes out from the piece, thus the name. It is believed to be either Bohemian or possibly English. The color is cranberry with vaseline applied feet. Photo courtesy of the Keathleys.

LaBelle

This is the name given to me by the owner and I'm happy to honor it. The shape is a toothpick holder shown in vaseline opalescent, the only color and shape reported. It resembles the Inside Ribbing pattern but without the ribbing. I have no indication as to the maker at this time. Thanks to the Sandemans for sharing it.

Lady Caroline

Lady Caroline was made by Davidson in 1891 as their Pearline pattern in blue and canary opalescent glass. Shapes are an open sugar (shown) and creamer, baskets, a two-handled spill, and several novelties from this mould.

Lady Chippendale

This is now known to be from Davidson and Company in England. It was incorrectly labeled Greener in pervious editions. Some additional shapes have been found including baskets, compotes, pitcher, salt holder, bowl, tumbler, an open sugar, and creamer, as well as advertising and promotional pieces. The pattern dates from 1881 and in opalescent glass is found in either blue or canary, all marked RD 176566. Thanks to the Petrasichs for the new information.

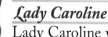

Lady Finger Spill Vase

Like other patterns with these feet, I strongly suspect this spill vase is English from George Davidson & Company. I've seen it in vaseline as well as the blue shown.

Lady Slipper Vase

Here is another of those English vases with a flair that can only be found on glass of the Victorian age. It was made by Davidson and is only 4½" tall. It is shown in canary but was also made in blue and white opalescent glass. It was probably made in other sizes as well.

Late Coinspot

Here is a Fenton version of the famed Coinspot. This one, dating from the 1925 – 1929 era, was called an iced tea set in advertising and had a taller tumbler with it. As you can easily see, it has a semi-cannonball shape and the handle is rather thick. In 1931 Fenton made this same pitcher with a dark, contrasting handle, and teamed it with mugs with the same handle treatment.

Lattice (English)

The owner of this nice vase in vaseline tells me it's English and I have no reason to believe otherwise. This cylinder shaped vase with bulbous base has an interesting pattern of elongated lattice work throughout the entire piece. This is the only shape reported to date. Thanks to the Sandemans for sharing it.

Lattice and Daisy

This tumbler is likely a Dugan product before it became Diamond Glass Co. in 1913. It is a bit tough to find, especially in vaseline. No opalescent pitchers or other shapes have been reported to date but the pitcher would certainly be a welcomed site to see. Thanks to the Sandemans and Ruth Harvey for the photo submissions.

Lattice and Points

This Dugan pattern is pulled from the same mould that produced the Vining Twigs plates and bowls that were made in carnival glass as well as the vases. In opalescent glass, the vases are usually short and haven't been pulled or swung as most vases are. White and scarce blue examples are known. Production of the opalescent pieces dates from 1907.

Lattice Medallions

This very graceful pattern is from the Northwood Company and is sometimes marked with the famous "N." It can be found primarily in bowl shapes, often very ruffled and ornate. This pattern can be found in the standard opalescent colors of white, blue, and green. Shown is a very pretty white opalescent bowl with the tri-corner shaping.

Laura (Single Flower Framed)

Here is another example of poor naming. The Laura name is from Rose Presznick but the pattern has long been called Single Flower Framed by carnival glass collectors. It is a Dugan pattern, found only on the exterior of nappies, bowls, and this very rare ruffled plate. These scarce items date from the 1909 period of Dugan production.

Laurel Swag and Bows

While I've searched every reference I could find about this pattern, it doesn't seem to be shown anywhere. I know it was made by the Fenton Company about 1908, for they made the only amethyst opalescent glass around that time. As you can see, there are laurel swags tied with a ribbon and bow, as well as cosmos-like flowers and an unusual bull's eye with a swirl of connecting leaves. I would appreciate any information about this pretty gas shade.

Leaf and Beads

Just why Northwood made two variant treatments to this pattern is unclear, but both are shown here. One has twig feet and a few changes in leaves while the other has a dome base. The latter should be called a variant. Production of the twig-footed bowl began in 1905, but by 1906 both styles were being advertised.

Leaf and Diamonds

This pattern was first made in 1907 and was shown in a 1908 Butler Brothers ad that included other Jefferson Glass items. Leaf and Diamonds can be found in three colors, and may well be a companion pattern to Jefferson's Hearts and Clubs opalescent bowl pattern. Bowls have three large spatula feet and show an interior design of three diamond patterns separated by three fans of leaves, with a leaf circle in the center of the bowl.

Leaf and Leaflets

Here is another of those patterns that appeared first in Northwood's lineup (1907 ads) and later became part of the Dugan production line. The opalescent examples in blue, white, and goofus are Northwood. Dugan made this pattern in other glass treatments where it is called Long Leaf.

Leaf Chalice

Leaf Chalice was made by Northwood while a part of the National combine. It appears in a May 1903 Butler Brothers ad that featured three shapings of the piece. Colors usually found are white and blue, but green was also made and is considered rare in this pattern.

Leaf Garland

This 4½" tall by 6" wide blue opalescent compote is from Greener & Co. and has the Rd. #176239 (1891). It is also known in a small vaseline opalescent bowl. I'm sure other shapes may exist but they haven't been reported to date. Thanks to the Petrasichs for the name and photo.

Leaf Garland and Ribs

Although it isn't marked I feel that this little 3" creamer may be a product of Davidson (compared to the Lady Caroline pattern) judging by the looks of it, although Greener & Co. has also been mentioned as a possible maker. Vaseline is the only color and the small creamer is the only shape reported at this time. Thanks to the Petrasichs for sharing it.

Leaf Rosette and Beads

Made by the Dugan/Diamond Company beginning in 1906, this pattern seems to be a cousin to Blocked Thumbprint and Beads with the addition of the chain of leaves. And if you take a look at the Single Poinsettia pattern, you will see just how similar these patterns are. It has been reported only in three colors to date.

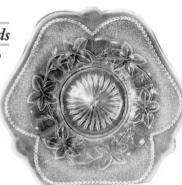

Leafy Stripe

Measuring 9" long, 7" wide, and 4½" tall, this beautiful honey-amber bowl was probably made to fit into a bride's basket or to be a hanging bowl. It has a pontil on the base and I strongly suspect it is from England. Besides the opalescent stripe design, there is a mould pattern of leaves around the bowl. Photo courtesy of Bill Walter and Laurel Walton.

Lily Pad

Other than to say it's English, I have no information to offer on this beautifully done epergne. I really love the way it is arranged and can picture water flowing out of the lily down into the bowl, perhaps with flowers floating in the water. Vaseline is the only reported color and I do thank the Sandemans for sharing this super piece of glass with me.

Lily Pool Epergne

This item is not a one-piece item as I originally thought; the lily pulls loose from the bowl base. It was just a matter of my misunderstanding the owner's description and I'm happy to get it straightened out. At any rate, it appears to be an American product and I'd guess from the Northwood Company. It is reported only in vaseline.

Lily Vase

This interesting cranberry vase has odd light green feet applied, but also a stem sticking up from the feet toward the top of the vase at the front. I have no idea of its purpose. This is the only example reported at this time. Photo courtesy of Ruth Harvey.

Lined Heart

This 1906 Jefferson Glass Company vase pattern can be found in white, blue, and green opalescent glass. The examples shown haven't been swung as many are and are about 7" tall; some range to 14".

Linking Rings

Linking Rings was made by Davidson in 1894, and most pieces bear Rd. #237038. Shapes in opalescent glass are a water set, oval 8½" x 7" tray, juice glass, bowls, a compote, 7½" plate, 3" creamer, and an open sugar. Colors in the opalescent treatment are a deep blue, a softer blue, and canary (vaseline). Thanks to Jan Horne and Harold White for the nice photo.

Little Nell

Despite being very plain, this vase is still a very cute item. Except for the threading above the collar base, there is no design at all and whatever the vase has going for it comes from the shaping and fine opalescence. The maker isn't certain at this time, and I'm not sure it really matters.

Little Swan (Dugan)

Dugan's version of Little Swan is slightly larger than the Northwood swan shown elsewhere. It came along in 1909 and can be found in white, green, and blue opalescent glass.
The Fenton Company also made a version, but the breast feathering is quite different from the two versions here, more like flower petals than feathers.

Little Swan (Northwood)

The Northwood version of this pattern is virtually the same design as the Dugan Little Swan, but came first and is slightly smaller. It can be found in blue and white; green may be a possibility but I've only seen Dugan ones in that color. Some examples have been gilded on the head, along the rim of the opening, and down the tail.

Looped Maze

I'm not sure if this is considered a milk pitcher or a banquet size creamer, but none-theless, it is has a very interesting pattern of loops which inconsis-tently run about the piece. This is the only reported example to date. Photo courtesy of Bill Walter and Laurel Walton.

Loops with Ring Top

I have no idea of the maker of this interesting handled piece but assume it to be Euro-pean. It has a nice white opalescent coverage with light pink handles and flat base. Any information on this piece is welcomed. Photo courtesy of John and Mary Petrasich.

Lords and Ladies

Lords and Ladies was made by Davidson in England (their Rd. #285342) and can be found in blue and canary (vaseline) opalescent glass. Shapes include a 2¼" salt, covered butter dish, a 3" creamer, small sugar, one-handled nappy, cake plate, creamer and sugar on feet, a celery boat, platter, and a 4" x 6" oval bowl. The date of manufacture is October 2, 1896.

Lorna

This should be called the traveling vase since it was first made at Model Flint in 1900, then at North-wood as their #562 the same year, then by Dugan/Diamond when Northwood left the plant, and finally by West Virginia Glass! Most stand about 6½" to 7" tall and can be found in white, canary, and blue opalescent. Photo courtesy of Samantha Prince.

Lotus

This Albany Glass pattern is found only in the rose bowl shape with an attached underplate. It was made from 1900 to 1902 in three opalescent colors as well as in other types of glass. Speculation is this was made by Model Flint during their last years at Albany. It is also called Lotus Blos-som by some collectors.

Love Flower

I had this photo for some time before I was told its name and that is was English in origin. It has three handles like a loving cup, so that may be the source of the name. The flowers that wind up the center are somewhat like those of Dugan's Windflower pieces as well as the Tree of Love pattern. Thanks to Richard Petersen for sharing this piece with me.

Lustre Flute

Northwood's Lustre Flute, also called Waffle Band or English Hob Band, is found sparingly in carnival glass and decorated glass. The opalescent colors reported are white and blue. Opalescent production began in 1907. Shapes are various. The pattern is a bit on the plain side and certainly not one of the better remembered ones from this company.

Many Diamonds

This likely European ruffled candy ribbon edge bowl on a metal stand is heavy opalescent with a sapphire colored crest. It is very similar in appearance to the Peacock Tail bowl, also on a metal stand. Any information would be appreciated. Thanks to Marty Vogel for sharing it.

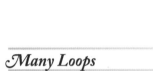

Many Loops

Jefferson Glass Company's #247 pattern was confined to novelty bowls, rose bowls, and banana bowl shapes all from the same mould. This spirograph-like pattern of overlapping loops bordered by zigzag threading is a distinctive design. It is found in three opalescent colors.

Many Rays

The maker of this 8½" – 9" bowl has not been established but I believe it to be an American product. No other colors or shapes have been reported. Photo courtesy of Roger Lane.

Many Ribs

This very distinctive vase with a columnal base was made by the Model Flint Glass Company of Albany, Indiana, in 1902. It can be found in three opalescent colors. This particular vase measures nearly 8" and has the typical slightly flared top.

Maple Leaf

Maple Leaf was apparently first a Northwood pattern (at least in custard glass), and then a Dugan product in opalescent and later carnival glass. The opalescent glass dates from 1908 to 1910. Colors in this glass are green (scarce), white, and blue, with a very rare example in vaseline. The only shape reported in opalescent glass seems to be the jelly compote, but others may certainly exist.

Maple Leaf Chalice

This very pretty vase is a naturalistic piece from the Northwood Company made in purple slag and opalescent glass. It dates from the 1903 – 1905 era. Opalescent colors are white, blue, green, and vaseline. It is often confused with Northwood's Leaf Chalice.

Markham Swirl Band with Opal Cobweb

What a name! Actually there are other Markham Swirl designs with various opal designs in white, blue, cranberry, and possibly canary. The piece shown is a finger lamp but standard oil lamps are also known.

Mary Ann

While this vase is well known to carnival glass collectors, it comes as a surprise to many who collect opalescent glass. It came from the Dugan Company and received its name from Fanny Mary Ann Dugan, sister of Thomas E. A. and Alfred Dugan. In carnival, the vase is known in an eight-scallop and ten-scallop top, and a three-handled, flat-topped loving cup. In opalescent glass, the only colors reported are white and blue, and both are considered rare. This pattern has been reproduced.

Mary Gregory

Normally I wouldn't consider this small lidded piece as opalescent, but if you look closely at the lid you will see it has an opalescent stripe in the glass. The piece stands only 4" tall and I suspect it is from Europe where most of the Mary Gregory type enameling was done.

Mavis Swirl

This 1901 Model Flint Glass pattern is sometimes called Opal Swirl but the correct name is as I list it. It is found in various shapes and colors. Photo courtesy of Rick and Debbie Graham.

May Basket

Jefferson Glass Company's May Basket was shown in ads as their #87 pattern. For years some collectors thought this was a Northwood pattern since it has the same design as the Pump and Trough pieces. May Basket can be found in four colors and three sizes.

93

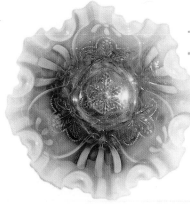

Meander

The moulds for Jefferson's #233 were obtained by the Northwood Company after its move to the Wheeling location. The opalescent pieces in white, blue, and green are attributed to Jefferson, and the carnival bowls with Three Fruits Medallion as an interior pattern are strictly Northwood.

Medieval Arches

This 4" square bowl has so much opalescence in the bottom that it gives the appearance of having skim milk in it. Vaseline is the only color and this is the only shape reported so far. I have no idea of the maker at this time although the owner states it is flint glass and dates from the mid 1800s. Thanks to the Sandemans for sharing it.

Meisenthal Swan

Although similar to the swans made by Burtles and Tate, this is believed to be a French-made example by Meisenthal. Additional information is welcomed. Photo courtesy of the Petrasichs.

Melon Optic Swirl (Jefferson)

This very beautiful, tightly crimped bowl has a melon rib exterior that has been shaped into a swirl with cranberry edging. This bowl appears to be quite close to a series of pieces shown in a 1902 Jefferson ad, showing Stripe, Swirl, and Coin Dot items. The ad lists colors of white, blue, green, yellow (vaseline), and cranberry.

Melon Swirl

I'm convinced this very beautiful water set may well be early Dugan production from Indiana, Pennsylvania. Examples of handles just like the one on the water set shown are found in 1904 ads showing decorated sets. In addition, the enamel work is very similar to that found on several Dugan sets made between 1900 and 1905. These sets, more elaborate than most in this enameling, are consistent with Melon Swirl. I certainly hope someone out there can shed more light on this fantastic pattern.

Melon with Bars

I can only speculate that this light amber pitcher is either English or a late production piece. Either way, this nice pitcher with reeded handle is a pattern I have not seen to date. Thanks to Ruth Harvey for sharing it.

Melon with Sprig

This circa 1892 Northwood pattern is found in four opalescent shapes, mostly in white opalescent, but a rare blue pitcher is known. Photo courtesy of Ruth Harvey.

Mermaids and Shells

What a beautiful design this piece is. It is from Burtles, Tate, and Company and is reported in white opalescent as well as the vaseline opalescent shown. It measures 7½" long and 3" deep. Thanks to John and Mary Petrasich for sharing it with me.

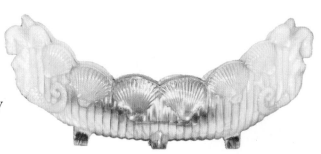

Mica Spatter JIP Vase

This 4½" vase is shaped just like the Rubina Verde JIP vase shown elsewhere, is on clear glass, and has a beautiful spatter treatment with flecks of mica in the pattern. Hobbs, Brockunier & Company used this treatment on vases, tumblers, and pitchers, and I suspect the vase shown is theirs. Dates of production were from 1883 to 1885. This glass was later produced at Northwood and Bonita Art Glass Company.

Mirror Frame

This rather interesting round frame has the look of flower petals surrounding a border of beads. Only vaseline opalescent is reported to date. Additional information would be appreciated. Thanks again the Steve and Radka Sandeman for sharing this nice piece.

Monkey (Under a Tree)

This 1880s pattern is found mostly in crystal, but occasionally turns up in white opalescent glass. A host of shapes are known, but not all shapes are found in opalescent glass. Opalescent pieces are very collectible and expensive.

Morning Glory

This well designed tab handled basket, or open sugar as some may call it, is the only shape and green the only color reported. Thanks to Ruth Harvey for the name and photo.

Murano Floral Vase

This squat vase has applied rigoree and opalescent glass flowers that are typical of this Italian producer's work. The vase has a hammered look in clear glass. I appreciate Ruth Harvey sharing this item with me.

Mystic Maze

This blown vase of very thin glass is similar to Jefferson's Swirling Maze design, although I believe it to be of English origin. The color is a soft canary yellow. I certainly welcome any information about his vase from readers and I thank Bill Walter and Laurel Walton for sharing it.

Nailsea

Nailsea is actually not the name of any pattern design, but comes from a particular section of England where several glass factories were in operation. This is just one of the many designs referred to as Nailsea type glass. This individual creamer stands 3⅝" tall and white is the only reported color.

National's #17

This rather scarce 8" vase was created at the Northwood plant in Indiana, Pennsylvania, for the National glass combine. It is shown in a 1901 catalog ad called a bouquet vase. It can be found in three opalescent colors.

National Swirl

I have no proof this pitcher is from National but a similarly shaped pitcher appeared in a1900 G. Sommers & Company catalog. A vase with this same shape, known as Fenton's #39 Swirl, is shown in Fenton ads in 1939. I've never seen a Fenton ad showing the pitcher however. As for National, their ad showed reeded handles and listed colors of crystal, blue, and green, so perhaps these pitchers evolved from this earlier treatment.

Nesting Robins

In the second edition I said the bowl shown was marked EZAN as well as Made in France. I now know of a bowl in this pattern that is marked Sabino, also a French company, making glass in the 1920s and 1930s. The quality of workmanship is quite good, and only time will tell more about this piece. The bowl shown measures 10" across and was purchased in France.

Netted Cherries

While I have no proof, I feel confident this pattern was made by Dugan/Diamond. It is found only on bowls in crystal or opalescent glass where the colors are white and blue. Shapes are round, tri-cornered, and banana shape, all from the same mould.

Netted Roses

This 1906 Northwood bowl pattern is another of those with one name for opalescent glass and another for carnival. In carnival, the pattern is called Bull's Eye and Leaves, and it is an exterior pattern also. In opalescent glass as Netted Roses, the colors are blue, green, and white, often with a goofus treatment. Thanks to Wayne and Joan Jolliffe for the photo.

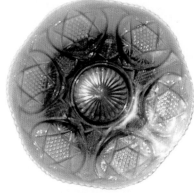

Northern Star

This very nice 1908 Fenton geometric pattern is most often found in carnival glass or crystal but can rarely be found in large plates in white, blue, and green opalescent glass. Just why the small bowls and plates were not made in an opalescent treatment is a mystery since 5" bowls, 7" plates, and 11" plates are all known in crystal.

Northwood's Mikado

Perhaps this should be called Northwood's Poppy since that is the interior design, and most pattern names originate from the interior design unless there is only an exterior pattern. If you'll compare this very rare nappy to the Blossoms and Blooms pattern earlier in this edition you'll see that only the exterior is the same. The difference in this piece, besides it being round and in vaseline, is that it carries a Poppy interior pattern and the base has a full flower in the center as opposed to the rayed base seen on the Blossoms and Blooms pieces. This could possibly be a prototype due to the design and since it's the only reported example to date. Nonetheless it is considered a very rare variant. Thanks to Dave Peterson for sharing this rare and interesting item.

Northwood's Poppy

This is the first example of this pattern in opalescent glass I've seen. The shape is called an oval pickle dish. It does not carry the Northwood trademark. It is possible other colors were made in the opalescent treatment, and all would be rare and desirable.

Northwood Swirl

Since Northwood Swirl is found primarily in carnival or decorated glass, it was a bit of a surprise to see this tumbler in opalescent glass. It has also been reported in vaseline opalescent glass. It is 3⅞" tall and the ribs are all interior. Thanks to the Petrasichs for sharing it.

Ocean Shell

Ocean Shell is still another of the naturalistic compotes. It has three variations of twig-like supports for stems. Some go all the way to the bowl, others are short and not connected, while still others are longer but remain unattached at the top. Ocean Shell was made by Northwood Company circa 1904.

Ocean Wave

I believe this piece was made by Jefferson for the Oneida Silver Mfg. Company since the bowl is labeled: O.S.M. CO. — NY — ONEIDA. It was obviously made to go into a bride's basket or some sort of holder for the silver company. If anyone has additional information on this item, I'd like to hear from them.

Ohio State Seal

This lettered 3⅜" white opalescent cup plate is embossed "The Great Seal Of The State Of Ohio" around the outer edge. It shows a bright sunrise coming up between a mountain range. White is the only color and the small cup plate is the only shape reported. Thanks to the Petrasichs for sharing it.

Oktoberfest

This very attractive German ale glass may have another name but I haven't found one. It has a very active pattern of birds, people, flowers, crowns, and German writing. The coloring is a very good vaseline with a fine opalescent edging (the lip tilts as you can see). I'd appreciate any information on this item.

Old Man Winter

This Jefferson pattern, shown in the two sizes made, was advertised as #135 (small) and #91 (large). Some are marked Patent 1906 and Patent March 18, 1902. The very interesting handle treatment is a design giveaway and harkens back to Victorian baskets.

Onyx

This well-known Findley Glass treatment, first made in 1889, isn't often thought of as opalescent ware but it really is (just look at the handle of the pitcher shown). It can be found in various colored effects, the base glass is white or tannish with a white casing inside. The floral design can be silver lustre, gold lustre, ruby lustre, or bronze lustre. A similar design from the same mould is known as Floradine but it isn't considered Onyx ware.

Opal Bull's Eye

I've yet to learn the maker of this pattern but I'm reasonably certain it is English and do hope someone has additional information to share. The only color reported is vaseline opalescent. The shapes known are a mustard with lid and spoon and a 1½" tall open salt in a metal holder. Thanks to Joan and Wayne Jolliffe for the photo.

Opal Daisy

These two strange pieces are a real mystery. The smaller is 2" tall and the larger 3½". Both have brass bound tops and both slant. At this time I have no idea who made them or even what they were used for. I certainly welcome any information readers may have on these pieces.

Opal Dot

This generous size vaseline water tray is the only shape and color I've heard about at this time. I believe this to be English in origin but have no proof of such. Additional information would be appreciated. Thanks to the Sandemans for sharing it.

Opalescent Swirl

This shade, which I am assuming is English, can be found in at least two different shapes, but is reported only in vaseline at this time. All of these diagonal swirl patterned shades that I've seen have been ruffled. I urge anyone with additional colors, shapes, or information to contact me. Thanks once again to the Sandemans for sharing with me.

Opal Flower

This English cylinder shade (maker unconfirmed) is very well done, with large and small flower groupings and vines throughout the pattern. The color seems to be a white opalescence with cranberry top, but may in fact be rubina verde (I have no information on the actual color). This is the only color and shape reported to date. Thanks to Steve and Radka Sandeman for the photo.

Opaline Brocade

In an earlier edition this was given the name Barbed Wire. Since then the correct name has been brought to my attention. It was made by John Walsh Walsh and is thin blown glass. Shown in vaseline are a rather large shade and the Walsh signature "twisted stem" compote. Thanks to Dave Peterson for the new information and photos.

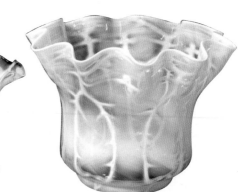

Opal Loops

I understand this pattern was made by one of the smaller English glass companies in the 1880s. Pieces known are a decanter, a flask, a vase, and a glass pipe. Pieces like the one shown are mistakenly called Nailsea glass by some collectors, but they were made in Sunderland or Nailsea or Newcastle plants perhaps.

Opal Open (Beaded Panels)

Carnival glass collectors have long known this pattern as Beaded Panels. Opalescent glass collectors call it Opal Open. It was shown in a Northwood ad in 1899, so I know they made it. But it shows up in Dugan ads after 1907, and I know the iridized items are Dugan. To add to the complication, Westmoreland made a reproduction in the 1940s and 1950s that has a solid stem rather than one pierced like the originals. Old pieces in opalescent glass were made in four colors.

Opal Stripe

This vaseline striped vase has applied feet and beautifully done applied flowers in a rose pink color. It is obviously of European origin (no maker confirmed to date). This would enhance any opalescent or vase collection. Additional information would be appreciated. Photo courtesy of the Sandemans.

Opal Urn Vase

I now know this fine 7½" vase is Jefferson Glass's #18, made in 1902. The distinctive features are the flaring above the 2½" base and the striping ending before it reaches the base.

Open Blossom Vase

This pale green opalescent vase stands nearly 6" tall and has the shape of an open blossom, hence the name. The owner feels it is from England (as do I). Additional information is appreciated. This is another fine pattern from the Petrasichs.

Open Edge Basket (Fenton)

Introduced into the Fenton line in 1910, this novelty item has been a part of Fenton's production throughout the years, being made in many glass types and colors. Shapes are bowls of three sizes, plates, candleholders, and vase whimsies. Carnival items sometimes have interior patterns. Early opalescent production colors are white, blue, green, and canary, but later production offered cobalt or royal blue and emerald green. These later examples date from the 1930s.

Open O's

Open O's was advertised by Northwood as early as 1903. This very unusual pattern is known mostly in short, squat vase shapes, but it was also made in novelty bowls and a handled ring bowl. It is possible Dugan continued production of this pattern once Northwood moved to Wheeling, but I can't confirm this at this time. The ring bowl is known as Heart Handled Open O's.

Optic Basket

This mould blown basket has a ten-panel interior optic pattern, six crimped ruffles, and a twisted vaseline handle that is one piece of glass doubled. It measures 5" tall, 5½" across, with a base diameter of 3". The glass is quite thin and there is a pontil mark. I suspect this is from an English glassmaker.

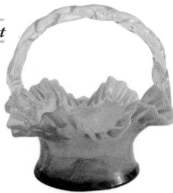

Optic Panel

This beautiful vase is truly a work of art with its applied cranberry edging. It is 6" tall with a 2¾" foot. It is mould blown and has eight optic panels that run from the applied base to the top. Coloring is a super vaseline. I believe this pattern dates from the 1890s and may well be British.

Orange Tree

Orange Tree is very much like the Wild Daffodils mug shown elsewhere in this book. It has custard-like opaqueness with a good deal of opalescence. Needless to say, it is a real rarity. One can only speculate if other shapes in this pattern were made in opalescent glass since both bowls and plates are found in carnival glass with opalescent edges.

Oscar's Legacy

This Art Nouveau vaseline opalescent glasier tile is in the shape of an iris, but other shapes and colors were also made. This tile was made by Oscar Haase, who lived in New York City and made these glass tiles for stained glass windows sometime between 1905 and 1915. The tiles were exported to Italy and one of those tiles was found at an old window company with a paper label still attached. All of the shapes and colors have been named in honor of the maker, who was a contemporary of Louis Comfort Tiffany. The particular iris-shaped tile measures 4¾" left-to-right and 4½" top-to-bottom. Special thanks to Siegmar Geiselberger and Dave and Vickie Peterson for their research on this pattern.

Oval Windows

I haven't found this pattern in any Hobb's or Beaumont catalog reprints so I can't say it came from either factory, as the regular windows patterns did. It's possible that this could be English but this is pure speculation. The piece shown has oval windows rather than round ones seen on the regular windows pattern shown elsewhere in this edition. The particular piece shown is in vaseline opalescent and has a metal flower frog lid. Many thanks to Ruth Harvey for sharing it.

Over-All Hobnail

This is A. J. Beatty's #100 pattern which was later made by U.S. Glass. The pattern can be identified on most shapes by the small feet (tumblers are the exception). A wide variety of shapes are known in three colors. Photo courtesy of Rick and Debbie Graham.

Overlapping Leaves (Leaf Tiers)

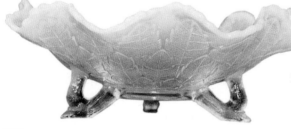

While it has been reported as a Northwood product, this pattern has long been known by carnival glass collectors as a Fenton pattern called Leaf Tiers. Three shapes are known, all footed from the same mould, and three colors are reported.

Palisades (Lined Lattice)

Here is yet another pattern first credited to the Northwood Company but now known to be a Dugan/Diamond product. Carnival glass collectors call this pattern Lined Lattice where it can be found in stretched vases and even a light shade for a table lamp called the Princess Lamp. Vase and novelty bowls are from the same mould. Photo courtesy of Rick and Debbie Graham.

Palm and Scroll

Although credited to the Northwood Company in 1905, Palm and Scroll is actually a product of the Dugan Glass Company. It was produced in opalescent glass beginning in 1906, in blue, green, and white. Shapes are various bowls on feet and a neat rose bowl from the same mould. The design is easily recognized: three palm leaves over the curled and ribbed feet and three very artistic feather scrolls between these designs.

Palm Beach

Palm Beach is a U.S. Glass pattern dating from 1906. It is found in various types of glass. In opalescent glass numerous shapes are known, but only in three colors (not all shapes are found in all colors).

Pan American

This interesting vase is found with "Pan American 1901" embossed on the front in the emblem. All examples have applied rigoree surrounding the neck. It was made by National Glass at the Northwood factory in Indiana, Pennsylvania. Colors are blue, white, and vaseline opalescent. The shape of the tops will vary. These are quite hard to find, so consider yourself fortunate if you locate one. Photo courtesy of Bill Walter and Laurel Walton.

Paneled Acorn Vase

This is a tiny 3" tall English vase with root-like feet and an acorn cup in the middle with a paneled top. I can't pin the maker down but strongly suspect it was Thomas Webb. The coloring is a strong canary. Thanks again to Ruth Harvey.

Paneled Cornflower

Shown in an 1882 ad from the Sowerby Glass Works of England, this two-handled bowl is typical of the opalescent glass produced by this company. The Paneled Cornflower design was also used on bowls with knob feet and on a vase shape in other types of glass, as well as opalescent ware.

Paneled Fronds

This 5¾" basket is likely a Greener and Co. product. The pattern consists of a series of panels with a frond at the top of each panel. The rustic handle has two open sections with the usual bumpy protrusions sticking out from around the edges. Blue is the only color reported. Photo courtesy of the Petrasichs.

Paneled Holly

Paneled Holly was made by the Northwood Company in various types of glass. Shapes in opalescent glass include a water set, table set, a berry set, novelty bowls, shakers, and some pieces whimsied from the table set items. Opalescent colors are white and blue, and either can be found with gilding.

Paneled Lattice Band

This beautiful tumbler has a band that is similar to that found on Dugan's Lattice and Daisy tumbler shown elsewhere, but I have no information to link the patterns. The Paneled Lattice Band tumbler is about 4" tall, has a many-rayed base, and panels from the base to the banding. Any information on this pattern would be appreciated. Thanks to the Sandemans for this piece.

Paneled Sprig

This 1894 pattern was made by Northwood and perhaps later by Dugan. It is found in white opalescent glass only. Shapes known are a cruet, toothpick holder, and salt shakers. It was also made in other types of colored glass, where it was widely reproduced.

Panels with Draped Crimp

This rather plain pattern comes from the Jefferson Glass Co., circa 1905. If you look at the distinct edge crimp on the Carousel pattern you can see that both are the same. I've seen no other edge crimp from any other factory that I recall. Photo courtesy of Ruth Harvey.

Panels With Spiral Band

This paneled vase with rigoree applied in a spiral fashion and found with various shapes to the top is certainly European. The only color is vaseline and a vase is the only reported shape. Thanks to Ruth Harvey for sharing this nice piece.

Peacock Basket

This very nice handled and footed basket shows peacocks and flowers around the top section of the piece and a ribbed section below. I believe this to be a Sowerby product. This is the only shape and white is the only color I know of. Photo courtesy of Ruth Harvey.

Peacock Feathers

I don't know the maker of this bowl on a metal stand but it certainly has a European flavor and somewhat resembles some of the carnival glass Aurora Pearls pieces from Austria. This bowl on a metal stand has a peacock tail feather design and is shown in white opalescent with a rose pink edging. Any information would be appreciated. Thanks to Marty Vogel for sharing it.

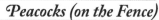

Peacocks (on the Fence)

Peacocks on the Fence is perhaps one of Northwood's best known patterns, especially in carnival glass. It is found only on bowls or plates. The pattern dates from 1908. In opalescent glass it can be found in white, blue, and cobalt to date. All these opalescent colors are quite scarce.

Peacock Tail

This rare tumbler is quite different than the pressed Drapery. Note the octagon base and design that ends about ¾" below the lip. Just why the Fenton Company decided to make this one item in opalescent glass is a mystery.

Pearl Flowers

This aptly named Northwood pattern from 1903 or 1904 isn't appreciated as much as it might be. All shapes are from the same mould with short knobby feet that are nearly ball-shaped. Several shapes and colors are known.

Pearline Rib

This Davidson Company bowl has no flat base so it has to sit in a holder. I have seen these in a chain ring and hung by windows as a bulb bowl. In the middle of the ribbing is a standing line of scallops that holds the piece in the holder. This was part of Davidson's Pearline run and can also be found in blue opalescent glass.

Pearls and Scales

This often seen pattern is now known to be from the Jefferson Glass Company from 1905 – 1906. It appears on stemmed pieces all from the same mould. Shapes include a compote, a scarce rose bowl, and a banana bowl shape. Five colors are known in opalescent glass. Sometimes a cranberry frit edge is present.

Pedestal Salt

This 1¾" tall salt is the first I've seen and I assume I am correct in calling it a salt dip. I welcome any information readers may have on this neat little item. Photo courtesy of the Petrasichs.

Peppermint Stripe Epergne

This beautiful cranberry single lily epergne is likely from either Stevens and Williams or Richardson, circa 1885 – 1890. The base of the lily and the rigoree appear to be a light vaseline color. It is one of my favorites. Photo courtesy of the Keathleys.

Petals with Cupped Pearl

This piece looks English to me, perhaps Richardson's or John Walsh Walsh, but I have no proof of such at this time. The design has several five petal flowers, which go up as well as down toward the base, along with a "U" shaped cup with reminds me of a pearl. Vaseline is the only reported color so far. If anyone has information on this pattern I urge you to contact me. Many thanks to Ruth Harvey for sharing it.

Phoenix Coinspot

The owner of this exciting pitcher has been told this was a Phoenix Glass product and I've found nothing to contradict that statement. The shape of the pitcher is very unusual as is the ruby throat treatment of casing. The glass color is a strong canary and the whole piece is about as pretty as this pattern ever gets.

Phoenix Drape

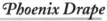

This pattern was made by the Phoenix Art Glass Co. in the mid 1880s. It has been reported in blue and cranberry opalescent. Shapes reported are a butter dish, celery vase, punch cup, pitcher, and tumbler. Thanks to the Petrasichs for the photo and information.

Phoenix Honeycomb

If you'll compare this pitcher with the Phoenix Coinspot pattern earlier in this edition you will notice the same edge crimping as well as the same style reeded handle. I'm told that both are made by Phoenix Glass. This blue opalescent pitcher is the only reported color and shape to date. Thanks to the Petrasichs for sharing it.

Piasa Bird

After reviewing a copy of Cyril Manley's *Decorative Victorian Glass*, I can say this pattern is English, probably by Sowerby. Manley shows it in a ruby glass with applied decoration, but the feet and design above them can't be mistaken for anything else. In opalescent glass, it is found in both white and blue but certainly vaseline was made. Shapes are bowls, vases, and several whimsey shapes, all footed, from the same mould.

Picket

This very well done square vase is English and is credited to the King Glass Company of London (1890), according to Heacock, but Sheilagh Murray declares it to be part of the Pearline ware from George Davidson. I can report it is certainly from England, and found in canary, white, and blue opalescent glass. It can be found in two sizes.

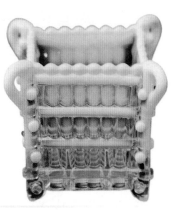

Pig Novelty

This Thomas Webb novelty can be found in several sizes in vaseline only. These were obviously popular items with Webb as indicated by the Swan shown elsewhere in this edition. Photo courtesy of Ruth Harvey.

Pilgrim

The information I was given is that this flint candlestick in white opalescent was made by the New England Glass Co. from 1868 to 1869. Reproductions were done for the Metropolitan Museum of Art and all are marked MMA. Thanks to the Petrasichs for the photo and information.

Pillared Vase

This is the first of these vases reported to me. This interesting vase has square type feet and opal stripes from top to bottom. Thanks to Roger Lane for the photo.

Pineapple

This English compote (or open sugar) measures 5¼" tall by 5¾" wide and is blue opalescent. This is about the only information I've received on it currently. Additional information would certainly be appreciated. Photo courtesy of the Petrasichs.

Pineapple and Fan

This A.H. Heisey Company pattern from 1898 is well known in crystal, ruby stain, gilded, and green glass. This was their #1255 pattern, and in opalescent glass, it is a very rare item indeed. Here I show the extremely rare vase in vaseline opalescent glass. I want to thank Douglas S. Sandeman for sharing the photo with me.

Pinwheel

I have no information about the maker of this very attractive stemmed 12" cake plate but suspect it may be English because it has that soft look. The stem is short and the whole piece is only 2" tall. I'd appreciate any further information. Thanks to the Petrasichs for sharing it.

Pistachio

This 8" vaseline opalescent pitcher is believed to have been made in the 1890s by Harry Powell of James Powell and Sons, London (which later became Whitefriars Glassworks). Only the pitcher and tumbler shapes have been reported at this time and only in vaseline opalescent. Photo courtesy of the Petrasichs.

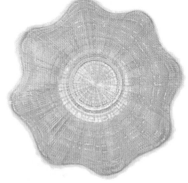

Plaid

Here is the first opalescent bowl in this Fenton pattern that has been reported. It is shared with me by Ruth Harvey. This pattern is also known as Granny's Gingham by some carnival glass collectors. The example shown is a ruffled 8½" bowl.

Plain Jane

I'm relatively sure this pattern came from the Dugan Company. This assumption is based on shape, color, and similarity to other Dugan pieces, chiefly nappies. Over the years I've seen several Dugan Leaf Ray nappies with exactly the same shape. Production was most likely from the 1906 – 1909 period.

Plain Opal

Other than a slight scalloping around the top, this the pattern has no mentionable features. The color is a light vaseline and the creamer shown is the only reported shape to date. Thanks to the Sandemans for sharing it.

Plain Panels

Plain Panels was made by Northwood in various types of glass, and later by Dugan/Diamond in carnival glass. The opalescent production by Northwood dates from 1908. There are six ribbed panels with plain panels between each one. The ribs run from near the base to the top, forming knobby flames. Sizes range from 9" to 14" tall.

Plume and Acorn

This nice 5" bowl is said to be a product of Barlow but I have no proof. I can only assume that other shapes are known. Additional information is appreciated. Photo courtesy of the Petrasichs.

Plumes and Scrolls

I have no information on this bowl at all, not even the size. The only thing I can positively say is that it's a ruffled bowl in blue opalescent. So I guess its open season on any information readers can supply me on this mystery pattern.

Poinsettia

This Northwood pattern, also known as Big Daisy, is found in various shapes. The pitcher shapes vary from a semi-cannonball type to three other tankard styles, and even a ring-necked one. Poinsettia dates from 1902 and can be found in four colors, with vaseline being rare. The tumblers are found in both pressed and blown examples and the bowl, which was made for use in a bride's basket, is most often found without a metal frame. Both the shaker and syrup are quite rare in any color and the tall tankard pitchers are very desirable. Photo courtesy of Rick and Debbie Graham.

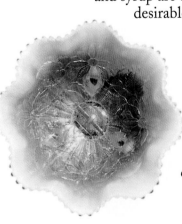

Poinsettia Lattice

This very beautiful Northwood bowl pattern is also known as Lattice and Poinsettia. Three opalescent glass colors are reported. Production at the Northwood factory dates from 1907. The latticework is exactly like that of a sister pattern called Cherry Lattice that followed a few years later in other types of glass.

Polar Medallions

I'm told by the owner that this milk pitcher is German in origin. I feel certain that other shapes were made but none have been reported to date. Vaseline is the only color found so far. Additional information is appreciated. Thanks to the Sandemans for the photo and to "gbarnm99" for the name.

Polka Dot

This West Virginia Glass Mfg. Company pattern, shown in an 1899 ad, was copied by Northwood and reproduced by L.G. Wright. A wide variety of the vintage shapes are known, but only three colors are known in opalescent glass. The pitcher shown is called the West Virginia mould.

Polka Dot with Thorn Handle

The 5" mug shown was purchased in the Czech Republic so I believe it may be from that area, Germany, or even England. The most interesting feature is, of course, the thorn handle, making it more an object to see rather than to hold. The date of production is unknown.

Popsicle Sticks

This is Jefferson Glass Company's #263 pattern. In design, it is a simple series of wide unstippled rays that fan out from the center of the bowl shape. Bowl shapes may be widely varied including ruffled edges, a banana bowl shape, and even a squared shape.

Poseidon

I suspect the maker of this very well done pattern is either German or English. The shapes reported are bowls of various sizes and shapes, butter dish with lid, and a plate. All pieces reported so far have been in vaseline opalescent, with the exception of one bowl in white opalescent. Anyone having additional information is requested to contact me. Thanks to the Sandemans for the photo and to Thom from the Vaseline Glass Group for giving this pattern its name.

Poseidon Shell

This rather large blue bowl with a beaded shell design from Greener and Co. measures a whopping 8½" x 4¾" and is of very thick glass. It has two scroll type handles at each end and sports four bracket style feet. The Rd. #113896 indicates a production date of November 15, 1888. This is the only color and shape reported at this time. Thanks to the Petrasichs for sharing this very nice piece.

Pram

Here is a really neat novelty piece from Greener and Co. that should be considered fairly tough to find. It measures in at 6½" long by 3" wide. Is has Rd. #150277 which indicates a production date of June 3, 1890. This is the only size known and blue opalescent is the only reported color. It is also known as Carriage. Many thanks to the Petrasichs for the photo and information.

Prayer Rug

I am pleased to show the vase in this Fenton pattern. While the bonbon can be found in either blue or vaseline opalescent, the vase has only been reported to date in vaseline opal. Both date from 1914. Thanks to Donna Drohan for sharing it. Please note that most of these pieces once had a paint or gilding that has long since worn off.

Preakness

I've eliminated some of the single lily epergnes shown in previous editions since the lily was interchangeable with various metal holders. Most could be grouped together, which I've done in the price guide under Universal Epergne. However, I felt this unique epergne should be shown with its allover diamond pattern and cranberry edge treatment. Thanks to Marty Vogel for sharing this nice piece.

Pressed Coinspot (#617)

This compote (advertised as a card tray) first showed up in a 1901 National Glass catalog, and then showed up in a Dugan ad for an Oriental assortment, labeled #617. The vase shape later became known as Concave Columns and in carnival glass it is simply called Coinspot. Shapes from the same mould are tall vases, compotes, goblets, and a stemmed banana boat shape. Colors are the standard opalescent ones.

Pressed Diamond

The owner of this 13" x 5" boat shaped bowl tells me that Central Glass is the maker and I have no reason to doubt that attribution at this time. This very large piece has only been reported in white opalescent. Thanks to the Petrasichs for sharing it.

Primrose Scroll

This is another beautiful pattern from England. It has both flowers and a scroll as well as occasional filler dots. It has a 6" diameter and a glass applied ring to fit in a holder of some sort. Additional information would be appreciated.

Primrose Shade

This rubina verde shade with opalescent treatment is a wonder to behold. I've also seen a water pitcher in this same design in canary opalescent. Hobbs, Brockunier introduced this process (vaseline and cranberry with opalescence) in 1884, but I suspect this is English, possibly by John Walsh Walsh. The pattern is similar to the Daffodils pattern shown elsewhere.

Prince Charles

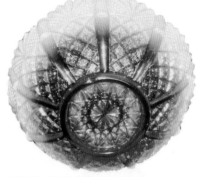

This English pattern, similar to both Princess Diana and Queen's Crown, can be found in amber as shown, an indication it may have been made at Greener & Company. The 4" bowl shown has a metal holder. Photo courtesy of Mary and John Petrasich.

Princess Diana

This Davidson of England pattern was from 1890 and is also known as Suite 1890 or Queen Anne. Shapes include a crimped oval plate (8", 10", and 12"), crimped round plate (7", 8½", 10½", 12"), crimped round dish (6", 7½", 9", 10½"), crimped oval dish (10½"), covered butter dish, creamer, footed sugar, biscuit jar and plate, water set (pitcher in both pint and half-pint), salad bowl, and water platter. Colors in opalescent glass are blue and canary.

Prince William

This pattern, made by Davidson in 1893, carried an Rd. #217752. It is found in an oval plate, a creamer, open sugar, child's water set, and the rare handled basket shown. This piece is 6½" long and stands 3½" tall. Colors are either blue or canary for pieces in this pattern as far as I know.

Prism Hobnail

This nice little creamer is interesting in that each hobnail has a distinct scoring added to it. The color is vaseline and I believe it to be English but have no concrete proof to date. Additional information would be appreciated. Photo courtesy of the Petrasichs.

Pulled Coinspot

This mug is a puzzle in a couple of ways. First the design has been pulled into ovals rather than the usual dots and then the coloring blends from a cranberry glass at the base to a clear glass above. The maker is unknown and I welcome any information about it. Thanks to Mary and John Petrasich for sharing it.

Pulled Loop

This pattern was made by Dugan/Diamond as early as 1906 in opalescent glass. Pieces are limited and found in white, green, and blue. Sizes range from 9" to 14" in height and there are at least two base sizes, 3" diameter and 5" diameter. There are six ribs with very extended tops and six rows of panels that contain the loops. The Pulled Loop pattern was advertised as #1030.

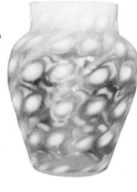

Pump and Trough

This pattern was shown in a 1900 Pitkin and Brooks catalog along with other Northwood Glass Company items. The very interesting Pump and Trough pieces are listed as #566 and #567, respectively. The design of these items typifies the trend toward naturalism in so many Northwood glass products (Grapevine Clusters, Ocean Shell, Leaf Chalice, and even the Dolphin compote), a trend that continued into their carnival production to some degree with the famous Town Pump. Of course, as with many good things, the Pump and Trough has been widely reproduced, so beware of pumps with flat tops!

Pussy Willow

This little vase stands 4½" tall. The shape is somewhat like one in the Dugan/Diamond Pompeian and Japanese assortment advertised in 1906, but this one has an opalescent design of ovals on the diagonal, connected by a fine line of opalescence. Probably other colors were made and there may be another name for this piece, but this name is what the owner calls it.

Queen's Candlesticks

Greener & Company's Rd. #17637 is very similar to the Queen's Spill shown elsewhere. These date from 1891 and stand 2½" tall. They were probably made in blue opalescent also.

Queen's Crown

This very scarce English pattern was made by Davidson in 1898 as their #320124 registered design. It can be found in four shapes and two opalescent colors. Here I have to pleasure to show the very rare and beautiful towering epergne with five bowls and a top lily in vaseline. The proud owners are Dave and Vicki Peterson and I greatly appreciate them allowing me to show this exquisite piece here, as well as on the cover of this edition.

Queen's Spill

This very pretty Greener & Company spill (vase) stands 4" tall and is 3¼" wide at the top. It was part of the Pearline glass production in 1891. It is similar in design to the Quilted Daisy Fairy Lamp.

Queen Victoria

The pattern on this Davidson ruffled plate is actually one I show elsewhere in this book called Somerset. Here, the pattern was registered in 1895 as #254027. This piece with the Queen's portrait was obviously made to honor the Golden Jubilee of her reign in 1887. The portrait seems to be a form of photo transfer. Since Somerset was made in blue opalescent, this piece was possibly also made in that color.

Question Marks

It is difficult to use only one name for this well-known Dugan pattern because it is actually three patterns. The interior is called Question Marks, the exterior pattern is known as Georgia Belle, and the stem has a Dugan pattern called Puzzle! It was reproduced in vaseline.

Quilt

This 5¼" bowl is a real mystery. Only the opalescence gives a clue that it is possibly a Sowerby product. It is oval (many English bowls are), has an oversized collar base, and the opalescence is almost uniform over the piece rather than on the high spots as on American glass. I'd appreciate any information on this pattern.

Quilted Daisy Fairy Lamp

This pattern is English, I feel sure, and has a superb canary color. The base is hard to see since it is a plain color without any milky finish. The design is one of diamonds bordered by sections of daisy filler with a skirt of points below a similar band of points. This piece was made by Greener in 1891.

Quilted Diamonds

I can only assume that this nice piece in white with a cranberry edge is European. Any information is welcomed. Photo courtesy of Bill Walter and Laurel Walton.

Quilted Phlox Lattice

This Northwood piece is on a Quilted Phlox mould but has the lattice opalescent treatment. It was probably an experimental combination, dating from the 1895 to 1905 era. It may have been made in blue or cranberry as well. Four shapes and two colors are reported.

Quilted Pillow Sham

Quilted Pillow Sham, also known as Pattern 900, was made by Davidson in 1893. The design is distinctive with a petticoat base, an allover diamond quilting, and a collar of glass below the top of each piece.

Quilted Rose

I've learned very little about this interesting pattern except that it is probably European. The pattern is an allover one on the tumbler shown and I must assume there is a matching pitcher. I welcome any information about this design.

Rainbow Stripe

This pattern is believed to be from England and has a usual shading of opalescent striping that varies from vaseline to cranberry. The basket shape shown and a compote are also known. I thank Ruth Harvey for sharing it and welcome any information about its origin.

Raised Rib

This was Fenton's #857 pattern, made in cameo opalescent in 1929. An 11" flared bowl on a dome base is shown here, but ads show a deep cupped bowl from the same mould. Thanks to the Petrasichs for this piece.

Raspberry Prunts

This interesting vaseline creamer is the first of its kind I've seen and it is believed to be from Stuart and Sons Limited of England. The applied handle, rolled feet, and applied prunts make for an unusual design. I'd appreciate any additional information about this piece. Photo courtesy of the Sandemans.

Ray

This pattern was from Co-operative Flint Glass and was advertised in 1904, even though the company isn't known for making opalescent glass until the 1920s. I've seen this vase in three opalescent colors. The example shown is 13" tall and has a 3½" diameter base.

Rayed Heart

Although often credited to the Dominion Glass Company of Canada, the opalescent pieces certainly came from Jefferson Glass in this country before the moulds traveled north. This pretty compote dates from 1910 and came in three opalescent colors.

Rayed Jane

This Dugan/Diamond nappy is similar to the Plain Jane stemmed nappy shown elsewhere in this book, except that it has scalloped edges and interior rays. The Rayed Jane nappy comes from the 1909 – 1914 era and was made in white and green opalescent.

Reeds and Blossoms

The Petrasichs have given this bowl its fitting name. It has the look of English glass with a collarless base and the design extending below it. The pattern is a simple one with waving stems and leaves and small flowers.

Reflecting Diamonds

Reflecting Diamonds is not the same pattern as Compass, as some believe. It appears only in bowl shapes, and has been found as early as 1905 in Butler Brothers ads featuring Dugan/Diamond patterns. Like so many geometric patterns, this one has a series of diamonds filled with a file pattern, bordered by fan shapes standing back-to-back between the diamonds. The base has the exact overlapping star design found on the Compass base.

Reflections

This Dugan design is a difficult pattern to locate. It is found on footed novelty bowls, sometimes round or sometimes squared, like shown. It can be found in three opalescent colors. The pattern was continued from Dugan into Diamond production (it is signed with the Diamond-D mark on some pieces). Thanks to John Loggie for sharing it.

Regal

This pattern is certainly rightly named for it has a regal look. It was made by the Northwood Company in 1905, and some pieces are marked. Regal can be found in a host of shapes and three colors, some with gilding. The pattern was also known as Blocked Midriff, but the Regal name is more widely used.

Regalia

This is one of the more interesting shades in opalescent glass. It's the first I've seen and I assume it to be English but can't be sure. I welcome any information readers may have. Photo courtesy of the Petrasichs.

Reverse Drapery

This Fenton pattern (also called Cut Arcs in carnival glass) is sometimes confused with Boggy Bayou from the same maker. It is found in bowls as well as vases (shown in a regular and a pulled vase). Opalescent colors are white, blue, green, and amethyst.

Reverse Swirl

This well-known Buckeye Glass and later Model Flint Glass pattern dates from 1888. It is found in a wide variety of shapes and in four colors. Items may be satin finished on some places too. Photo courtesy of Rick and Debbie Graham.

Reverse Swirl Spatter

This pattern is from the same maker as the regular Reverse Swirl, but has a rolled frit spatter added to the glass. Various shapes and colors are known. Photo courtesy of Rick and Debbie Graham.

Rib and Big Thumbprints

This vase was shown in a Butler Brothers ad in 1906 for Dugan/Diamond and in a 1908 Jefferson ad in the same catalog. The design of four ribs in five columns with spots of opalescence between must have been a popular one for both companies. It appears to be another example of copying what sells.

Ribbed Beaded Cable

This is just like the regular Beaded Cable pieces made by the Northwood Glass Company in 1904, except it has added interior ribbing. This ribbed version is much scarcer than the plain interior pieces.

Ribbed Coinspot

Ribbed Coinspot was made by Northwood in 1888, in several shapes and colors in opalescent glass. It is actually the Coinspot pattern blown into a ribbed mould. Thanks to the Petrasichs for the photos.

Ribbed Enameled Epergne

I'm told that this nice vaseline epergne is possibly a product of Mount Washington, but have no proof. It stands a towering 22½" tall. Photo courtesy of the Keathleys.

Ribbed Epergne

I can only imagine the original cost of this exquisite five-lily epergne in its very fancy base. It is most certainly European. This is the first time I've seen these particular ribbed lilies. Vaseline is the only reported color. Photo courtesy of Dennis Crouse.

Ribbed (Opal) Lattice

This is probably a Northwood Glass pattern but may have been an earlier La Belle Glass product. It is found in water sets, a cruet, salt shakers, syrup, table set, berry set, toothpick holder, sugar shakers in two sizes, and a celery vase. Photo courtesy of Rick and Debbie Graham.

Ribbed Opal Rings

Ribbed Opal Rings is sometimes called Ribbed Opal Spiral. The pattern is believed to be from the Northwood Company and is found on water sets, as well as a sugar bowl.

Ribbed Optic

The Fenton Company made this pattern in 1927 in the bedroom set or tumble-up (the tumbler is missing) in green, vaseline, blue, and the light cranberry shown. The water bottle is 6" tall and has a base diameter of 3½".

Ribbed Pillar

This Northwood pattern is also called Northwood Pleat by some collectors. Like the Apple Blossom mould, the name of this pattern refers to the mould shaping. It was Northwood's #245 pattern. A variety of shapes are known, but the only color is cranberry opalescent with a frit spatter.

Ribbed Spiral

This was #911 from Model Flint Glass (1899 – 1902). It is found in three opalescent colors. Shapes include 4", 7", 8", 9", and 10" bowls (either round or square), a table set, celery vase, 7¾", 9¼", and 11" plates, a salt and pepper, toothpick holder, water set, custard cup, jelly compote, lemonade glass, and vases that range from 4" to 21" tall.

Ribbed Triangle and Fans

Although this pattern resembles Davidson's Victoria and Albert pattern, it is a registered Greener and Co. piece. The Rd. #284639 gives it a date of September 23, 1886, which was 11 months before the Victoria and Albert pattern was registered. This blue opalescent oval 9½" x 7½" bowl is the only reported shape and color. Thanks once again to the Petrasichs for sharing it.

Ribbon Wave

This nice salt in a metal holder is likely from England and dates from 1880 to 1890. It has a wave band applied around the center. The only reported color is the rubina verde shown. Any information would be appreciated. Photo courtesy of the Sandemans.

Richelieu

Richelieu was made by Davidson of England with Rd. #96945 or #96943. This pattern is found in a wide variety of shapes and in three opalescent colors.

Ric-Rac

This unusual blown vase in vaseline stands 8¼" tall and has a pontil mark on the base. The glass is very thin, and I suspect it is English. If anyone knows it by another name, I'd be interested in hearing from them.

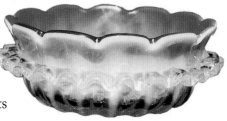

Rigoree

This very attractive sauce bowl is probably English, made in the 1890s. It is a ribbed optic stripe opalescent piece in rubina verde with a vaseline rigoree (ribbon) ring applied. I don't need to tell anyone this is opalescent glass art at its best and the piece shown would be a standout in any collection.

Rigoree Spill

This beautiful spill vase has just a touch of Rubina at the top and ribbons of rigoree along the sides and top. I suspect it is English but can't determine the maker. I certainly welcome any information and thank Ruth Harvey for sharing it.

Ringed Barrel

The owner of this piece (it is either a toothpick holder or a spittoon shape) pointed out its similarities to the Sowerby Triangle piece I show elsewhere in this book. I believe they are both from that concern. This piece has no Rd. number but surely dates to the 1890s.

Ringed Flute with Beaded Medallions

The owner of this basket tells me it is likely Greener and Sons. The basket stands 5¾" tall by 6" at the widest point. Blue is the only reported color. Any additional information is appreciated. Thanks to the Petrasichs for sharing it.

Ring Handled Basket

This fine center-handled basket has the same basic design as Opal Open (Beaded Panels). The same design is found on salt shakers. It can be found in four opalescent colors and measures 7½" wide. It was made by Dugan/Diamond, I believe, but may have also been a Northwood product.

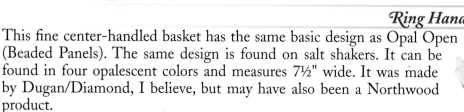

Rings and Arches

I have no information on this bowl but believe it to be English. The design consists of two sets of fine cut rings within double arches and the base is a star pattern. This is the only shape and color reported. I urge anyone with information on this pattern to contact me. Thanks to the Petrasichs for sharing it.

Rings With Wave Band

This 5¾" vase certainly has an English flavor with its applied wavy band, rings circling the stem from top to bottom, and the finecut pineapple look to the base. I would appreciate any information on this piece. Vaseline is the only reported color. Thanks to Joan and Wayne Jolliffe for sharing this very nice vase.

Ripple

This scarce Ripple vase, made by Imperial, has a many rayed base and is more flared at the top. Colors reported so far are blue, vaseline, and green, but surely white was also made. This was a very popular carnival glass design, made in at least four base diameters and many carnival colors.

Roaring Lion

The owners of this goblet (a cordial and pilsner style glass are also known) tell me that the pattern was made by Pukeberg, Sweden, in the mid to late 1920s. All pieces to date have been in vaseline opalescent. The same design appears on the stem of each drinking vessel. Additional information is appreciated. Thanks to the Sandemans for sharing it.

Rococo

Thanks to the research of Siegmar Geiselberger of Germany, I can now say this pattern was a product of the Fenne Glassworks in Saarland, Germany. Pieces known are a bowl that fits a bride's basket, a 6" plate, and the 10" ruffled plate shown. There are some variations to the design and the Casbah pattern seems to be one of these. Photo courtesy of the Sandemans.

Rolled Wide Stripe

This English piece was previously listed as a tumbler but is shown here in its original holder. It stands 2½"tall without the holder. I do not know the maker at this time. Thanks to the Petersons for sharing it.

Rose

This pattern, also called Rose & Ruffles, was first made at Tiffin and later at their U.S. Glass factory. A variety of shapes are known, but only two opalescent colors are found. This pattern has been copied by Fenton in several shapes and treatments so beware of reproductions and look for the Fenton logo.

Rose Bush

This extremely well done 5¼" wall pocket with flowers, leaves, and twig handle has been reported on white opalescent only. Probably from the early 1880s, the possibility of makers includes Burtles, Tate & Co., and Molineaux Webb & Co. Anyone with additional information is urged to contact me. Thanks to John & Mary Petrasich for sharing this nice piece with me.

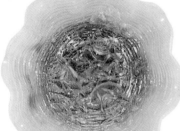

Rose Show

Although known primarily as a carnival glass pattern, this very beautiful bowl can also be found in limited amounts of white and blue opalescent glass. Rose Show is reputed to be a Northwood pattern. The bowl has a reverse pattern of Woven Wonder, a spin-off design of Frosted Leaf and Basketweave.

Rose Spatter

While I still feel the water set I showed in a previous edition is either Buckeye Glass or Beaumont, I feel the Northwood Company had a try in this same coloring. Here is a ruffled vase that certainly looks like Northwood. It is the first reported and I'm happy to show it.

Rose Spray

Although found mostly in carnival glass, this Fenton compote can also be seen on rare occasions on opalescent glass. Production dates from 1910 to 1914. The design of a stem, leaves, and a rose is little more than a line drawing and is very hard to see.

Roulette

Roulette was made by the Northwood Company and shown in one of their ads in a Lyon Brothers 1906 glass catalog. This is not one of their better designs, consisting of a series of ovals that are bordered by beading, with a stylized three-petal flower between each. All pieces are dome based and from the same mould, despite a variety of shapings.

Royal Fan

This small whimsey posy has an overall coverage of overlapping fans. Other than the top being ruffled, it has the look of a ladies' cuspidor in some respects. Vaseline is the only color reported and this is the only shape I've seen. I feel certain it is English and would love to hear from anyone having additional information. Photo courtesy of the Sandemans.

Royal Jubilee

This British pattern, credited to Greener & Company, can be found in three opalescent colors. The shape is a footed novelty basket with a scroll curling on each end of the elongated piece. The pattern somewhat resembles a zipper design.

Royal Scandal

This superb English wall pocket vase is one of four designs I've seen, and all are well above the ordinary in the glassmakers' art. Royal Scandal has no Rd number but most of these pieces were made in the 1880s or early 1890s by various makers. The design is a series of rope-like strips over a shell and flower pattern. Royal Scandal is known in three opalescent colors and some are found with felt-backed mounting pieces.

Royal Sunburst

I'm certain this is English but haven't found any information about it to date. Only the bowl shape has been reported at this time and vaseline is the only color. Any information about this pattern would be appreciated. Thanks to the Sandemans for the photo and name.

Rubina Diamonds

I'm not sure that this pattern was made by Hobbs like the regular Rubina Verde pattern shown next. I'm not even certain of its age. The pattern is an overall coverage of diamonds and the shape is a jack-in-the-pulpit with candy ribbon edge (notice the twist at the bottom of the edge treatment). If anyone knows anything about this piece I urge you to contact me. Photo courtesy of Marty Vogel.

Rubina Verde

Rubina Verde was made by Hobbs, Brockunier & Company in the 1880s. It is actually a combination of canary and ruby glass, with the ruby plated over the canary or portions thereof. Some pieces are acid finished. Shown is a 6½" tall jack-in-the-pulpit vase with opalescence on the reverse of the throat. Other patterns such as Dewdrop (Hobnail) were made in this formula.

Ruffles and Rings

Ruffles and Rings is another of the Jefferson Glass patterns that came into the Northwood production orbit. The opalescent version appears to have been made in 1906 and after. In carnival glass, the pattern has been found as an exterior one with such designs as Rosette and even on a rare flint opalescent bowl with no interior pattern, marigold iridizing, and an added floral border edging.

Ruffles and Rings with Daisy Band

Just why the Northwood Company decided to do this variant of the Ruffles and Rings pattern is a mystery, but here they've added a classy banding of daisies along the outer edge. Since both Jefferson and Northwood are credited with Ruffles and Rings, perhaps the unbanded pieces are Jefferson's that were later made by Northwood who then added the band. At any rate, Northwood later made both versions in carnival glass and a very rare example of marigold with an opalescent daisy band exists. Opalescent colors are the usual white, blue, and green.

Salmon

According to Cyril Manley in his book *Decorative English Glass*, this fish bowl was made by Molineaux Webb Glass Works in 1885 with a registry number of 29781. It is found in white opalescent glass as well as the canary opalescent shown. Manley calls it a posy bowl. It is also known as Pink. Molineaux Webb was a glass factory in Manchester, England.

Scheherezade

While the maker of this very pretty pattern has not been confirmed, I really believe I need look no further than the Dugan/Diamond Company. It is found in bowls in three opalescent colors. The design of file triangles, finecut triangles, and hobstars is a close cousin to Dugan's Reflecting Diamonds, but has more than enough difference to distinguish it from any other pattern.

Scottish Moor

This pattern is attributed to the West Virginia Glass Company by some collectors. It is found in only a limited number of shapes (pitcher, tumbler, cruet, cup, celery, cracker jar, and vase). It was made in the usual opalescent colors of white, amber, and blue, as well as in cranberry, rubina, and a light amethyst color. Here I show the water pitcher and you will note the handle is reeded. Production may have been as early as 1890 or as late as 1900, but I have no evidence of an exact date.

Scroll

This 4½" high by 6⅛" bowl is very light vaseline opalescent and the glass is quite thin. The design is similar to Buttons and Braids but without the buttons. I certainly don't think it's a Fenton product, but believe it is possibly English in origin. It does have somewhat of a Model Flint Glass look, but this is only guesswork. Any information is welcomed on this pattern. Thanks to the Petrasichs for sharing it.

Scroll Fluted

Imperial's #721 pattern was made beginning in the late 1920s and continuing into the late 1930s. This was made in several types of glass. In opalescent glass, four shapes and colors are known. Photo courtesy of Bill Walter and Laurel Walton.

Scroll with Acanthus

Credited to the Northwood Company, Scroll with Acanthus can be found in a host of shapes and three opalescent colors. Production dates from 1903.

Scroll with Buttons

I've given this pattern a name unless I find out a name already exists. The intricate pattern on this white opalescent 4⅜" creamer is very nicely done and I only wish I knew more about it. Additional information is requested. Photo courtesy of Len Galloway.

Scroll with Cane Band

This pattern was made by the West Virginia Glass Company in crystal, ruby stain, and possibly gilded glass. I was very surprised to see this wonderful green opalescent bowl. This pattern dates from 1895 and could possibly have been a treatment testing, but no other pieces have been reported. Thanks to the Petrasichs for sharing it with me.

Sea Scroll

I've seen this piece in a book section devoted to Davidson glass so I now know it was made by that company in England. Pieces include the compote shown as well as one on a very short stem that would be called a dessert in this country. The compote shape measures 4¾" tall, with a base diameter of 2⅝". The shorter piece is 3¼" tall.

Sea Shore

This blue opalescent bowl looks to be American but I have yet to find it in any old catalogs or other reference material. The pattern reminds me of waves rolling in on a sandy beach with a shell inside a shell being the center of attention. This is the only shape and color I've heard of at this time. Thanks to the Sandemans once again for the nice photo.

Sea Spray

This is Jefferson Glass Company's #192 pattern made from 1906 to 1907. It is found in only one shape and in three opalescent colors. The design is somewhat similar to the S-Repeat but it has an interesting beading added below the "S" design and sections of line filler above. Photo courtesy of LouAnn Novak.

Seaweed

This pattern was first made by Hobbs, Brockunier in water sets, a salt shaker, a syrup, table sets, berry sets, a barber bottle, a sugar shaker, a pickle caster, a cruet, and two sizes of oil bottle. It has become confused with a pattern called Coral Reef. The differences lie in the shaping of the small bulb and line patterns and if you will make a comparison of both, you will be able to instantly tell them apart. Hobbs made both patterns and Coral Reef was also made by Beaumont and possibly Northwood a few years after the Hobbs production. Photo courtesy of Rick and Debbie Graham.

Seaweed Variant

This pattern is somewhat different than the regular Seaweed pattern. Some may consider this Rubina Verde (and they may be right) but in my opinion it is white opalecent with cranberry edging. I hope someone can shed more light on this nice pattern. Photo courtesy of the Sandemans.

Serpent Threads Epergne

This stately epergne stands 23" tall. The glass is very thin and fine, and each lily fits into a brass holder. This epergne was made in vaseline opalescent with or without cranberry frit on the edges, and can be found with a ruffled or a candy ribbon edged base. The lilies are decorated with glass banding. It is likely European and possibly Bohemian, but I have no proof. Thanks to Marty Vogel for sharing this beauty.

Shamrock

This is the first one of these lamps I've seen and I do think the name is fitting. The font is vaseline opalescent and shows what certainly would pass as a shamrock design. The base is of black glass. This is the only color reported and I've seen no other sizes of this lamp to date. Photo courtesy of the Sandemans.

Sharks Tooth

Items reported in this pattern are a spooner and oil lamp in vaseline opalescent and a smoke shade in rubina verde; a process which combined vaseline and cranberry with opalescence added. Hobbs, Brockunier introduced this treatment in 1884 but I have no proof this rare shade is from that company. John Walsh Walsh is another possibility. This pattern is also known as Christmas Trees. Thanks to the Sandemans for the photo and the name.

Sheldon Swirl

This Buckeye Glass Company lamp is, of course, the Reverse Swirl pattern, and is highly desirable to collectors. Colors are white, blue, canary (shown), and cranberry, and are sometimes found with a satin finish or with a speckled treatment. The distinctive stem design gives this lamp its name.

Shell

These two shell dishes were made by Geo. Davidson. They both appeared in a 1912 catalog that featured various items for the soda fountain. I am told these are ice cream dishes but haven't confirmed this. The blue one is 4½" long and the vaseline is 5½" long. It is not known if the blue came in the long size and the vaseline in the short size, as they are so rare. Thanks to David Peterson for the photos and John Bell for the catalog reference source.

Shell and Dots

Shell and Dots, made by the Jefferson Company, is nothing more than the well-known Beaded Fans pattern with a series of bubble-like dots on the base. This 1905 pattern can be found in white, green, and blue opalescent.

Shell and Wild Rose

This 1906 Northwood pattern is called Wild Rose by carnival glass collectors. The Wild Rose pattern is exterior, but the interior can be plain or have a stippled ray design of which there are two variations. The open edged inverted heart border is a real piece of mould maker's art.

Shell Ink Well

This very nice double ink well (missing the lids) is the first example I've seen. The maker is unknown to date and I do welcome any information readers may have on this nice piece. Photo courtesy of the Petrasichs.

Shoe

This Burtles, Tate and Co. English novelty shoe had an Rd. #65455 indicating it was made in 1887. It is a simple shoe design with a bow near the top of the opening. Photo courtesy of the Petrasichs.

Silver Overlay Vase

Several companies made silver overlay treatments of glass, including Westmoreland, Cambridge, and Heisey. The vase shown here was made at the Dugan/Diamond factory and has an added treat of opalescent glass. The example here is about 7" tall and is really the Dugan's Junior JIP vase with a silver overlay treatment. Photo courtesy of Bill Walter and Laurel Walton.

Simple Simon

Carnival glass collectors know this pattern as Graceful. It was a product of the Northwood Company dating from 1908 to 1909. It is found in three opalescent colors. While the design isn't too well planned, the compote's shape adds class, and the workmanship is quality.

Singing Birds

Singing Birds is one of Northwood's best-known patterns. The mug is also found in rare opalescent pieces in white, blue, and vaseline. In addition, tumblers have been reproduced.

Single Poinsettia

With the evidence of this bowl in amethyst opalescent glass, I can now declare the maker of this pattern is Fenton. Bowls are found in ruffled or the squared shape shown. Thanks to John Loggie III for sharing this find.

Sir Lancelot

Sir Lancelot was advertised in a Butler Brothers ad in 1906 along with several well-known Northwood patterns. Only bowls are known, and only in three opalescent colors. The design, three fleur-de-lis and three starburst figures on a stippled background, is very interesting and quite attractive. The dome base is rayed.

Six Petals

This is the first example of opalescent glass I've heard about in this Dugan pattern from before 1910. It is a ruffled 7½" bowl and the opalescence is very heavy over most of the surface. Thanks to the Hollenbachs for sharing it.

Skirted Dots

I'm uncertain what the function of this piece is; some are calling it a salt dip, some an open sugar, and others a marmalade. I have no dimensions to make a call either way. The looks indicate it being English but this is only a guess. This vaseline piece is the only item reported but I feel others may turn up eventually.

Smooth Rib

Since I first showed this simple bowl pattern, I've seen it with a cranberry frit edge like the example shown, so I now suspect this was a Jefferson Glass pattern. The bowl, on a collar base, has 20 interior panels. The collar base (marie) measures 2½" across and the exterior is completely plain. There is also a bowl in a metal holder known.

Snail Loop and Ball

I'm told that this English creamer (maker and origin are uncertain) is known by the name I've listed, but some collectors also know it as Porpoise. White is the only color I've seen and the creamer is the only reported shape. Photo courtesy of the Petrasichs.

Snowball Royale

The owner of this rare Christmas ornament (vaseline opalescent only found to date) is likely correct in saying that this pattern is of British origin, due to the fact that the previous owner bought three examples at the Newark Antique Fair in England. These ornaments can be displayed in various ways, either on a table stand, a table wire hanger, or on a tree by the attached wire loop. If you locate one of these be prepared to pay a hefty price. Many thanks once again to Dave and Vickie Peterson for sharing another rarity from their fine collection.

Snowflake

This pattern is actually from Hobbs, Brockunier & Company. It is called Daisy or Clover Leaf in trade papers. Date of production was 1891, and shapes and sizes include flat and footed hand lamps, a sewing lamp, a night lamp with matching shade, and five styles of stand lamps. Shown is a table lamp in cranberry. Photo courtesy of Rick and Debbie Graham.

Snowflakes and Icicles

This enameled pitcher is the first I've seen in this pattern. I'm told it comes from England, circa 1890. Additional information would be appreciated. Photo courtesy of the Petrasichs.

Snowflake Spatter

If you compare this vase and its treatment with other pieces of spatter ware, you will see this piece has a much finer allover opalescent look, rather like a snowstorm. This is a Dugan vase and sometimes this treatment is called granite. It is known in white, green, and blue as far as I know.

Solar Flare

The outer flames of this piece appear to be flame activity coming off the surface of the sun. This vaseline plate is the only piece I've had reported to date and vaseline is the only reported color. Photo courtesy of the Sandemans.

Somerset

Somerset was made by Davidson in 1895 with an Rd. #254027. This pattern is found in a host of opalescent shapes and in two colors. Around 50 shapes are shown in an 1896 catalog, but are unreported in opalescent glass at this time. The pattern is considered highly collectible.

Sowerby Basket

This dainty little basket measures only 3½" by 2" and is a real treasure. The looped handles are ribbed and step up from bottom to top. This is a Sowerby product that has the diamond lozenge dating it to 1879. I like the tight shape between the handles and would love to see it in another color, however white opalescent is the only color I've seen at this time. Thanks again to the Petrasichs for sharing it.

Spanish Lace

This pattern, introduced by the Northwood Company to American collectors in 1899, has also been known as Opaline Brocade (or just Brocade in some ads). It was originally made by John Walsh Walsh and known as Opaline Brocade. Over the years this pattern, from all makers, was given the generic name of Spanich Lace and I will leave the Northwood version under that name. Many shapes are known in the Northwood version and it is found in most standard opalescent colors. A few items in a canary are of the English origin (which will be listed under Opaline Brocade). A handled basket, a cruet, and a rose bowl have recently been made by Fenton in cranberry, but these are the only items that are not old.

Spatter

This treatment was used by both Northwood and Dugan/Diamond on water sets, bowls, and vases, but I feel from both the shape and top design, this piece is from Dugan/Diamond. It stands 9" tall, and the random opalescent swirling through the glass is quite attractive.

Spattered Coinspot

The shape of this very beautiful pitcher seems to be the same ball shape that Northwood used on the Daisy and Fern pitcher, but it may belong to another maker. I'm confident it is old, dating from the late 1800s, and as far as desirability is concerned, it would have to be quite high. The coloring is simply beautiful with spatters of cranberry mixed with flecks of white.

Speckled Celery Vase

Although very similar in appearance to Dugan's Venetian line, this is reported to be a product from the Northwood factory. This shape in the speckled treatment has been reported in four opalescent colors.

Speckled Chrysanthemum Base (Northwood)

This pattern was first made at American, Buckeye, and then Northwood in their speckled treatment in berry sets, table sets, water sets, a finger bowl, cruet, syrup, toothpick holder, sugar shaker, mustard jar, celery vase, and a lidded straw holder.

Speckled Stripe

This Model Flint Glass pattern is distinguished by the stripe being broken and not solid. It was made in the pitcher shown, a barber bottle, finger bowl and underplate, sugar, and three sizes of vases.

Spiny Cactus Vase

The Hollenbachs named these vases and say a former owner of the small one acquired it in England in the 1940s. I believe they are called thorn vases and are mould blown with applied feet. I've heard of them in canary as well as white. The large vase is 5" tall and the small one is 3⅛" tall.

Spiralex Vase

If you compare this vase and the Twisted Rib vase shown elsewhere in this edition, you will see it swirls to the right and the Spiralex swirls to the left. In addition, the latter has thinner ribs and less of a ball on the top of each rib. Both are from Dugan and then Diamond Glass.

Spiral Optic (Fenton)

Fenton's Spiral Optic was made with the same treatment as the Stripe pieces from other companies. This is the first example I've heard about in amethyst opalescent glass. I believe this piece dates from the 1915 production of this color. Amethyst opalescent glass was first made in 1908 and continued until 1918 or 1919.

Spiral Web

This corseted marmalade bowl was made in the Stourbridge region of England, circa 1900s and is also know as Cascade. It has an interlocking spiral opalescent pattern reminiscent of a spider web. The maker is believed to be Thomas Webb. The glass is vaseline, with a vaseline petticoat retaining skirt to hold it suspended in the frame. The top rim is cranberry, with opalescent highlights on the outside edge. The base has a polished pontil. Many thanks to Dave Peterson for the photo, name, and information provided.

Spokes and Wheels

This well-known 1906 Northwood pattern is found primarily in bowls or plates. Please compare this design to the Spokes and Wheels Variant below. This piece is a tri-cornered plate with ruffled edges.

Spokes and Wheels Variant

Just why this variant was made after the first version is a mystery, but a close comparison of the two patterns shows the variant has the area between the top of each oval notched out, omitting the blossom and stem that were there. This variant is found mostly on the plates or ruffled plates in four opalescent colors.

Spool

Spool is very similar to the Spool of Threads compote, but without the vertical ribs. The Spool piece surely came first and then the mould was retooled to produce the other design. Both patterns are credited to Northwood and both can be found in the usual opalescent colors. Shapes of the top may be flared or in a standing candy ribbon ruffle.

Spool of Threads

This pattern was made by the Northwood Company in opalescent glass in 1905. Primarily a compote pattern, this stemmed piece can be shaped in several ways, sometimes ruffled and sometimes not. The design is simple but easily recognized.

Square

This companion pattern to Sowerby's Triangle vase, shown elsewhere, has four sides and feet. The two patterns are exactly the same size but beyond that, I know little. Both blue and white examples are reported and these 4" tall pieces are considered spills or match holders.

Square Horn Epergne

This towering 23" epergne in rubina verde is a product of Thomas Webb. It has two side lilies, a tall center lily, and two hanging baskets on opposite sides. It is indeed a beautiful and rare epergne. Photo courtesy of the Keathleys.

Square Windows

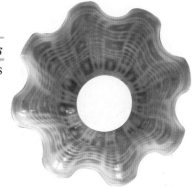

I don't recall seeing this pattern on any other shape except a shade. I suspect it is English but have no proof to date. Additional information is appreciated. Photo courtesy of Ruth Harvey.

Squirrel and Acorn

Here is one of the most appealing patterns in opalescent glass and in the whimsey section I show the vase. At this time, I do not know the maker of this pattern but can tell you it is quite rare, especially in blue and white. It was also made in a very scarce green. All shapes, a footed bowl, the compote, and the vase are from the same mould showing six panels with alternating designs of a frisky squirrel, acorn, and leaves. The base has a raised scale-like pattern. I'm sure the pattern dates from the 1904 – 1910 era. Photo courtesy of Bill Walter and Laurel Walton.

S-Repeat (National)

This pattern was first advertised in a Butler Brothers ad from the newly formed Dugan Glass Company. S-Repeat (or National as it was then called) seems to be a pattern designed while the plant was still operated by Northwood as a part of National Glass, but only released once Dugan had taken over. The ad dates from May 1903. Shapes and colors in opalescent glass are limited.

Star Base

Thanks to Ron Teal's excellent book about Albany Glass, I now know this pattern was Albany's #21 or Plain Pattern. It can be found in several shapes, all in blue opalescent. The catalog cuts show round bowls too, as well as a spooner and a creamer.

Starflower

The 7¼" tall vase shown is quite similar to both the Daffodils and the Crocus patterns but is definitely a different design. It is on canary glass and very thin. I suspect this piece may be from either England (maybe John Walsh Walsh) or Europe (possibly Czechoslovakia) but have no proof. This may be known by another name to some collectors.

Star in Diamond

This little 5⅜" by 3½" oval bowl is the only shape reported in this pattern, and is found only in blue opalescent. I have no information as to the maker but believe it to be English. Photo courtesy of the Petrasichs.

Starry Night

So far this white opalescent bowl is the only shape and color reported. The maker hasn't been established, but I do want to alert readers not to confuse this with the 1902 Westmoreland pattern Star Berry. They are close in appearance, except the Westmoreland pattern has a rayed base and a deeply scalloped and serrated edge. Additional information is appreciated. Photo courtesy of the Petrasichs.

Stars and Bars

Glass furniture knobs were the first pieces of pressed glass made in this country beginning in the 1820s, so it isn't surprising to see examples of opalescent knobs like the one shown. Today, these are scarce and finding a complete set is next to impossible. The example shown has a series of stars in prisms around the top and rows of bars on the sides. It is but one of many designs known and is found in at least two sizes. Most of these knobs are white but cranberry opalescent is also known.

Stars and Stripes

This pattern has been reproduced by the Fenton Company for the L.G. Wright Company, particularly in tumblers, a pitcher, and a small milk pitcher with reeded handle. The design originally came from Hobbs (1890) and later from Beaumont (1899). The Wright reproduction cruets can be found with both ruffled and tri-cornered tops, and both have reeded handles. Some of the repro items, especially the new water pitchers in blue, are very poorly done and the matching tumblers have thick, splotchy coloring.

Stippled Ivy

Although the maker has not been firmly established on this nice basket, the handle almost certainly indicates it being a Greener & Co. product. The basket is 6⅜" long and 3" wide and has been reported in blue opalescent only. The leaf and vine pattern is accented by a stippled background and it has a basketweave bottom. Thanks to the Petrasichs for sharing this beauty.

Stippled Scroll and Prism

After receiving a long letter from Seigmar Geiselberger, a glass researcher in Germany, I am now able to place this pattern as one made in either Saxonia or Bohemia. The date of production was around 1900, in a style the Germans call Second Rokoko. In addition more than one size in this piece is known (5¼", 7½", and 9"). The larger piece is also found with a lid.

Stork and Rushes

This quite scarce mug and a tumbler are the only shapes known thus far in opalescent glass. Colors reported from Dugan Glass Company ads dating from 1909 are white and blue. There are two border bands on this pattern but as you can see, the opalescent pieces have the diamond file designed band at the top and bottom. The second banding, a series of dots, seems to appear only on carnival items.

Stork and Swan

This very attractive syrup seems most likely to be of English origin. The handle is applied and the piece measures 5½" tall with a base width of 2¾". The metal lid is marked Patd. Nov. 16th 1869. On one side is a very attractive swan design featuring cattails and the floating swan, and on the reverse side, a stork (or crane) stands among cattails with a blooming tree on the opposite area. The rest of the piece is filled with vertical ribbing.

Stourbridge

This pattern is thought to be from the Stourbridge region of England around 1890 and was named by the owner. Shapes are a 5¼" creamer and a 4¼" sugar, and the only color reported is vaseline opalescent with green/vaseline crested edges around the top of each piece. Thanks to the Petrasichs for sharing these pieces.

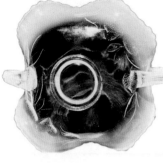

Strawberry

This pattern was made by the Fenton Art Glass Company in the 1915 – 1919 period. For some reason, only the two-handled bonbon shape is known in either carnival glass or opalescent glass (in the latter, only white opalescent is reported).

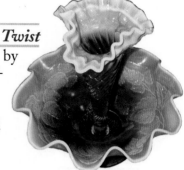

Strawberry and Dahlia Twist

This is somewhat of a mystery. This Strawberry design was made by Dugan and the Dahlia Twist Lily was originally a product of Jefferson. In fact the carnival version of this epergne has a different lily and was advertised in 1910 while the opal version came along in 1916 (after Dugan had purchased the Dahlia Twist Lily and mated it with their Strawberry base).

Stretched Diamonds

I have no idea of the maker of this vase and can only speculate that it may be English. The enameling is nicely done in white and light blue with a gold bow. I welcome any information readers may have on this item. Photo courtesy of John and Mary Petrasich.

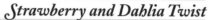

Stripe

Stripe, or Oval Stripe as it is also known, was made by many glass companies including Northwood, Nickel Plate, Jefferson, Buckeye, Beaumont, and even of English production. It dates from 1886, and continued at one concern or another until 1905. Many shapes and various colors are found in opalescent glass. Reproductions are well known in the barber bottle, small 5" – 7" pitchers, and perhaps other shapes. I believe the example shown is Nickel Plate glass.

Stripe Bracket Lamp

This seldom found bracket lamp is a beautiful example of just how many uses the makers of glass could find. It rested in this metal holder or bracket that was attached to the wall. It is shown in cranberry but was also made in white, blue, or canary. I have seen these with new burners and in new metal wall brackets which look a bit suspicious, so beware as they are possibly being reproduced. Thanks to Kelvin Russell and Debra Jennings for sharing it.

Stripe Condiment Set

First advertised in an 1889 Butler Brothers ad, this very fine condiment set was made by the Belmont Glass Company, not Hobbs or Northwood as previously stated. The set consists of a white opalescent base or server, a white mustard pot, a cranberry vinegar bottle (stopper is not original), and a pair of shakers, one in blue and one in white.

Striped Lemonescent

This color was made by Thomas Webb, circa 1900s. The color combination is similar to rubina verde opalescent by Hobbs, Brockunier & Co. Lemonescent was Webb's trade name. A small gather of cranberry, followed by a larger gather of vaseline opalescent glass, then the opalescent is obtained by returning the piece to the glory hole. These are three shapes, but an epergne horn has also been seen. Although the primary color the eyes see is cranberry, the entire outside layer is covered with a thin layer of vaseline opalescent glass and glow green under a UV light. Thanks to Dave Peterson for sharing this information and photo.

Stripe With Fan

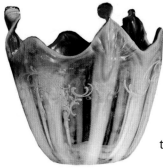

This interesting bowl shaped piece in cranberry opalescent shows a fan near the top of every other point and these points are twisted in a very eye-catching fashion. The yellow enameled decoration is very similar to some pieces listed as being made by Consolidated Glass, although recent information has been given to me which may indicate that Harrach Glass in the Czech Republic may in fact be the maker of many of these type pieces, but further research and time will be the deciding factor. Thanks to Ruth Harvey for sharing the photo.

Stripe With Fly

This frame was obviously made for this vaseline creamer, as the silver-plated holder is marked Western Silverplate, which would indicate a U. S. manufacturer. Just why a fly was incorporated into the holder design is unknown. I'd be interested in hearing from readers who may have this creamer in another color, shape, or with a different variation in the holder design. Thanks to Dave Peterson for the photo and information.

Sunburst-on-Shield

This fine Northwood pattern, originally called Diadem, was made in crystal in 1905 and in opalescent glass the following year. A host of shapes are known in only three opalescent colors to date.

Sunderland

This 1889 Greener and Co. pattern, Rd. #138051, has been reported in a basket, handled nappy, and tumbler shape in blue opalescent, as well as a compote shape in vaseline. Photo courtesy of Bob Lamoureux.

Sunk Honeycomb

This novelty bowl is a bit of a mystery. It is reputed to be from McKee Glass but they aren't known for producing opalescent glass. The only color reported is vaseline opalescent. The bowl is considered a rarity. Thanks to the Hollenbachs for sharing it.

Sunset

I am told by the owner of this piece it is from Duncan-Miller and the coloring is called Sunset. I do know this firm began making opalescent glass in the 1920s and continued with this treatment for more than a decade. The bowl shown is 9" across at the widest point and the color ranges from orange to pink to clear.

Surf Spray

This Jefferson Glass Company pattern (their #253 pickle dish), which is similar to their Sea Spray pattern, is found only in the shape shown. The pickle dish was first advertised in 1906 and can be found in white, blue, and green opalescent glass.

Sussex

To the best of my knowledge, this English pattern by Greener and Company hasn't been previously listed anywhere. It has an Rd. #103434, indicating a date of July 11, 1888. Thanks to the Petrasichs for the Rd. number, maker, and date.

Swag with Brackets

Swag with Brackets is a product of the Jefferson Glass Company and dates from 1904. It can be found in a host of shapes and in four opalescent colors.

Swan Novelty

This Thomas Webb piece would look nice sitting with the Pig novelty pieces shown earlier in this edition. This is the only free-hand swan I've seen from Webb but suspect other sizes were made. Photo courtesy of Ruth Harvey.

Swastika

Shown on the Diamonds and Clubs mould, this Dugan/Diamond opalescent pattern can also be found on a ball-type pitcher mould, as well as on tumblers and a syrup. The syrups can be found in both paneled and ball shapes. All pieces date from 1907 production and are currently demanding a premium price. Thanks to Frank and Melissa Keathley for sharing this rare item.

Swirl

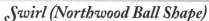

Virtually every glass company who made opalescent glass had a Swirl design, and it is quite difficult to distinguish one maker's examples from the others except by shapes known to have been favored by some companies. It is for this reason I believe this pitcher and tumbler shown came from the Jefferson Glass Company, since it matches the shape of pitchers they made in both Swirling Maze and Lattice. Notice that the handle is not reeded as on the Lattice pitcher in this shape. (The Swirling Maze also has no reeding.)

Swirl (Northwood Ball Shape)

Here's another look at one of the many Swirl patterns. This one is on Northwood's ball shape in the water set. This shape was also made by the Dugan Company and dates from 1890 (Hobb production). The Northwood version is sometimes called a variant. Colors are primarily white, blue, and cranberry, although rare examples of canary are known.

Swirled Interior Flute

Like the Interior Flute vase I show elsewhere in this edition, this one has the interior pattern swirled. The coloring on the vase shown is a very deep blue with good opalescence and I've heard of no other colors to date. I thank Ruth Harvey for sharing this and many other items.

Swirling Maze

Apparently the questions about this pattern still persist and I am no closer to all the answers than before. I do know that Jefferson Glass showed this pattern in ads as early as 1903 and into 1904, but just who advertised the water sets after that is still a mystery. There are three distinct pitcher shapes as well as the 6" milk pitcher. In addition, salad bowls are known. I was recently told that Fenton made this pattern after 1910 so that would dispel some of the mystery, if true.

Swirl Lamp

I'm told that this oil lamp is of English origin. The top seems to fit quite well but doesn't have the intense opalescence as the bottom. There is some question as to whether this was a marriage between two pieces, but this is speculation only. With its bold applied feet and overall look, this is certainly a worthy addition to any lamp or vaseline glass collection. Photo courtesy of the Keathleys.

Swirl with Enameled Bird

I have no idea of the maker or date of this vase, but it is an interesting piece. It appears that this piece not only has enameling, but also applied frit incorporated into the decoration. I welcome any information readers may have on this piece. Photo courtesy of Bill Walter and Laurel Walton.

Target

This Dugan/Diamond vase pattern was made in various types of glass, but in opalescent glass it is considered very scarce. Sizes range from 7" tall to 14", depending on how much the vase was swung or slung out, once it was taken from the mould.

Target Swirl

Because the design and shapes in this pattern are similar to some Harlequin pieces, it is now speculated that this pattern is Bohemian in origin. Shapes known are a tumbler, a bottle, a tall vase, hard to find salt in metal holder, and the squat vase shown. It is found in several opalescent colors.

Tazza

This very attractive English compote shows a very intricate pattern design and a lovely flowered style foot. The interesting part of this compote, which happens to be the stem, can't be seen but it comes up from the base and makes a pigtail loop before it attaches to the top portion. The maker is somewhat uncertain at this time, although the stem was registered by John Walsh Walsh and probably copied by other factories. Thanks to the Sandemans for sharing it.

Thin and Wide Rib

This Northwood pattern is found in several types of glass, but is a bit scarce in opalescent glass. The design is one of a wide or thick rib with thinner ribs on either side. Sizes range from 7" to 13" in opalescent glass and it comes in the standard colors.

Thistle and Wreath

The owner believes this 3½" diameter cup plate may well be English. I certainly welcome any information on this pattern and its maker. I thank the Petrasichs for sharing it.

Thistle Lily Vase

The silver holder, with its thistle and leaf pattern, is just as impressive as this rubina verde glass lily. I thank Ruth Harvey for sharing this fine vase. I believe the entire piece is English.

Thistle Patch

This was first a 1906 Northwood pattern called Poppy Wreath, then it was produced by Dugan/Diamond as Intaglio Poppy. Unfortunately, Heacock didn't look for these previous titles and tacked on a third title of Thistle Patch. It is found in three opalescent colors.

Thistles

Like the beautiful Primrose shade shown elsewhere, this one has the rubina verde treatment. The design of thistles runs up and down the shade. The base coloring is a good vaseline and the opalescent treatment is just superb. The maker of this fine item is unreported at this time.

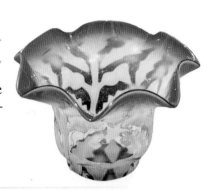

Thomas Webb Crocodile

What a great English novelty piece this is, and I love the detail. (Some examples will have tails that are pulled longer than others) This 1890s Richardsons piece would certainly be a conversation piece in any collection. Vaseline is the only reported color so far. Photo courtesy of the Keathleys.

Thorn Lily Epergne

This 21" tall epergne, with three side lilies and a tall center one, is probably from Europe or Britain. It has metal fittings, much like those found on British pieces. The design of pulled thorn-like projections along the lilies and the peachy interiors of their throats add appeal to this piece. It is reported only in vaseline to date.

Thorn Vase

This pattern is credited to Thomas Webb & Sons of Stourbridge, England. Shown is the vase with a twisted stem, running leaf foot, and thorns on the body in a pinkish hue with white opalescence. It is also known in vaseline and white opalescent. It is a blown item and very collectible. Thanks to Ruth Harvey for sharing it.

Thousand Eye

Thousand Eye was first made in 1888 by Richards and Hartley and later by U. S. Glass once they had absorbed the factory in 1892. It is only found in white opalescent glass, but is known in other types of glass. A host of shapes are known. Thanks to Bill Walter and Laurel Walton for sharing the photo.

Thread and Rib

Harry Northwood patented Thousand Rib in 1906, Wide Rib in 1909, and the universal receiving tube in 1916. This is his #305 Flower Stand. This epergne has been reproduced by L.G. Wright in the 1940s, so be sure of what you are buying. The originals came in blue, white, and canary opalescent glass. Wright's reproductions are found in these treatments as well as opaque ones of white, pink, and blue, all with casing on the lily openings!

Threaded Grape

This smaller than average fruit compote is a real beauty, as is the harder to find banana boat shape. It was made in 1909 by the Dugan Glass Company. The pattern is all exterior with the grape and leaf clusters fanning out from the center of the bowl, and the base has a teardrop and beading design. A band of eight threads circle the piece around the outer rim of the bowl.

Threaded Melon Basket

This very pretty basket with a twisted handle and candy ribbon edge is a real beauty. The glass is a beautiful blue opalescent treatment with a cranberry handle and edge casing. I believe this piece to be English but have no proof. Thanks to Ruth Harvey for sharing it with me.

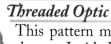

Threaded Optic

This pattern may be a spin-off pattern from the well-known Inside Ribbing pattern made by the Beaumont Glass Company of Martins Ferry, Ohio, but it has the look and coloring of a Dugan product. I've only seen the rose bowl in blue opalescent glass, but it comes in other glass types also. The ribbing or optic is all interior and the threading or horizontal rings are on the outside. The marie is plain and slightly raised. It is also called Band and Rib. Three sizes of bowls are known.

Threaded Stripe

The name for this pattern comes from the band of threading that runs around the body of the bowl. The color is a very strong amber and I believe this piece is English, possibly from Greener & Company who made a fair amount of amber opalescent glass. I welcome any information on this pattern. Photo courtesy of Bill Walter and Laurel Walton.

Three Fruits

This 1907 Northwood pattern is mostly known in carnival glass production, but it was also made in limited amounts in opalescent glass in white and blue. The exterior pattern is called Thin Rib, and the interior pattern of cherries, pears, and apples with leaves is an attractive one.

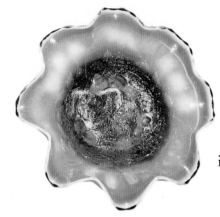

Three Fruits with Meander

In carnival glass this pattern is known as Three Fruits Medallion because of the leaf medallion in the interior's center. The Meander pattern is on the exterior and shows through nicely with the pattern of fruits and leaves on the inside. In opalescent glass, this Northwood pattern in found only in two colors.

Three Lily Waterfall Epergne

These America and English multi-lily epergnes are found in both opalescent glass and carnival glass. The one shown here is English. They are known with three, four, five, or six lilies. The example shown has vaseline lilies (or trumpets). Thanks to Ruth Harvey for sharing it.

Tines

This pattern was named Tines after the fork-like ridges that run vertically on the exterior from top to bottom. It also has a nice interior optic or ribbing. The opalescence is around the neck where the glass color is actually blue instead of the green found on the rest of the vase. This beauty stands 9½" tall and is very graceful indeed.

Tiny Rib

This pattern comes as a real surprise to me and I can't be sure of the maker (Northwood or Jefferson? Dugan, perhaps?). The bowl sits on three scroll feet and the only pattern is the interior ribbing. It measures about 6" across. I'd welcome any information on this piece.

Tiny Tears

Very little information seems to be available for this vase although it appears to have the same coloring as so many vase patterns from either Northwood or Dugan/Diamond. The example shown stands 14" tall, has a marie with 28 rays, and an extended ridge above the base with fine ribbing on the inside, all around the base. I'm sure this was made in the usual opalescent colors and must have come from the 1903 – 1910 era.

Tokyo

Jefferson Glass Company's Tokyo is a very distinctive pattern that can be found in a variety of shapes and in three opalescent colors. Some years ago Tokyo was reproduced in several shapes including the compote, so buy with caution. Photo courtesy of Frank and Melissa Keathley.

Trafalgar Fountain Epergne

Trafalgar Fountain epergne is smaller than some of the epergnes previously shown and it has no large under-bowl but sits on a wide, slightly ruffled base. The lily holders are also glass, rather than metal, but I still think this is from England and have named it accordingly.

Trailing Vines

Trailing Vines was made by the Coudersport Tile & Ornamental Glass Company in several types of glass, as well as blue, white, and canary opalescent. Opalescent shapes seem to be only novelty bowls with various tops. All pieces, though heavily produced, are considered somewhat rare today.

Tree Form

This posy from Thomas Webb reminds me of a harp and you can also see a resemblance to the Thorn vase from Thomas Webb shown elsewhere. This piece has branch or root like feet commonly seen on many English pieces. Photo courtesy of the Sandemans.

Tree of Life

I am now reasonably sure this pattern is from the Dugan Glass Company. It is now known in the vase shape in blue opalescent as shown, as well as white opalescent.

Tree of Love

Siegmar Geiselberger, a glass researcher in Germany, has traced this pattern, as well as the Casbah and Rococo patterns, to the Fenne Glassworks of Saarland, Germany. So if some pieces are marked Sabino as reported, the moulds must have traveled from Germany to France before 1920.

Tree Stump

While this very interesting mug is usually called just Stump, the formal name is Tree Stump. The mould work is very good as are the coloring and the opalescence. Most collectors feel this item is from the Northwood Company, and I agree it certainly has all the attributes of Harry Northwood's quality. In size it is shorter than most mugs and the very realistic tree branch handle and the knots on the bark add real interest.

Tree Trunk

This well-known Northwood vase is sometimes marked and was made in several sizes in various types of glass. In opalescent glass, I know of only the standard size (3¼" base) that can be stretched from 7" to 14" in height. Three opalescent colors are known, and date from 1907 – 1908.

Trellis

This stemmed tumbler stands 4½" tall. Aside from that, I can offer very little information. The opalescence forms a diamond quilting and there is an optic effect, but the difference from the Diamond pattern is evident. Origin may be England, but I can't be sure. I base this opinion on the heavy opalizing and the general shape.

Triangle

There may well be another name for this 4" tall match holder, but I haven't heard it. The sides measure 3" across. The pattern relies on the three-corner columns and the bands at the top and bottom; the rest of the glass is plain. The entire piece stands on ball feet. It was made by Sowerby of England.

Trident

This pitcher was named by the owner and I really love the design and overall look. The bottom has a smooth polished pontil and the height is 9½" tall. I'm going to assume a tumbler exists although I have not seen one. The only color to date is a nice amber opalescent. The maker is unknown. Many thanks to the Petrasichs for sharing it.

Tri-Fold Epergne

This 21½" epergne looks somewhat like a Thomas Webb signature design: two side lilies and one center lily with two hanging baskets opposite the side lilies. The color is vaseline with cranberry edging. It is another really nice epergne to add to any collection. Once again I want to thank Frank and Melissa Keathley for sharing their many epergne photos with me as well as other pieces from their nice collection.

Tri-Footed Spill

This rather plain looking item is actually very nice and I believe it is a tough piece to find. Two possible makers have been given to me: Alfred and James Davies and John Walsh Walsh. I have no information to substantiate either, but would like to know more about this interesting piece. Thanks again to Ruth Harvey for sharing glass from her nice collection.

Trumpet Vase

It's a pleasure to show these two vases. First is the 42" tall vaseline example in a non-glass base (maker uncertain) and second is the wonderful 37" cranberry example from Frederick Carder (before coming over to Steuben). It is rare to find this vase or any of these tall examples with their original base. Both are real beauties and I appreciate Frank and Melissa Keathley for sharing them with me.

Tulip

This cylinder shade in rubina verde is almost certainly English, although I have no confirmation of the maker at this time. The design consists of four tulips within a shield, all linked together with a scroll-like design near the bottom. This is the only shape and color reported to date and I'd love to hear of others. Thanks to the Sandemans for sharing it with me.

Tulip Vase

Made by Richardson's of England in the 1890s, this 6" tall vase is a masterwork of design. It stands on a vaseline stem and leaf-work base, but the bowl is wide-striped in opal and has an amethyst tint to the glass. I thank the Sandemans (Steve and Radka) for this exciting piece of glass.

Tut

While these very plain stemmed pieces may have another name, this is the one I've heard them called. The maker hasn't been confirmed as far as I know, but Northwood and Jefferson seem likely candidates. They can be found in various shapes and four opalescent colors.

Twigs

First advertised in 1898 as a Northwood product in opalescent glass, the Twigs pattern was another of those patterns later produced by Dugan/Diamond once Northwood left the Indiana, Pennsylvania, plant. In opalescent glass, Twigs is found in a smaller 5" size and a slightly larger 6½" example. The smaller size can be found in various shapes and colors.

Twigs and Leaves

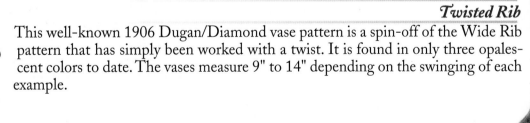

This basket with twig handles was made by Greener & Co., England, and was registered on March 27, 1888. The piece is unmarked, but was issued the Registration number 96775 for the unique twig handles. It was never named by Greener & Co. The mold was manipulated into various twig basket shapes, all having the distinctive twig handles. Thanks go to Dave Peterson for this photo and information.

Twist

As a part of the National Glass Company, Model Flint Glass of Albany, Indiana, produced this very collectible miniature table set consisting of the covered butter, sugar, creamer, and spooner. A secondary name for this pattern is Ribbed Swirl.

Twisted Rib

This well-known 1906 Dugan/Diamond vase pattern is a spin-off of the Wide Rib pattern that has simply been worked with a twist. It is found in only three opalescent colors to date. The vases measure 9" to 14" depending on the swinging of each example.

Twisted Roots

I really love the name of this vase. Judging by the looks of this piece I would have to assign it to John Walsh Walsh; his signature looped stem design gives it away. Thanks to Ruth Harvey for sharing this nice piece.

Twisted Rope

Shown are two examples of this very rare vase, now known to be a product of Jefferson Glass. These vases are 8" tall and have a 3" base with only a flattened ball stem. To date there are two vaseline, three blue opalescent, two white, and one green, and I'm told there is one pink example without opalescence on the edge. Thanks to Dave Peterson for sharing these vases and the information.

Twisted Trumpet

What a joy epergnes were and this is one of the most imaginative examples. The stem has been twisted while the glass was still hot and then pulled into the graceful lily shape. I suspect it is English and is only found in vaseline glass to date. Please note that the top of the lily goes from opal to clear vaseline again in the twisting.

Twister

Twister was shown in a 1908 Jefferson Glass Company Butler Brothers ad. It is found in bowls, plates, and whimsey vases, all from the same mould. Plates are scarce in this pattern, even more so than the whimsey vase.

Universal Epergne

These are available in such a wide variety of single lily epergnes, I decided to lump them all into one category. They can be found with many different bases and a host of lilies from various makers as well as a variety of base designs: Single Spool Lily (plain lily), Cherub base (Dahlia Twist lily) epergne, Elephant base (Thorn lily) epergne, and this list goes on and on.

Universal Northwood Tumbler

When the Northwood Company produced Alaska and Klondyke (Fluted Scrolls or Jackson), the same tumbler mould was used for both patterns. By adding an enameled design (forget-me-nots for Alaska, daisies for Fluted Scrolls), the company not only saved money but also produced similar but distinctive patterns. I am showing one of these tumblers without the enameling to show the design as it came from the mould. Naturally it came in all colors of each pattern and was made in opalescent glass, custard, crystal, and emerald green. In addition to the tumbler, a similar universal salt shaker was produced for these patterns.

Venetian (Dugan)

This well-known Dugan pattern can be found in a host of shapes, sizes, and colors. Here are two sizes of the crimped rose bowl, with the smaller one being quite rare in any shape or color. Photo courtesy of Rick and Debbie Graham.

Venetian Beauty Night Lamp

This 3¼" miniature lamp is now felt to have been a product of the Buckeye Glass Company. It was shown in an 1890 Butler Brothers ad. The shade on the example shown is not original, but a matching chimney was advertised in opalescent glass. Photo courtesy of Rick and Debbie Graham.

Venetian Drape

Here is a pattern that is appropriately named because the glass is from Venice. It is blown Italian opalescent glass with a hand-applied gold decoration of drapery and a rim of beading. I thank Ruth Harvey for sharing it with me.

Venice

This very beautiful table lamp, shown in the 1888 *American Potter and Illuminator*, had a matching shade and is said to have been made with either a blue or white opalescent stripe on the fonts. They came in 8", 9", and 10" sizes.

Vertical Stripe

This vase has enameled flowers and a nice silver band around the base and top edge. The maker and date have not been confirmed. I'd appreciate any additional information. Photo courtesy of Bill Walter and Laurel Walton.

Vesta Venetian

This pattern, shown here in a ruffled lamp shade, was registered in 1908 by John Walsh Walsh. The only other shape reported is a compote, and the only color reported is vaseline opalescent. Photo and information is courtesy of Dave Peterson.

V-Hatch

I have no idea of the maker or date of this vase but would love to know more if anyone can shed some light on it. The color is white opalescent with a cranberry edge. Photo courtesy of Ruth Harvey.

Victoria and Albert

Victoria and Albert was made by Davidson of England as Rd. #303519 in 1897. This pattern is found in both blue and canary opalescent glass. Shapes include a biscuit jar, a creamer, an open sugar, a crimped plate (6½" x 9"), a water set with a matching platter, a 4" plate, and a compote. Davidson was one of three major English glass factories that produced opalescent wares. The others were Sowerby & Company and Greener & Company.

Victorian Hamper

This very pretty novelty basket was listed in an 1882 Sowerby pattern book as #1187½. It measures 5" long and 2½" tall. It has two rope-like handles and a woven pattern that goes from the rope edging to the ground base. The coloring is very soft like so much of the glass from England and it has good opalescence. It was probably made in canary as well as the advertised crystal (flint), opal, turquoise, Patent Queen's Ware, and Blanc de Lait treatments. Queen's Ware is an opaque glass with a yellow tint, similar to custard glass, and Blanc de Lait is milk glass. The hamper was also made in malachite or slag glass.

Victorian Stripe with Flowers

While this is certainly pure art glass like so many items of the 1890s, I felt one piece of decorated glass with applied floral sprays might be in order to set a bit of perspective as to where the opalescent glass craze started before it progressed into the mostly pressed items I show elsewhere. This beautiful 10" vase is likely British and is tissue-paper thin, with stems of applied clear glass and flowers that have a cranberry beading. Notice the flaring base, much like many Northwood tankard pitchers that came later.

Victorian Swirl with Flowers

Although very much like the Victorian Stripe with Flowers vase shown above, this one has the swirl pattern and is shaped differently. Both are blown vases and both have applied glass flowers and leaves. Thanks to Ruth Harvey for this piece.

Viking

This beautiful 8½" boat-shaped piece is obviously from England. I am told by the owners, the Petrasichs, that they believe it is from Greener & Company and may have been made in amber as well as blue. The design is very strong with leaves and roping covering much of the piece. I welcome any information about this piece.

Vintage (Fenton)

Seen mostly in carnival glass, this very distinct Fenton pattern dates from 1909 – 1910 and can be recognized by its large leaf center as well as the five bunches of grapes that are grouped around the bowl. The exterior is plain, as is the marie. All colors are hard to find and well worth the search.

Vintage (Jefferson/Northwood)

This was an opalescent pattern from Jefferson Glass found on the exterior of dome-based bowls that was later used by Northwood as a carnival glass pattern exterior. Jefferson called this their #245 pattern. Jefferson pieces date from before 1907 and Northwood used this pattern after that time.

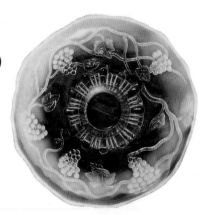

Waffle

I know very little about the origin of this attractive epergne except it originally came from Germany, carried by hand aboard a commercial airline a few years ago. It stands some 20" tall on an ornate metal base and the lily fits into a metal cup. The beautiful waffle design is olive green, shading to an attractive pink just before the opalescent edging starts. The glass is very fine and thin and is mould blown.

War of the Roses

War of the Roses was made by George Davidson & Company in England, has Rd. #212684, dates to 1893, and can be found in blue or vaseline opalescent glass. Shapes include the boat shape (7½" and 9½"), novelty bowls, four-pointed star dish, a two-handled posy trough, and a three-pointed star dish. Be aware, however, that the canoe shape was reproduced by L.G. Wright in all sorts of glass treatments in the 1940s, but not in opalescent glass that I'm aware of.

Waterlily and Cattails (Fenton)

The Fenton version of this pattern in opalescent glass is known in a host of shapes and in blue, green, white, and a scarce amethyst opalescent.

Waterlily and Cattails (Northwood)

In carnival glass, Northwood made this pattern in only a water set, so it isn't surprising to find it showing up in opalescent glass. Blue is the only color I've heard about. This pattern in opalescent glass dates from 1905. Shown is the rare pitcher in blue, which carries the Northwood mark. Thanks to Dennis Crouse for the nice photo.

Waves

This pattern was named by my former co-author Bill Edwards and the name fits quite well. The coloring is a soft vaseline. Blue is also reported as well as a cranberry pitcher, and I suppose a tumbler in that color was made too. I'm told that John Walsh Walsh is the maker. The shade is mould blown and is very thin. Anyone with additional information about this pattern is urged to contact me. Photo courtesy of Frank and Melissa Keathley.

Webb Centerpiece

Reportedly from Thomas Webb in 1900, this centerpiece, with three lilies, is a beauty. The feet and stem are rough worked while the lilies are white opalescent glass. I certainly thank Ruth Harvey for sharing it.

Webb Drapes

This interesting 10½" vase was from Thomas Webb and Sons Limited, circa 1900. It is actually of light "uranium" base glass with cranberry drapes on the inside, which adds up to a great combination: vaseline, cranberry, and opalescent glass (not to mention the fact that only a handful are known). I'd like to thank the Sandemans and the Petersons for photos and information on this vary rare item.

Wedding Bell

This interesting bell with the ringed top is believed to have come from James Powell, England. This interesting bell stands 12" tall and would add to any collection. Photo courtesy of the Keathleys.

West Virginia Stripe

I am listing this pattern under this title as iffy. The shape is the same as the West Virginia Glass Company's Polka Dot and Fern pitchers so I feel confident it was from that short-lived company and was made between 1893 and 1895. I'd appreciate any information about this pattern.

Wheat

This short stem oil lamp, complete with chimney and shade resting on what is referred to as the spider, has an English look but no maker has been established. The only color reported is vaseline opalescent. Additional information would be appreciated. Photo courtesy of the Sandemans.

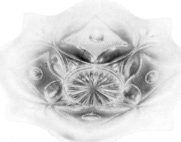

Wheel and Block

Wheel and Block was shown as early as 1905 in ads with other Dugan Glass patterns. It has been seen in deep bowls, a vase whimsey, and a square plate, all from the same mould. Colors are blue, green, and white with the latter sometimes having a goofus treatment as on the square plate shown.

Wide Panel

Here is the second Northwood epergne design, called Wide Panel or Colonial by some collectors. It is well known in carnival glass and is equally respected in opalescent colors of green, white, and blue. Notice that the four lily receiving tubes have been moulded into the glass and the whole design sweeps in a wide paneling from lily to base. It is less formal than the first epergne design, Thread and Rib, and has no metal in the fittings at all.

Wide Rib Vase

The carnival version of this vase was made by the Northwood Company and is so marked, but I strongly suspect the opalescent vase with the frit top was a product of Jefferson Glass. It is 13½" tall and has the heaviest frit I've ever found. Perhaps this is another of those moulds Northwood obtained from Jefferson and then marked with the Northwood trademark.

Wide Stripe

I believe this shade was made by the Nickel Plate Glass Company about 1890. Four opalescent colors are known. While both Fenton and Imperial made similar versions of these shades in the late 1930s, the shaping was different. Wide Stripe is known in several shapes.

Wild Bouquet

Apparently Northwood first made the opalescent pieces in this pattern while a part of National, and the design was then continued by Dugan/Diamond. Various colors are known. Thanks to Roger Lane for sharing this odd Persian blue tumbler photo with me and also to Rick and Debbie Graham for the toothpick holder photo.

153

Wild Daffodils

While similar to the Wild Rose pattern by Fenton, this one has a different flower altogether. The shape of the mug and its handle are exactly like the Fenton Orange Tree mug. Production probably dates from 1909 or thereabouts.

Wild Grape

Only a bowl and compote are reported in white in this pattern. The compote is 4½" tall, has a 3¼" base, and is 4¾" across the top. I believe other colors in opalescent glass were made but haven't confirmed them, and possibly other shapes may exist.

Wild Rose (Fenton)

Wild Rose was made at the same time as the Wild Daffodils mug from the Fenton Company using the same technique. It can be found in three opalescent colors. The pattern consists of four groups of roses and leaves sections, very realistically done, with buds and thorned stems.

Wild Rose Shade

This shade is found in both the electric style and the gas shade as shown. It is not to the same as the Wild Rose pattern in other types of glass. This is the first I've seen in opalescent glass and I thank Ruth Harvey for sharing it with me.

William and Mary

This Davidson Company of England pattern was first made in 1903 and has a registration number of 413701. It is found in several shapes including a table set, compote, biscuit jar, celery vase, handled nappy, oval salt dish, round salt dish, 9" cake plate, and oval or round bowls in several sizes.

Willow Reed Basket

I believe this handled basket is English, possibly Greener, but I have no proof. The design is a good one with a natural reed, binding, and ribbing. Thanks to Ruth Harvey for sharing it with me.

Wilted Flowers

This Dugan/Diamond pattern is called Single Flower by carnival glass collectors. It was part of their 1909 Intaglio line. Besides bowl shapes, there are handled baskets, tri-cornered bowls, banana bowls, rose bowls, and whimsied nut bowl shapes found in three opalescent colors. The flower design is a weak one and looks best with the goofus treatment as shown.

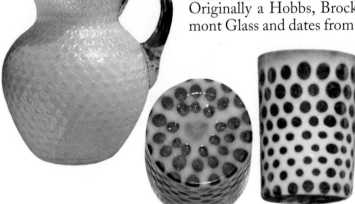

Windflower

Windflower is known to be a Diamond Glass Company product that is better known in carnival glass than in opalescent, where it is considered rather rare. First advertised in 1907, the opalescent pieces are known in white and blue. In a 1914 Butler Brothers ad they can be seen along with equally rare opalescent patterns like the Mary Ann vase, the Constellation compote (pulled from the S-Repeat or National goblet shape with an added interior pattern), a Fishscales and Beads bowl, and Stork and Rushes mug and tumbler.

Windflower Nappy

This Diamond Company nappy is a real rarity in opalescent glass. I've seen only a few examples in white. The bowl in this pattern, shown above, is part of a very small production run. I would surely like to hear from anyone knowing of additional opalescent colors in this piece.

Windows (Plain)

Originally a Hobbs, Brockunier pattern, Windows was later produced by Beaumont Glass and dates from 1889. Shapes known are water sets, finger bowls, bitters bottles, a crimped bowl, oil lamps in several shapes, and two sizes of miniature lamps. Notice on the tumbler shown that the windows continue onto the bottom of the piece, where on the late piece they stop at the bottom edge.

Windows (Swirled)

This Hobbs, Brockunier pattern is sometimes called Hobbs Swirl. The swirl is in the moulding of the glass. It is found in a host of shapes but in only three opalescent colors. Strangely, the shapes in this pattern all seem to have an oval shape. Production started in 1889. Photo courtesy of Rick and Debbie Graham.

Windows on Stripe

I have no information on this Windows pattern oil lamp other than to say the only reported color is vaseline opalescent. It has some resemblance to the other Windows patterns, however I don't think it is a product of Hobbs, Brockunier or Beaumont. I urge anyone with additional information to contact me. Photo courtesy of the Sandemans.

Windsor Stripe

I feel sure this stripe pattern is English, and I've added the Windsor to establish this. The vase is cranberry with a great amount of opalescence. It stands 4¾" tall and has a six-scallop top and a pontil mark.

Winged Scroll

This 1888 A.H. Heisey pattern is normally found in crystal or custard glass, but can sometimes be found in milk glass. A very rare 4" berry bowl in vaseline opalescent glass is shown here. A creamer is also known. I want to thank Douglas S. Sandeman for sharing this find with me through his son, Steve.

Winter Cabbage

This Dugan pattern very closely resembles Cabbage Leaf, also made at Dugan. Both patterns date from 1906. The difference is the number of leaves. Winter Cabbage has only three and Cabbage Leaves has overlapping leaves. Winter Cabbage is known in bowls that rest on three vine-like feet that bend back and join the drooping marie of the bowl.

Winterlily

This very pretty vase was first made in 1906 and was shown in Dugan ads in 1908 in white, blue, and green opalescent glass. The mould work is superior with twig feet turning into rows of vertical beading and a leaf vining around the vase. The lily shape has a glass twist at the top, much like the Cleopatra Fan vase. All colors are scarce.

Wishbone and Drapery

Jefferson Glass's 1903 Wishbone and Drapery is found on bowls and plates in white, green, and blue opalescent. While the design is a pleasant one, it didn't take much imagination and could not be called exciting. However, the coloring is nice, especially on the blue pieces.

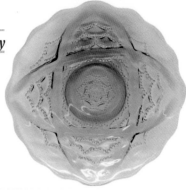

Wood Vine Lamp (Gaiety Base)

It has been speculated that this smaller size oil lamp is a Northwood product but I have no information to confirm such. This ribbed lamp has a variety of opalescent designs running throughout the font with no particular theme in mind. This is the only size reported and white is the only color. Thanks to the Petrasichs for sharing it.

Woven Wonder

Northwood's Woven Wonder is actually the same pattern as the exterior of the Rose Show bowl and even the same as Frosted Leaf and Basketweave without the leaf. Perhaps the latter's sugar base was flared for these exterior patterns, but I can't prove it.

Wreath and Scroll

This oil lamp's very busy pattern has almost total coverage consisting of an alternating wreath and scroll, two each around the font. The design seems to be English but I have not proof of such at this time. The color is vaseline. This lamp would certainly grace any opalescent or oil lamp collection. Thanks to the Sandemans for sharing it.

Wreath and Shell

This pattern was originally named Manila by Model Flint Glass (their #905). It was made in 1900 in crystal (rare), colored glass, and opalescent glass (sometimes decorated). A variety of shapes are known and the standard colors are found in opalescent glass.

Wreathed Grape and Cable

Fenton's #920 was made in 1911 and named for the wreath of leaves around the collar. This was It can be found on opalescent or crystal glass (the leaves were removed before carnival glass production) and is rare in either treatment. I am greatly indebted to both the late Jack Beckwith and Kathryn McIntyre for sharing this fine item. The footed fruit bowl shown measures 5" tall and has a diameter of 10".

X-Hatch

I love this name and expect it may very well be the only pattern listed in the "X" area of the alphabet for some time. A series of interlinking X's with a background of vertical bars, although simple, make for a pleasing pattern indeed. The color is rubina verde and this is the only reported shape to date. Thanks to the Sandemans for the photo and name.

Zinfandel

This is a really lovely water set which I believe may be from Consolidated Glass, although I have no solid evidence yet. The enameled pattern consists of a grape and leaf design on the pitcher with an added circle of beads around the hip section of the tumblers. I've heard this color referred to as rose opalescent and will stick with that color designation unless I hear different. Photo courtesy of John and Mary Petrasich.

Zipper and Loops

Apparently this vase was the only shape made in this pattern by the Jefferson Glass Company in 1908. It may have been intended as a celery holder, but if so, there should have been other table pieces. Sizes are 7" or 11½". Additional information would be appreciated.

Zippered Flute

Not only does this vase have an interesting shape with three corners pulled into flames but the design of flutes that have an edging of zipper-like cuts is one I haven't seen before. The color is dark green and I welcome any information from readers about this pattern.

Part II: Whimsey Pieces

Webster's Dictionary defines a whimsey as an odd fancy and that definition certainly fits the glass items in this section.

Generally speaking, the glassmakers were very skilled artisans and liked nothing better than to show off these skills. Often, when they grew bored or tired of the same shapes being turned out, they produced one of these odd fancies that was not a part of regular production but could nevertheless be sold as either a novelty or sometimes given to a friend or loved one as a special gift. Many whimsies were made to be slipped out of the factory by the glassmaker at the end of the day, to be taken home and presented to a wife or family member.

For these reasons, whimsies have become a much loved part of glass collecting and it is a pleasure to show a few examples here, so that the collector of today may understand just what whimsies are and how attractive they may be.

And perhaps I should also say that some whimsies were so popular they did go into limited production from pattern to following pattern. Such examples of lady's spittoons as I show here became very popular and were produced over the years on many types of glass, especially in the years of carnival glass production, until they were no longer considered whimsies!

Many whimsies, however, are a bit grotesque in their shaping and seem strange indeed. Just remember, every one of these odd fancies was the product of a master craftsman in the days when glassmaking was an art.

*As I mentioned at the beginning of this book, you will note that a good deal of the whimsies shown in previous editions have been removed, as they were not true whimsies, but rather production pieces. This was also done to allow for the growth of this edition as well as future editions.

Astro Hat

This hat whimsey, made from the common bowl shape, is actually much prettier than the original shape and could have even been pulled into a vase. It just shows what a little imagination and a good bit of skill can do in adding to the design.

Barbells Vase Whimsey

This vase whimsey stands 5½" tall and is pulled from the regular Barbells bowl, made by Jefferson Glass in 1905. I've called the bowl undistinguished, and it certainly is when compared to this very beautiful vase shape. Thanks to Richard Petersen for sharing this whimsey.

Blooms and Blossoms Proof Nappy

Occasionally, you will find a piece of old glass that has only part of the design finished. These are called "proofs" and they are very collectible. On the nappy shown here, the outline of the blossoms and the leaves are there, but the detail of the design is missing. Since only a few of these pieces were produced before the finished design was completed, these proof pieces are always scarcer than the normal pattern.

Cashews Whimsey Bowl

It is hard to imagine a bowl more whimsied than this one. The rim is pulled into three extreme peaks and the rest is rolled into a low flowing sweep that gives the piece an almost unusable shape. It does have a strange appeal however and certainly would be a conversation piece.

Cherry Panel (Dugan)

Here is the Dugan Cherry Panel three-footed bowl with the edges ruffled into a JIP shape that is tri-cornered. Please notice the ruffling is a variety called candy ribbon edge. The same pattern is also found in white, blue, and vaseline opalescent glass.

Cherry Panel Nut Bowl Whimsey

This piece is one of the nicer shapes in this Dugan pattern. It was pulled from the stemmed bowl and is deep, with straight sides, making a nut bowl shape.

Cherry Panel Vase Whimsey

This Dugan pattern, pulled from the large footed bowl shape, is usually found in a ruffled bowl. Here I show a rare vase whimsey, pulled up to a three-sided vase with the top edges in an arc-and-point edge. Since the bowls are found in blue and canary opalescent glass, perhaps this vase whimsey was also made in those colors. Thanks to Arthur Van Curen Jr. for sharing this fine item.

Compass Whimsey Rose Bowl

This Dugan/Diamond pattern, also known as Dragon Lady, is mostly found in bowls, but here I show one pulled up and crimped into a nice rose bowl shape in a rich green (white is also known).

Concave Columns JIP Whimsey

As I've said this was originally the #617 design in National Glass ads (later continued at Dugan Glass). In carnival glass it is called Pressed Coinspot and is found in a compote, goblet, and vase. Here is a JIP top shape but with the front not turned down.

Coral Reef Rose Bowl Proof

Here are two proof rose bowl whimsies which you will notice are quite different. Note that the pattern goes to the collar base on one but not the other. I would consider these to be quite hard to find. Vaseline is the only color reported to me at this time. Thanks to John Schertz for the photos and information.

Daffodils Whimsey Bowl

What a beautiful whimsey this piece is. The top has been pulled out into v-folds, giving it a flower-like shape. The color is vaseline but white or blue must have been made also.

Daisy and Plume Basket Whimsey

This is the first of these I've seen and it has to be a scarce item. It was made by Dugan, from the footed rose bowl mould and simply turned out on two sides, turned up on the other two, and a handle was added to form a basket.

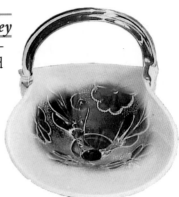

Daisy and Plume Whimsey

This Dugan version of the pattern has holes in the legs. It had been whimsied with the top flared out into a bowl shape that could almost be called a nut bowl. Thanks to the Petrasichs for sharing it.

Davidson Shell Ruffled Whimsey

While I've showed this piece previously as Davidson Shell, it is really a whimsey with the top ruffled. The original shape is shown in the first section and as you can see, it has no ruffling and the top is straight, making it a true spill vase.

Diamond and Daisy Rose Bowl Whimsey

This Dugan pattern, called Caroline by carnival glass collectors, was made in 1909 and is usually found in ruffled bowls where the exterior design is unimpressive. Here is a rose bowl whimsey shape and the design actually shows. Photo courtesy of the Petrasichs.

Diamond Stem Vase Whimsey

This Northwood and Model Flint Glass vase is shown in one of three whimsey shapes. On this one the front three edges are pulled down and the rear three are turned up, giving the vase a JIP shape as well as a square look. This vase was made in 6½", 8½", and 10½" sizes in four opalescent colors.

Feathers Bowl Whimsey

Since the second edition of this book, this bowl whimsey has shown up in all colors (white, blue, and green), so it was less rare than I thought. It was made from the same mould as the well-known Northwood Feathers vase. The bowls may be deep or shallow, but all I've seen are ruffled.

Fenton's #220 Stripe Vase Whimsey

This 8" tall Fenton Stripe vase whimsey was made from the same mold as the water pitcher in the same four opalescent colors. Thanks to Phil Barber for sharing this piece.

Finecut and Roses Bowl Whimsey

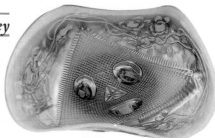

Shown in a 1908 Butler Brothers ad for Jefferson Glass patterns, this whimsey is really a production item, flattened and rolled out and up on four sides. This pattern later became part of Northwood's patterns purchased from Jefferson, then made in carnival and custard glass by that company.

Frosted Leaf and Basketweave Whimsey Vase

This pattern is now known to have been produced by the Chicago Flint Glass Company of Chesterton, Indiana. These vase whimsies are pulled from the spooner shape and are very hard to find. Most measure from 9½" to 11".

Interior Panel Rolled Rim Whimsey

Here's the Fenton vase I've previously shown in a fan shape. This example too, is in a cameo opalescent treatment, but with a rolled rim. There are also other whimsey shapes made from the same mould. Courtesy of John and Mary Petrasich.

Inverted Fan and Feather Large Whimsey Rose Bowl

This true delight is a rose bowl whimsey shaped from the large berry bowl. It was made by Dugan/Diamond and probably in the usual opalescent colors, with green being scarce. The piece shown measures 4" tall and 5½" across the top.

Inverted Fan and Feather Spittoon

Here is one of the very attractive spittoon whimsey pieces pulled from the spooner shape. In carnival glass, these pieces are called ladies' spittoons, for rumor has it that women actually were the users. I can't verify this, but the possibility certainly does exist.

Inverted Fan and Feather Vase

Shown in a 1908 Butler Brothers ad, this very scarce Dugan/Diamond vase was a carry-over at the factory and was made in limited amounts in blue, green, and white opalescent glass.

Iris with Meander Whimsey Vase

The vase shown is 13½" tall and has a base diameter of 3" to 3¾". I believe this vase was either pulled from the spooner mould or the master bowl mould. I've seen these vase whimsies in four colors of opalescent glass, so they aren't rarities but they are very collectible.

Jefferson Stripe Whimsey Bowl

Jefferson Stripe is normally found in bowl or vase shapes. This has been pulled from a vase and is almost a ruffled compote whimsey. It has the typical cranberry frit decoration.

Jewels and Drapery Bowl Whimsey

This whimsey, like the Feathers bowl shown elsewhere, was made from the vase mould. Both patterns are from the Northwood Company so it isn't surprising to find these pieces. It can be found in three opalescent colors.

Keyhole Rose Bowl Whimsey

To date, three of these whimsey pieces have been reported, all in blue opalescent. This is a Dugan/Diamond pattern made in opalescent glass in 1905. Opalescent pieces sometimes have a goofus treatment.

Lady Caroline Whimsey Piece

This Davidson novelty or whimsey shape has three handles and has been pulled up and crimped into an almost unusable shape. Other novelty shapes include a two-handled basket with the tops crimped in and a vase shape.

Lattice Medallions Nut Bowl

What a pretty whimsey this nut bowl shape is. And while Northwood was not known for items whimsied into this shape, a few examples are known, especially in carnival glass. Please note the unusual knobby feet on this pattern.

Lattice Medallions Rose Bowl Whimsey

Like the nut bowl I show, this Northwood pattern is much prettier on these whimsey shapes, and this rose bowl whimsey is the top of the line.

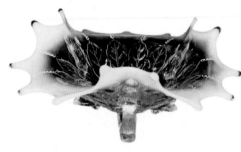

Leaf and Beads (Flame)

Shaped much like the regular tri-cornered bowl in this pattern, this example has the flames on the edging pulled into much exaggerated points, making this an attractive and unusual piece.

Leaf Chalice Four-Cornered Whimsey Bowl

Unlike the regular chalice shape elsewhere in this book and the rose bowl whimsey shape following, this piece is pulled in at four corners, forming a deep square bowl shape that is quite attractive.

Lorna Vase Whimsey

Actually, both this shape and the one shown elsewhere in this book could be called whimsies since the tops are often fashioned into these odd shapes. Here I show a vase with the tops tightly ruffled and then flared. Lorna is from Model Flint Glass.

Meander Nut Bowl Whimsey

While this pattern was produced first by Jefferson (their #233) and later by Northwood, the nut bowl shown is most likely from Jefferson. Without question, it shows the design to a far better advantage than the bowl shapes.

Ocean Shell

Not as obvious as some whimsey pieces, this Ocean Shell relies on the one edge being pulled out to form a tail-like section while the opposite side has been scooped into a small spout.

Open O's Rose Bowl Whimsey

What a pleasant surprise this pretty rose bowl was when I first saw it. I debated whether to call it a rose bowl whimsey or a spittoon whimsey, but since the top is turned in, it must be a rose bowl. It is a product of the Northwood factory.

Palm and Scroll Rose Bowl Whimsey

Again, here is a whimsey shape that is much nicer than the original bowl shape. Dugan/Diamond is the maker, and they certainly made the right move when they made this piece. The feather-like palms seem to be made just for this shape.

Palm Beach Card Tray Whimsey

What a wonderful and rare item this is! Pulled from the rare jelly compote shape and flattened into a card tray on a stem, it has to be near the top of this pattern's desirability. Palm Beach was a U.S. Glass pattern (their #15119), found in both carnival glass and opalescent glass.

Piasa Bird Spittoon

Probably no other pattern in opalescent glass can be found in more whimsey shapes than this one. This one is the spittoon shape and while it became an in-line item, it is nevertheless a whimsey shape as are all spittoons. All whimsey pieces were created from the bowl shape.

Piasa Bird Vase

This whimsey has one top flame pulled into a grotesque spike and it is for this reason it has to be called a whimsey. Just what the glassmaker had in mind is hard to imagine. Only a few of these are reported.

Pompeian

These were made by Dugan and shown in old Butler Brothers ads from the 1905 – 1906 period. The Pompeian line is very similar to Dugan's Venetian and Japanese lines. Various colors, shapes, and sizes were made. Shown here is a whimsey jack-in-the-pulpit shape with a candy ribbon edge in white opalescent. Thanks to the late Casy Rich for the nice photo.

Popsicle Sticks Nut Bowl Whimsey

This Jefferson novelty shape is called a nut bowl. Colors are white, green, and blue opalescent.

Pressed Coinspot Rose Bowl Whimsey

Here is the white rose bowl whimsey pulled from the compote shape shown elsewhere. This pattern is also known as Concave Columns in the vase shape and was made in 1901, first by National (Northwood) and then by Dugan as their #617 pattern. It is also found in carnival glass.

Reflecting Diamonds

The ice cream bowl isn't an ordinary shape for this Dugan pattern, and in fact, few bowls from this company are found in this shape. For novices, ice cream bowls are round without ruffling and have a slightly turned-in edge.

Reverse Drapery Whimsey Vase

If you compare the Boggy Bayou vase shown elsewhere in this edition and the Reverse Drapery bowl (also shown in this edition), you will see just how this whimsey vase, shaped from the bowl, has been widely confused with the Boggy Bayou vase. The design on the marie is quite different however and starts higher above the marie. In addition, the top flaming is very different and usually has little flare.

Ribbon Swirl

Ribbon Swirl is found on vases, bowls, and rose bowls, but here I show a spittoon shape in vaseline. (Some may not consider this a whimsey, but I'll leave it for now.) This pattern is also found with cranberry decoration, so I feel there is a strong possibility this was made by Jefferson.

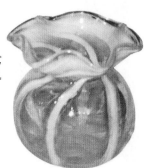

Squirrel and Acorn Rose Bowl Whimsey

This rose bowl whimsey is from the same mould as the other shapes in this pattern: a stemmed bowl, compote, vase, and vase whimsey. The maker hasn't been determined at this time but production seems to be in the 1904 – 1910 era. All pieces are scarce.

Squirrel and Acorn Vase

If you will compare this with the standard compote in this pattern shown elsewhere, you will see just how much of a whimsey this piece has become, especially with the three flattened flames that are almost comical. But despite this odd shaping, this piece is quite attractive and would add much to any collection, especially since the pattern is very rare.

Stripe Spittoon Whimsey

This beautiful piece of glass is 3" tall, 4" wide, and has a top opening of less than 1". It is blown glass and may well be of English origin although the shape seems to indicate it isn't. Many American companies made a Stripe product, and it could be from any of these, especially Northwood. Any information on this piece would be greatly appreciated.

Swirl (Handled Novelty Whimsey)

I suppose this 3½" tall piece started out as a creamer but somewhere along the way the top was ruffled and the spout was left out so it has become a novelty or whimsey piece that no one would pour from. Thanks to Ruth Harvey for sharing it with me.

Tree of Life Vase Whimsey

If you will examine the Tree of Life vase shown in the first section of the book, you will see just why I call this vase a whimsey. It has been pulled in like a corset in the middle and the top has been flared and ruffled. It can be found in three opalescent colors to date. There is also another ruffled vase without the pinched in middle section.

Tulip Compote Whimsey

This 1880s Richardson (England) vase form was pulled into a ruffled compote. The coloring is the same as the vase I show with wide stripes of opalescent glass and amethyst, while the stem and base are vaseline glass.

Twister Vase Whimsey

This vase, pulled from the bowl (or plate) shape, is a scarce item. It was made by Jefferson Glass and is shown as a bowl in a 1908 Butler Brothers ad for the Jefferson Company.

Waterlily and Cattails (Fenton)

This spittoon whimsey made from the bowl shape is quite hard to locate. To date blue is the only color reported. Photo courtesy of Rick and Debbie Graham.

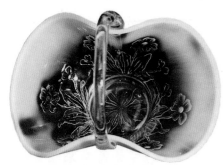

Wilted Flowers Basket Whimsey

This Dugan pattern is called Single Flower in carnival glass and the original design was part of Dugan's Intaglio line. Here I show the handled basket made from a standard bowl with an added handle.

Wreath and Shell Spittoon

This pattern was made by Model Flint Glass of Albany, Indiana, in several shapes and treatments. The spittoon whimsey is a very collectible item, especially for advanced collectors who recognize its rarity. Four colors are known in opalescent glass, as well as a very rare example with pink opalescence around the rim.

Wreath and Shell Whimsey Ivy Ball

Shaped from the flat tumbler (tumblers in this pattern can be flat based or footed), this whimsey is called an ivy ball and is one of my very favorite pieces in this pattern. It is rare and very collectible, and I wish I owned one!

Wreathed Grape and Cable Centerpiece Whimsey

Named for the wreath of leaves around the collar, this was Fenton's #920, made in 1911. It can be found on opalescent or crystal glass (the leaves were removed before carnival glass production) and is rare in either treatment. This somewhat whimsey piece is shaped from the same mould as the regular orange or fruit bowl in this pattern. This has been flared to become what collectors call a centerpiece bowl. I sincerely thank Ruth Harvey for sharing this bowl and many other fine items with me.

Cranes

I have little information on this piece, other than it is likely late opalescent glass and possibly French. Photo courtesy of the Petrasichs.

Cubist Rose

In the 1930s when the Art Deco craze swept America, glass products were radically changed. The bowl shown is certainly no exception. It is called Cubist Rose and is typical of glass in the mid-1930s. It was made by Jobling (Rd. #780719) in 1933.

Daisy and Button (Fenton)

This Daisy and Button pattern was made by Fenton in the 1950s and again in the 1980s and 1990s. It has panels of vertical bars. The rose bowl on a metal stand dates from the 1980s but various shapes are known. The rose bowl shown was their #1927 pattern, according to a catalog.

Daisy and Button with Thumbprint

This 1950 – 1960 L.G. Wright goblet was part of a huge Daisy and Button line. Shapes were made in many treatments including opalescent glass in both vaseline and some blue.

Dancing Ladies

Dancing Ladies was made by the Fenton Glass Company for about five years beginning in 1931. This very collectible pattern is also called Dance of the Veils by carnival glass collectors. The pattern was Fenton's #900 and #901 and can be found in opalescent glass as well as other glass treatments. Some pieces have lids and handles, and sizes range from 5¼" to 9¼". Vases, pitchers, bonbons, and compotes are known.

Deco Daisy

This Jobling plate has a registration number 777134, indicating it was made in 1932. The design is interesting with typical deco parts. It was named by the Petrasichs.

DeVilbiss Wide Swirl

This perfume bottle with matching stopper was made for the DeVilbiss Company in the 1930s and 1940s in a wide swirl pattern. It has a DeVilbiss paper label still intact as well as the original ribbon.

Diamond Optic Water Carafe

This Fenton Art Glass Company version of the Lattice (Bubble Lattice) pattern is found in many shapes. Production of this pattern began in the 1950s and continued for more than three decades. Shown is a water bottle or carafe in cranberry opalescent glass.

Dogwood

In 1910, Earnest Jobling Purser took over the Greener & Company plant in England, and began to produce a treatment he called Opalique, in an attempt to capitalize on the popularity of France's Rene Lalique in the art glass world. He called this glass Jobling's Opalique and produced it from 1910 to 1932. Many pieces were signed but some were not. The Dogwood bowl with the butterfly I suspect is Opalique but it isn't signed. Any information on this pattern would be appreciated.

Dot and Mitre

This late Fenton oil lamp is a well done example that could be mistaken for a vintage piece. The milk glass cut to cranberry look is a nice touch. Photo courtesy of Bill Walter and Laurel Walton.

Dot Optic (Fenton)

This vase shape was used to make an electric lamp. It was a popular late pattern for Fenton. It is found in a host of shapes and only a few colors. Several shapes of lamp shades are also known.

Duncan and Miller

This well-known firm was organized in 1874 and over the years made many types of glass. It is their opalescent items made in the 1920s and 1930s that most impress collectors today. For this reason I'm showing two examples of their work. First is an ashtray in vaseline opalescent glass from a line known as Sanibel. It has a very modern look, came in many colors, and certainly would not be confused with old glass. Next is a pale blue opalescent vase called Cocs et Plume. Its artistic quality is obvious and compares with items from Lalique glass.

Easter Chick (with Leaf & Scroll Border)

Plates like this, mostly in decorated milk glass, were very popular in the early 1900s, but the one shown here was made by Westmoreland for the Levay Company in the 1960s or 1970s. Other patterns made at the same time in blue opalescent glass were Contrary Mule and Cupid & Psyche. All are 7½" plates with decorative borders.

Ellen

Since I first showed this vase pattern, I've learned it is a bit newer than I thought and now falls near the 1930 time frame. It is 5" tall and has a scalloped base with six wide panels that run all the way to the top. It has also been seen flared out to a bowl shape.

Empress

Empress was made by Fenton in various types of glass. This vase is quite nice for late opalescent glass. Photo courtesy of the Petrasichs.

Eye Dot

This beautiful reproduction oil lamp from L. G. Wright is a quality item and would be an asset to any collector. Just don't pay old prices for it and you'll be fine.

Fenton Coin Dot Basket

This basket shape was first made about 1947. It has a lot of quality, as do nearly all Fenton products. The giveaway as to age is two-fold: the shape is not found in old American opalescent glass and the sectioned handle looks like bamboo. Remember, unless you are confident about age, always avoid reeded or sectioned handles.

173

Fenton Coin Dot Pitcher

Fenton called this their Dot Optic pattern and it dates from the 1940s in most shapes. Here I show the #1353 water pitcher in cranberry. Note that it has the reeded handle and the lip is pulled in to form an ice cube trap, a dead-giveaway of its age.

Fenton Hand Vase

This 3½" tall vase miniature was made by the Fenton Glass Company in 1942 or 1943 as their #38. It can be found in both blue or white opalescent glass as well as other treatments. It is still being made and recently I saw a Burmese glass example. And even though it isn't old glass, this is one of the very collectible items from Fenton.

Fenton Hobnail

This has been one of Fenton's most commonly recognized patterns.

Production started in the mid 30s and continued until 2007. It has been a long standing favorite with collectors. The number of colors and shapes is staggering, including lamps, bowls, shoes, vases, hats, baskets, candy jars, compotes, bonbons, and bells. Since this pattern is covered extensively in other works, the list here as well as in the price guide will be condensed.

Fenton Rib

This 1951 Fenton square ashtray was copied from the old Beatty Rib pattern. It was shown in their ads of the time as part of a four-piece smoking set. It can be found in both white and blue opalescent glass and the quality of the piece is very good. The boxed set was listed as their #1728 pattern.

Fenton's #37 Miniature Creamer

This 1942 Fenton piece was from the same mould as the vase shape shown elsewhere. It can be found in blue, vaseline, or white opalescent glass. On this piece a handle was added to make the creamer shape.

Fenton's #37 Miniature Vase

This often seen miniature was made by the Fenton Company from 1942 to 1944 in blue, vaseline (topaz), and white opalescent glass. It was fashioned as a creamer, a handled basket, the vase shown, and a toothpick holder. Tops can be straight or ruffled as shown, and some examples have a gilded rim.

Fenton's #894

This late 1930s vase can be found with various shaped tops. Shown here is a cranberry opalescent example with a JIP (jack-in-the-pulpit) shaped top.

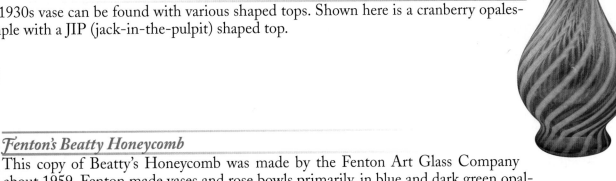

Fenton's Beatty Honeycomb

This copy of Beatty's Honeycomb was made by the Fenton Art Glass Company about 1959. Fenton made vases and rose bowls primarily, in blue and dark green opalescent. Here I show the vase reproduction in blue.

Fenton Spanish Lace

This very pretty Fenton reproduction is so well done it compares favorably with old pieces. Aside from being marked, this piece has a reeded handle that has to be a warning. Just remember, the Fenton Company has made many patterns and pieces over the years in opalescent glass and most have been well cataloged in several Fenton books, so there is little reason to mistake these pieces. Add to that the fact that Fenton began marking all their glass in 1970, and the task becomes simple.

Fenton Swirl

Swirl was made by the Fenton Art Glass Company from the 30s through to modern day. It was made in many shapes and colors. As with the Hobnail pattern, this one is shown in other works in its entirety and the list here will be condensed as well as in the price guide.

Flying Birds

The maker of this white opalescent piece is unknown at this time but it could be of French origin. This lidded dresser box has three sections and a design of flying birds on the lid and base. Thanks to Bill Walters and Laurel Walton for sharing the photo.

Fostoria Heirloom

Here is a very nice epergne and candle holder from Fostoria's Heirloom line, made between 1959 and 1970. Heirloom was produced in a host of shapes. The quality of all these items is outstanding and should be collected with the best of glass items of the 1960s and 1970s. Photo courtesy of the Keathleys.

Frisco (Fostoria)

This original pattern was called Frisco when it was made by Fostoria in 1904 (their #1229), but I don't believe Frisco was ever made in old opalescent glass. Here is a small rose bowl shape. I would love to hear more about this pattern from readers. The owner calls it Beaded Jewel.

Gibson Spittoon

This dark green opalescent spittoon was made by Gibson Glass and is clearly marked on the base. It is, of course, late glass. Still the coloring is good, the opalescence outstanding, and the design better than average. There are narrow ribs on the exterior that cover the piece and are swirled above the neck. I am uncertain as to the age of this pattern. Any information would be appreciated.

Grape & Vine

The latest information on this pattern tells me it was made by the Fenton Glass Company in 1990. It is a pretty piece of glass that may be part of the Paneled Grape pattern after all. The jack-in-the-pulpit shape does make it better than average.

Hobnail (Czechoslovakian)

Made in the 1950s, these two pieces, a cranberry puff box with cover and a vaseline tumbler, are very pretty examples of the world famous Hobnail pattern, this time made in Czechoslovakia. Note that the hobs go all the way over the bottom of these pieces. It is found in various shapes and colors.

Hobnail Variant

I've called this Hobnail pattern a variant because of the odd seam-like sections that are on opposite sides of the piece. I've named this a zipper mould because it looks just like a zipper's fittings to me. It looks to have been made in the late 1940s and early 1950s. Quality-wise, it isn't top-notch. The maker is uncertain at this time.

Hobnail (Westmoreland)

I'm told this is a Westmoreland pattern made around 1970. The color is a deep rich blue, and shapes include a creamer and sugar as well as a goblet. Photo courtesy of the Petrasichs.

Honeycomb with Flower Rim

This pattern had been widely reproduced, so I am placing this toothpick holder here with the glass after 1930. It is also known as Inverted Thumbprint with Daisy Band or Vermont Honeycomb. I'd appreciate any information about this piece and thank the Petrasichs for sharing it.

Jersey Swirl (L.G. Wright)

This goblet shape, made for L.G. Wright and advertised as Jersey Swirl, was made in an opalescent treatment in 1950. Others were a covered compote, low covered compote, 6" plate, 10" plate, salt dip, master salt dip, 4" footed sauce, and a wine.

Lace-Edged Basketweave

This Fenton pattern (their #992) was mislabeled in previous editions as being Imperial and I do apologize. This one has a strong basketweave as the exterior design. Here is a beautiful green opalescent example and it is known in white and blue opalescent too. Date of production is from the early 30s to the early 50s.

Lace-Edged Buttons

This Imperial pattern, also known as Sugar Cane, dates from 1937 and was still being made in 1942. I've seen more than one shape but all had the open-edged treatment. While attractive, the value isn't much more than it was when these items were made.

Lace-Edged Diamonds

Like its close companion Lace-Edged Buttons, this is another Imperial pattern made in the late 1930s and early 1940s. It is a very nice design made in white, green, and blue, but again the value is small and only slightly more than when manufactured.

Moon and Stars

This reproduction was made for the L.G. Wright Company, starting in the 1950s and continuing off and on until 1970. It was never made in old opalescent glass, It is found in several glass treatments as well as blue and vaseline opalescent glass. Various shapes are known.

Nautilus

The anchor stem gives this rare beauty its name. This 1935 Duncan Miller piece is seldom found and when it does show up it brings top dollar. The color is a strong vaseline. Thanks to the Sandemans for sharing it.

Needlepoint

This is a Fostoria pattern and is signed on the bottom in script. These tumblers were made in three sizes and at least three colors including green (shown), blue, and orange. They first appear in Fostoria ads in 1951 and have no other shapes listed.

Opalberry

Like the Dogwood bowl shown earlier, I believe this is an example of Jobling's Opalique ware made at the Greener plant in England between 1910 and 1935 by Ernest Jobling Purser. The plate shown has three clusters of leaves and berries that cover much of the surface with overlapping leaves in the center. It is a beautifully designed piece of glass. Further information about this pattern would be appreciated.

Open-Edge Basketweave

While Fenton made this very pattern in opalescent glass in 1911 – 1913, it wasn't made in this royal blue color until 1932, so I can be sure this is a newer piece. Old colors are blue (regular), green, white, and a pastel vaseline.

Panache

This 1940s Fenton atomizer was likely done for DeVilbiss. The pattern, also called Style, consists of six plumed panels and a scalloped base. The color is blue but I feel certain other colors were made. Thanks to Samantha Price for sharing it.

Peacock Garden Vase

This very beautiful 10" vase in French opalescent glass was a product of the Fenton Company (their #791) and was made in 4", 6", 8", and 10" sizes in 1934. The 8" and 10" moulds originally came from the old Northwood Company, it is believed, where a carnival version was made. It is thought that the 4" and 6" moulds were made at the Fenton factory. Since the early 1930s, Fenton has made this vase (in the 8" size mostly) in several dozen treatments. The 4", 6", and 10" examples are considered quite rare and are very collectible.

Petticoats

This very attractive perfume, also called Flounces, was made by the Fenton Art Glass Company for DeVilbiss in 1933. It can be found in white, blue, and canary (topaz) opalescent glass.

Pinecone and Leaves

This pattern was first made at Greener and Company in jet glass (black) bearing Rd. #777133. It was later made in Jobling Opalique opalescent glass in the beautiful bowl shown. Opalique was a glass made by Ernest Jobling Purser at the Greener Factory between 1910 and 1935 in the manner of Rene Lalique's famous French opalescent ware.

Pinecone Spray

This piece is similar to the Pinecone and Leaves pattern by Jobling, but it has fewer sprays and a more deco look. I believe this piece may also be from Jobling or even from Sabino, but have no proof and welcome any information from readers.

Plume Twist Atomizer

This 1940s DeVilbiss atomizer can be found in white opalescent, as shown, or in vaseline. It stands nearly 4" tall and has a series of feathers that wind around the bottle.

Plymouth

In 1935 Fenton made a large line of this pattern, all very useful items including plates, wines, highballs, old-fashioned glasses, a rare mug, and the pilsner shown. These were all done in their French opalescent glass and are quality all the way. Additional shapes were added, including a cocktail glass and a goblet.

Queen's Petticoat

Only after the first edition of this book came out did I learn this pretty little vase was made by Fostoria in 1959 as part of their Heirloom collection. It was listed as their #5056. I am sorry that I may have misled some collectors into thinking this was an old piece, but it is just that good!

Quilted Pinecone

This atomizer was made by Fenton for DeVilbiss. It can be found in blue and I'm certain other colors are available as well. Thanks to Wayne and Joan Joliffe for sharing it.

Ring

This 1933 Fenton Ring pitcher is actually very scarce and highly collectible. It stands 7" tall. I'm sure Fenton made this in their usual colors of the time, so green, blue, and vaseline are possibilities.

Ring and Petals

This blue Westmoreland butter is the only shape and color reported. Additional information is appreciated. Photo courtesy of Bill Walter and Laurel Walton.

Rosette

This lamp base was made by Fenton for L. G. Wright. It is found on several different lamps, some used for the base and others for the top section of a hurricane lamp. Photo courtesy of Bill Walter and Laurel Walton.

Seaweed and Shell

This small shallow bowl consists of six shells, three of which are surrounded by seaweed. The bowl measures 5¾" in diameter and is in blue opalescent. I'm told it is French and possible makers are Etling and Ezell. Any information is appreciated. Thanks to the Petrasichs for the photo.

Spiral Optic (Fenton)

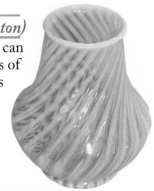

Fenton's Spiral Optic was made primarily from the 30s to the 50s (and into the 70s). It can be found in white, blue, and cranberry opalescent. A variety of shapes can be found: vases of various shapes and dimensions, hat shapes, candy boxes, and the list goes on. Since this pattern is covered extensively in other works, the list of shapes and the list in the price guide have been condensed.

Spiral Waves

I have no information on this pattern other than it was possibly made by Ezell or Etling of France. This large plate measures 15" in diameter and is found so far in only white opalescent. Thanks to Samantha Prince for sharing it.

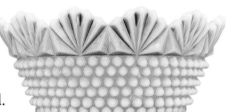

Stamm House Dewdrop (#1886/642)

This fine piece of new glasswork was made by the Imperial Glass Company in 1966 in large (10") and small (5") bowls in a beautiful canary opalescent glass. It has the look of old English opalescent glass and since Imperial made very little opalescent glass at any time, this is a collectible item indeed.

Stars and Stripes

Stars and Stripes was originally from Hobbs, Brockunier and then Beaumont. It was revisited in the 1940s by Fenton for L.G. Wright in tumblers, a creamer, barber bottle, cruet, basket, finger bowl, syrup, and other novelties in blue or cranberry opalescent glass. Shown are the cruet and barber bottle.

Swan Bowl

Apparently this bowl and its companion pieces (smaller bowls and candlesticks) were first made at the Diamond plant from 1926 to 1927 and later at the Fenton Art Glass factory from 1934 to 1939. The Dugan/Diamond version is known in pink, green, and black glass, and the Fenton pieces are advertised in opalescent colors so it appears the master bowl shown is a Fenton item despite its color matching so many of Dugan's blue opalescent items. At any rate, these blue pieces are considered rare, as are the green opalescent items.

Swirl

This well done Fenton pattern was made for the L.G. Wright Glass Company in cranberry in 1973 (other opalescent colors were made earlier). A wide variety of shapes are known. Note that the handle is reeded.

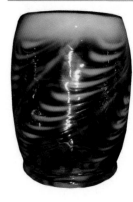

Swirled Feather

This 1953 Fenton pattern can be found in a fairy lamp, candy dish, vase, cruet, hurricane lamp, a vanity set, and a water set (tumbler shown). It was an attempt to reproduce the Blown Twist pattern.

Sylvan

Sylvan was shown in a 1943 catalog from Duncan Miller. This pattern, like the Canterbury pattern, is found in a variety of shapes including, but not limited to, bowls, relish trays, candy dishes, and vases. Photo courtesy of the Petrasichs.

Tokyo

If you look closely at the compote shown, you can see the color is light and the opalescence thin. The original pattern was made by Jefferson Glass in 1905, but this piece when held and examined is obviously not of that quality. I do not know of other shapes having been reproduced but it is possible.

Trout

When I first showed this pretty bowl, I had no information about it but speculated it might be French. It is, in fact, Verlys, made by the Holophane Company of France in 1931, so I've moved it from the old glass section. Fenton bought the mould in 1966 and has reproduced this piece. New treatments include an acid finish with opalescence. The bowl has an 8½" diameter and stands 3½" tall.

Twigs (Reproduction)

On close examination, you will see some differences from the regular Twigs vase. First, the lip has a cased edge, a clear applied edging. On some the area between the legs and the body of the vase is filled solid with glass. Beware of these and always know the dealer before you buy this pattern. Colors of the reproductions are vaseline, blue, and white opalescent (so far). The white opal ones are also being iridized to create copies in peach opal. The old vase was never made in this treatment.

Water Ballet

I'm told this low bowl or plate is from France and have no information to dispute it. The only color reported is a nice white opalescent. I have assigned a name, but if anyone knows it by a previously established named I'd certainly like to hear from them. Thanks to Samantha Prince for the nice photo.

Wildflower

This reproduction of the old U.S. Glass pattern was first sold by L. G. Wright in the 1940s and in an expanded line in the 1959 – 1960 era. It can be found in several treatments, including crystal, amber, blue, and green, as well as vaseline and blue opalescent glass. Reproduced shapes include covered compotes, a table set, goblets, square plates, salt dips (two styles), footed sauce, covered candy jar, and a 7½" footed vase. No old opalescent pieces exist.

Windows (L.G. Wright)

This was made in the 1950s by the Fenton Art Glass Company for L.G. Wright. Fenton called this Window Pane. Shapes reproduced include an epergne, lamps, fairy light, water set, syrup, vase, creamer, cruet, and a finger bowl. Colors were cranberry and blue, often satin finished.

Wreathed Cherry

Apparently all the opalescent items in this Dugan/Diamond pattern are new, made for and distributed by the L. G. Wright Company starting in 1963 and continuing for several years. Colors are blue and vaseline in opalescent glass, as well as some non-opalescent runs that include amber, red, emerald green, and blue.

Wright's Thread and Rib Epergne

In 1940 L. G. Wright reproduced the Northwood #305 (Thread and Rib) epergne from moulds from Island Mould and Machine Company. Fenton was the maker of the epergnes in several crest or cased edge treatments as well as plain blue or vaseline opalescent ones. These epergnes continued in production into the 1950s and were sold through a New York import dealer, Kosherak Brothers. Beware of all cased examples or ones with the flames pulled. They are all reproductions.

Price Guide

As in my past price guides, I've attempted to include in a complete and up-to-date manner American and English opalescent glass production from 1890 to 1930, a natural time frame for such glass, one that separated antique production from contemporary. In a few instances, prices have been averaged where several variations of a shape exist, but I've tried to list prices as completely as possible.

Values in this guide were determined from dealers' lists, shop taggings, antique guide listings, and personal observation. Auction prices played only minor roles due to their often inflated bidding value. All items are priced as in mint condition and with average opalescence; flaws or poor coloring reduces value. Please remember this is only a guide and prices herein are not set in stone. As with all my prices guides, this one is meant to advise the buyer rather than set prices.

Most pattern names conform to those most frequently encountered but where more than one name is commonly in use, I've included both names in the interest of clarity.

Or course, I welcome all constructive comments from readers and ask anyone with more information to contact me. Please include a self-addressed, stamped envelope with your correspondence. You may also feel free to email me at the email address located at the beginning of this book. I am always looking for information or photos of patterns I haven't covered in this edition. That's how I learn and how I improve these books with each new edition.

*Indicates pattern was reproduced.

Pattern Name	Blue	Green	White	Vaseline/ Canary	Cranberry	Other
ABALONE						
Bowl	45.00	35.00	25.00	50.00		60.00 Emerald
ACORN BURRS (NORTHWOOD)						
Bowl, sauce, very rare	175.00		100.00			
ACORNS						
Jar with lid	200.00		150.00			
ACORN WITH BEE						
Sugar with lid			250.00			
ADONIS PINEAPPLE						
Claret bottle						400.00 Amber top
Blue top 5% less than amber top						
ALA-BOCK						
Bowl whimsey, ruffled	115.00			130.00		
Candy dish	95.00			100.00		
Pitcher	235.00			250.00		
Rose bowl	130.00			140.00		
Tumbler	25.00			35.00		
ALASKA						
Banana boat	235.00		200.00	265.00		270.00 Emerald
Bowl, master	175.00		125.00	165.00		165.00 Emerald
Bowl, sauce	65.00		30.00	60.00		60.00 Emerald
Bride's basket	300.00		135.00	375.00		350.00 Emerald
Butter	415.00		300.00	450.00		375.00 Emerald
Celery tray	195.00		140.00	225.00		175.00 Emerald
Creamer	90.00		70.00	85.00		80.00 Emerald
Cruet	325.00		280.00	300.00		325.00 Emerald
Pitcher	425.00		350.00	450.00		500.00 Emerald
Shakers, pair	170.00		90.00	185.00		125.00 Emerald
Spooner	100.00		70.00	90.00		90.00 Emerald
Sugar with lid	165.00		150.00	175.00		175.00 Emerald
Tumbler	80.00		60.00	80.00		90.00 Emerald
ALBANY REVERSE SWIRL						
Bowl, 9"	65.00		45.00	70.00		
Butter	135.00		100.00	145.00		
Celery vase	70.00		55.00	75.00		
Creamer or spooner	60.00		50.00	65.00		
Pitcher	290.00		225.00	325.00		
Rose bowl	85.00		60.00	90.00		
Sugar	75.00		60.00	85.00		
Sugar shaker	125.00		90.00	135.00		
Syrup	200.00		125.00	235.00		
Toothpick holder	80.00		55.00	90.00		
Tumbler	50.00		35.00	60.00		
Water bottle	165.00		115.00	185.00		

Pattern Name	Blue	Green	White	Vaseline/Canary	Cranberry	Other
ALBANY STRIPE (ALBANY)						
Barber bottle	275.00		200.00	300.00		
Pitcher	425.00		325.00	500.00		600.00 Decorated
Sugar bowl	200.00		175.00	225.00		
Vase, 4¾"	250.00		225.00	250.00		
ALFRED AND JAMES						
Rose bowl				200.00		
ALHAMBRA						
Rose bowl	125.00		100.00	135.00	175.00	
Syrup	325.00		275.00	375.00	475.00	
Tumbler	75.00		55.00	70.00	100.00	
ALVA						
Oil lamp	250.00		220.00			
ARABIAN NIGHTS						
Pitcher	400.00		285.00	400.00	1,100.00	
Syrup	225.00		185.00	275.00		
Tumbler	65.00		50.00	75.00	125.00	
ARCHED PANEL						
Bowl, master	110.00	120.00	70.00	100.00		
Bowl, sauce	40.00	45.00	25.00	30.00		
ARGONAUT SHELL *(NAUTILUS)						
Bowl, master	150.00		125.00			
Bowl, sauce	65.00		50.00			
Butter	325.00		275.00			
Creamer	200.00		150.00			
Cruet	500.00		350.00			
Jelly compote	125.00		75.00	90.00		
Novelty bowls, tray, etc.	65.00		50.00	100.00		
Pitcher	500.00		375.00			
Shakers, pair	110.00		85.00	100.00		
Spooner	200.00		150.00			
Sugar	265.00		225.00			
Tumbler	125.00		100.00	100.00		
Whimsey banana boat	65.00		50.00	75.00		
Add 15% for script signed pieces						
ARGUS (THUMBPRINT)						
Compote	90.00	95.00	50.00	80.00		
ARROWHEAD						
Lidded jar				165.00		
Shade				125.00		
ASCOT						
Biscuit jar	175.00			160.00		
Bowl	55.00			75.00		
Creamer	85.00			90.00		
Open sugar	85.00			85.00		
ASTRO						
Bowl	55.00	50.00	40.00	50.00		60.00 Emerald
Hat whimsey	75.00	70.00	65.00	75.00		
AURORA BOREALIS						
Novelty vase	90.00	80.00	65.00			
AUTUMN LEAVES						
Banana bowl	50.00	70.00	40.00			75.00 Emerald
Bowl	75.00	95.00	50.00			
Nappy			125.00			
AZZURO VERDE						
Vase	150.00			200.00		
BABY COINSPOT*						
Syrup			140.00			
Vase		100.00	60.00	90.00		
BALL FOOT HOBNAIL						
Bowl			75.00			
BANDED HOBNAIL						
Dresser bottle	75.00		50.00			
BANDED LILY EPERGNE						
Single lily epergne				375.00		
BANDED NECK SCALE OPTIC						
Vase			55.00			

Pattern Name	Blue	Green	White	Vaseline/ Canary	Cranberry	Other
BANDED STAR AND FAN						
Bowl, 9" and 11"	95.00-150.00					
BARBELLS						
Bowl	40.00	50.00	30.00	45.00		
Vase, rare	100.00	120.00				
BEADED BASE VASE						
Vase	75.00		45.00			
BEADED BASKET (DUGAN)						
Basket, handled, very scarce			150.00			
BEADED BLOCK						
Bowl	65.00	60.00	35.00			
Celery vase	85.00	75.00	45.00			
Creamer			65.00			
Milk pitcher, rare				700.00		
Nappy, handled			40.00			
Rose bowl, scarce	65.00	70.00	55.00	85.00		
Sugar			75.00			
BEADED BUTTON ARCHES						
Compote				210.00		235.00 Blue pearline
Creamer				75.00		90.00 Blue pearline
Sugar				95.00		110.00 Blue pearline
BEADED CABLE						
Bowl, footed	50.00	45.00	35.00	45.00		
Rose bowl, footed	65.00	60.00	45.00	60.00		
Add 10% for interior pattern						
BEADED DRAPES						
Banana bowl, footed	50.00	50.00	45.00	40.00		
Bowl, footed	45.00	40.00	30.00	50.00		
Rose bowl, footed	55.00	55.00	40.00			
Add 10% for frit						
BEADED FANS						
Bowl, footed	40.00	45.00	35.00			
Rose bowl, footed	50.00	50.00	40.00			
BEADED FLEUR DE LIS						
Bowl, novelty	55.00	55.00	45.00			
Bowl, whimsey	90.00	95.00	75.00			
Compote	50.00	50.00	45.00			
Rose bowl	60.00	60.00	50.00			
BEADED MOON & STARS						
Banana bowl, stemmed	85.00	90.00	65.00			
Bowl	70.00	90.00	50.00			
Compote	80.00	95.00	60.00			
BEADED OVALS IN SAND						
Bowl, master	75.00	70.00	50.00			
Bowl, sauce	35.00	30.00	20.00			
Butter	300.00	250.00	185.00			
Creamer	90.00	80.00	45.00			
Cruet	250.00	225.00	175.00			
Nappy	55.00	45.00	25.00			
Pitcher	425.00	375.00	300.00			
Shakers, pair	100.00	85.00	75.00			
Spooner	100.00	85.00	65.00			
Sugar	250.00	225.00	165.00			
Toothpick holder	200.00	175.00	125.00			
Tumbler	100.00	85.00	60.00			
BEADED OVALS WITH HOLLY						
Spooner, rare	165.00		125.00			
BEADED SHELL						
Bowl, master	85.00	100.00	65.00			
Bowl, sauce	55.00	65.00	35.00			
Butter	500.00	675.00	400.00			
Condiment set, four pieces	800.00	900.00	700.00			
Creamer	150.00	180.00	145.00			
Cruet	500.00	700.00	400.00			
Jelly compote, very rare	900.00	900.00	700.00	900.00		
Pitcher	575.00	625.00	500.00			
Shakers, pair	350.00	400.00	300.00			

Pattern Name	Blue	Green	White	Vaseline/Canary	Cranberry	Other
Spooner	150.00	180.00	150.00			
Sugar	225.00	275.00	190.00			
Toothpick holder	475.00	675.00	500.00			
Tumbler	100.00	115.00	75.00			
BEADED STAR MEDALLION						
Shade	70.00	55.00	40.00			
BEADED STARS						
Advertising bowl, rare	350.00	400.00	275.00			
Advertising plate, rare	450.00	500.00	400.00			
Bowl	45.00	55.00	35.00			
Plate	100.00		60.00			
Rose bowl	60.00	60.00	40.00			75.00 Lime opal
BEADED V'S AND BUTTONS						
Creamer	80.00					
BEADS & BARK						
Vase, footed	135.00	100.00	70.00	125.00		
BEADS & CURLEYCUES						
Novelty bowls, footed	50.00	50.00	40.00			
BEATTY HONEYCOMB*						
Bowl, master	50.00		40.00			
Bowl, sauce	25.00		20.00			
Butter	225.00		175.00			
Celery vase	80.00		70.00			
Creamer	90.00		50.00			
Cruet	200.00		175.00			
Individual creamer & sugar set	150.00		125.00			
Mug	55.00		40.00			
Mustard pot	100.00		75.00			
Pitcher	200.00		150.00			
Shakers, pair	80.00		60.00			
Spooner	90.00		50.00			
Sugar	125.00		100.00			
Toothpick holder	200.00		150.00			250.00 Violet opal
Tumbler	50.00		35.00			
BEATTY RIB						
Bowl, master	55.00		35.00			
Bowl, novelty	75.00		65.00			
Bowl, sauce	30.00		20.00			
Butter	200.00		125.00			
Celery vase	75.00		65.00			
Cracker jar	125.00		100.00			
Creamer	60.00		40.00			
Finger bowl	30.00		20.00			
Match holder	50.00		35.00			
Mug	55.00		40.00			
Mustard jar	150.00		125.00			
Nappy, various	40.00		25.00			
Pitcher	200.00		150.00			
Shakers, pair	75.00		60.00			
Salt dip	60.00		45.00			
Spooner	60.00		40.00			
Sugar	145.00		100.00			
Sugar shaker	125.00		100.00			
Toothpick	65.00		55.00			
Tumbler	50.00		30.00			
BEATTY SWIRL						
Bowl, master	55.00		40.00			
Bowl, sauce	30.00		20.00			
Butter	175.00		150.00			
Celery vase	75.00		60.00			
Creamer	75.00		60.00			
Mug	65.00		35.00	85.00		
Pitcher	185.00		125.00	225.00		
Spooner	75.00		60.00			
Sugar	125.00		100.00			
Syrup	250.00		200.00	275.00		
Tumbler	40.00		30.00	50.00		

Pattern Name	Blue	Green	White	Vaseline/Canary	Cranberry	Other
Water tray	100.00		65.00	110.00		
BEAUMONT STRIPE						
Pitcher	325.00		285.00	350.00		
Tumbler	65.00		50.00	70.00		
BEAUMONT SWIRL						
Pitcher	350.00	325.00	300.00			
Tumbler	80.00	70.00	55.00			
BELL FLOWER CENTERPIECE VASE						
Vase, 16"						325.00 Amber opal
BERRY PATCH						
Bowl, square	55.00		40.00			
Novelty bowl, square	50.00	45.00	30.00			
Plate	75.00	75.00	50.00			
BIG DIAMOND						
Vase, with enameling						325.00 Amber opal
BIG DOT						
Bowl				125.00		
BIG WINDOWS SWIRLED						
Barber bottle	175.00		135.00		200.00	
Bowl, two sizes	60.00-125.00		40.00-95.00		75.00-145.00	
Butter	225.00		165.00		245.00	
Creamer	65.00		50.00		80.00	
Oil lamp	425.00		300.00		500.00	
Shaker	125.00		95.00		135.00	
Spooner	65.00		50.00		75.00	
Sugar	95.00		75.00		95.00	
Syrup	165.00		125.00		175.00	
BIRD IN A TREE						
Novelty bowl						250.00 Rose opal
BLACKBERRY						
Bonbon			50.00			80.00 Amethyst
Bowl			30.00			70.00 Amethyst
Nappy	40.00	45.00	30.00			60.00 Amethyst
Plate, 6"			30.00			85.00 Amethyst
BLACKBERRY SPRAY						
Hat	35.00		25.00			65.00 Amethyst
Hat, jack-in-the-pulpit shape	55.00		35.00			75.00 Amethyst
BLOCK						
Celery vase	60.00	60.00	40.00	55.00	80.00	
Novelty bowl	50.00	45.00	30.00	45.00	65.00	
BLOCK (ENGLISH)						
Pitcher	175.00					225.00 Amber
Platter	75.00					95.00 Amber
Tumbler, two sizes	60.00-85.00					75.00-95.00 Amber
BLOCKED THUMBPRINT & BEADS						
Bowl	35.00	40.00	30.00			
Nappy	25.00	30.00	20.00			
Plate	50.00					60.00 Emerald
BLOOMS & BLOSSOMS						
Nappy, handled	50.00	50.00	40.00			
Proof whimsey, scarce	100.00	65.00				
BLOSSOMS & PALMS						
Bowl	70.00	65.00	45.00	95.00		
BLOSSOMS & WEB						
Bowl, rare	225.00	175.00	150.00			
BLOSSOM TOP CASTER SET						
Caster set	275.00		200.00	350.00		
BLOWN DIAMONDS						
Pitcher, scarce				300.00		
BLOWN DRAPERY						
Barber bottle, rare		1,500.00				
Pitcher	550.00	500.00	350.00		900.00	
Sugar shaker	500.00	450.00	300.00			
Tumbler	175.00	150.00	165.00		300.00	
Vase	225.00	200.00	175.00			
BLOWN ROPE						
Whimsey vase				200.00		

188

Pattern Name	Blue	Green	White	Vaseline/Canary	Cranberry	Other
BLOWN TWIST						
Celery vase	400.00		350.00	450.00		
Pitcher	550.00	500.00	350.00	525.00	900.00	
Sugar shaker	200.00	185.00	175.00	200.00	600.00	
Syrup	250.00		200.00		400.00	
Tumbler	200.00	175.00	150.00	175.00	325.00	
BLUERESCENT WEBB						
Marmalade in metal holder, very rare						2,250.00 Blue/vaseline
BOAT WITH WHEELS						
Boat shape				235.00		
BOGGY BAYOU						
Vase	40.00	35.00	25.00			85.00 Amethyst
BOHEMIAN STRIPE						
Vase, decorated	150.00					
BOHEMIAN TULIP EPERGNE						
Epergne, single lily, rare						500.00 Cran/vaseline
BOUGH & BLOSSOM						
Rose bowl						175.00 Lavender
BRASS NAILHEAD						
Mug			75.00			
BRICK						
Novelty match holder			100.00			
BRIDESHEAD (DAVIDSON)						
Basket, handled	90.00					
Butter	100.00					
Celery vase	60.00					
Compote	70.00					
Creamer	65.00					
Novelty bowl	55.00					
Pitcher, two sizes	145.00-165.00					
Sugar	75.00					
Tray, oval	125.00		100.00	120.00		
Tumbler	100.00					
BRIDESMAID (GREENER & CO.)						
Bowls, various sizes, rare	65.00-100.00					80.00-140.00 Amber
Bowl, large oval, rare	125.00					165.00 Amber
Pitcher, rare	200.00					400.00 Amber
Tray, rare	100.00					175.00 Amber
Tumbler, rare	70.00					100.00 Amber
BRILYNACEE LACE (ALBANY)						
Pitcher	425.00		300.00			
BRITISH FLUTE						
Vase				140.00		
BROKEN PILLAR						
Card tray (from compote shape)	170.00		135.00	165.00		
Compote	160.00		125.00	155.00		
BUBBLE LATTICE						
Bowl, master	70.00	50.00	45.00	65.00	80.00	
Bowl, sauce	30.00	25.00	20.00	30.00	35.00	
Bride's basket	125.00	100.00	75.00	130.00	225.00	
Butter	225.00	200.00	150.00	200.00	725.00	
Celery vase					125.00	
Creamer	60.00	50.00	50.00	55.00	150.00	
Cruet, average pricing	175.00	160.00	135.00	170.00	400.00	
Finger bowl	45.00	40.00	25.00	45.00	125.00	
Lamp, 4"			250.00		325.00	
Pitcher, various	300.00	275.00	225.00	275.00	750.00	
Rose bowl	75.00					
Shakers, various	150.00	125.00	100.00	175.00	150.00-300.00	
Spooner	60.00	50.00	50.00	55.00	200.00	
Straw holder with lid, rare			500.00			
Sugar	125.00	100.00	75.00	100.00	425.00	
Sugar shaker	235.00	225.00	185.00	225.00	300.00	
Syrup, various	225.00	200.00	175.00	200.00	750.00	
Toothpick holder	300.00	275.00	200.00	350.00	300.00-550.00	
Tumbler, various	50.00	50.00	40.00	45.00	125.00	

Pattern Name	Blue	Green	White	Vaseline/Canary	Cranberry	Other
BUBBLE LATTICE LAMP						
Lamp			250.00			
BUCKEYE BUBBLE LATTICE						
Cylinder shade	125.00		85.00	175.00	200.00	
Pitcher	225.00		150.00	325.00	375.00	
Salt shaker	100.00		75.00	150.00	175.00	
Tumbler	65.00		75.00	90.00	110.00	
BULBOUS BASE COINSPOT						
Sugar shaker	125.00		90.00		175.00	
Syrup	160.00		110.00		225.00	
BULL'S EYE						
Bowl	50.00				65.00	
Shade	60.00		40.00			
Water bottle			175.00		265.00	
BULL'S EYE & FAN VARIANT						
Bowl		90.00				
BULL'S EYE & LEAVES						
Bowl	150.00		95.00			
*Add 10% for goofus treatment						
BUSHEL BASKET						
One shape, scarce	150.00	250.00	150.00	550.00		
BUTTERFLY (FENTON)						
Compote, either shape			40.00			
*Add 10% for colored butterflies						
BUTTON PANELS						
Bowl	45.00		35.00	50.00		
Nut bowl	45.00		40.00	50.00		
Rose bowl	45.00		40.00	55.00		
BUTTONS & BRAIDS						
Bowl	50.00	55.00	30.00		85.00	
Pitcher	350.00	400.00	175.00	900.00	700.00	
Tumbler	60.00	70.00	50.00	110.00	100.00	
CABBAGE LEAF						
Novelty bowl, footed	80.00	65.00	50.00			
CACTUS (NORTHWOOD)						
Shakers, each	85.00			100.00	135.00	
CALYX						
Vase, scarce	85.00		60.00	90.00		
CANARY/BLUE J.I.P.						
Vase, 6½"						450.00
CANE & DIAMOND SWIRL						
Stemmed tray	75.00			70.00		
CANE RINGS						
Bowl, 8½"	75.00			85.00		
Celery vase	55.00			65.00		
Creamer	60.00			65.00		
Sugar	65.00			70.00		
CAROUSEL						
Bowl	165.00	125.00	100.00			
CASBAH						
Bowl			120.00			
Compote			140.00			
CASHEWS						
Bowl	50.00	45.00	30.00			
Bowl, tricornered	65.00	60.00	45.00			
Rose bowl, rare	90.00	85.00	60.00			
Whimsey bowl	55.00	50.00	35.00			
CATHEDRAL						
Pitcher, 8"	275.00					
CENTIPEDE						
Bowl, scarce	125.00			160.00		
CHERRY						
Master bowl	70.00					
Small bowl	25.00					
Covered butter	225.00					
Creamer	110.00					
Sugar	125.00					

Pattern Name	Blue	Green	White	Vaseline/Canary	Cranberry	Other
Spooner	115.00					
Goblet	75.00					
Wine	80.00					
Plate, rare	160.00					
Open compote	90.00					
Covered compote	125.00					
Novelty bowls	60.00					
CHERRY PANEL						
Novelty bowl	70.00		55.00	70.00		
Nut bowl whimsey	90.00		75.00	100.00		
Vase whimsey			150.00			
CHIPPENDALE						
Bowl, 9½"	85.00			115.00		
Basket	60.00			80.00		
Compote	75.00			95.00		
Creamer	50.00			65.00		
Sugar, open	45.00			60.00		
Plate, 6¼"	75.00			95.00		
Pitcher	150.00			165.00		
Salt dip	40.00			50.00		
Tumbler	40.00			45.00		
Vase whimsey			175.00			
CHRISTMAS PEARLS						
Cruet	300.00	280.00	350.00			
Shakers, pair	165.00	140.00	175.00			
CHRISTMAS SNOWFLAKE						
Cruet			125.00			
Oil lamp, three sizes	325.00-600.00	275.00-500.00	225.00-400.00		400.00-650.00	
Pitcher, either	675.00	500.00	425.00		950.00	
Tumbler, average	110.00	100.00	90.00		125.00	
CHRYSANTHEMUM						
Bowl, footed, 11"	275.00		200.00			400.00 Amethyst
CHRYSANTHEMUM BASE SWIRL						
Bowl, master	55.00		45.00		120.00	
Bowl, sauce	35.00		25.00		50.00	
Butter	325.00		300.00		500.00	
Celery vase	140.00		115.00		225.00	
Creamer	100.00		75.00		400.00	
Cruet	225.00		200.00		500.00	
Custard cup	75.00		50.00		110.00	
Finger bowl	45.00		30.00		140.00	
Mustard pot	150.00		120.00		240.00	
Pitcher	400.00		350.00		900.00	
Shakers, pair	125.00		100.00		300.00	
Spooner	100.00		75.00		215.00	
Straw holder with lid	500.00		400.00		1,200.00	
Sugar	200.00		175.00		350.00	
Sugar shaker	200.00		175.00		275.00	
Syrup	200.00		175.00		500.00	
Toothpick holder	100.00		75.00		300.00	
Tumbler	100.00		75.00		125.00	
CHRYSANTHEMUM SWIRL VARIANT						
Pitcher, rare	400.00		275.00		925.00	375.00 Teal
Tumbler, rare	100.00		65.00		110.00	
CIRCLED SCROLL						
Bowl, master	175.00	150.00	125.00			
Bowl, sauce	55.00	50.00	35.00			
Butter	475.00	350.00	300.00			
Creamer	175.00	170.00	125.00			
Cruet	700.00	675.00	465.00			
Jelly compote	150.00	140.00	125.00			
Pitcher	475.00	425.00	400.00			
Shakers, pair	325.00	300.00	250.00			
Spooner	175.00	170.00	125.00			
Sugar	250.00	225.00	200.00			
Tumbler	100.00	85.00	75.00			

Pattern Name	Blue	Green	White	Vaseline/Canary	Cranberry	Other
CIRRUS FEATHER LAMP						
Oil lamp				550.00		
CLEOPATRA'S FAN						
Vase, novelty, rare	100.00	90.00	75.00			
COIN DOT CHEVRON BASE						
Oil lamp	300.00		200.00			
COIN DOT LAMPS						
Lamp, three sizes	225.00-325.00		175.00-250.00			
Finger lamp	250.00		185.00	450.00		
COINSPOT						
(Includes variants, prices averaged. Not all shapes made by all companies.)						
Barber bottle	175.00	170.00	125.00		300.00	
Bowl, master	50.00	40.00	30.00		70.00	
Bowl, sauce	30.00	25.00	15.00		40.00	
Celery vase	125.00	110.00	100.00	125.00	185.00	
Compote	65.00	45.00	35.00			
Cruet, various	250.00	225.00	125.00	250.00	400.00	375.00 Rubina
Lamp (from syrup)	300.00		250.00		900.00	
Novelty bowls	60.00	55.00	35.00			
Perfume	65.00	75.00	55.00			
Pickle castor	300.00		225.00		750.00	
Pitcher	275.00	250.00	175.00	200.00	400.00	225.00 Rubina
Shakers, each	150.00	100.00	75.00	100.00	200.00	
Sugar shaker	125.00	100.00	80.00	110.00	390.00	250.00 Rubina
Syrup	175.00	155.00	150.00		400.00	325.00 Rubina
Toothpick holder	275.00	250.00	150.00	240.00	275.00	300.00 Rubina
Tumbler	40.00	35.00	25.00	35.00	100.00	100.00 Rubina
Tumble-up	155.00	150.00	125.00		300.00	
Water bottle			150.00		350.00	
COINSPOT & SWIRL						
Cruet, rare	150.00		100.00		200.00	235.00 Amber
Syrup, rare	175.00		125.00		235.00	250.00 Amber
COINSPOT (PHOENIX)						
Vase, bulbous shape						250.00 Amber
COLONIAL STAIRSTEPS						
Creamer	100.00					
Sugar	100.00					
Toothpick holder	200.00					
COMMONWEALTH						
Tumbler			20.00			
COMPASS (DUGAN/DIAMOND)						
Plate, rare	250.00	225.00				
Bowl, scarce	150.00	150.00	80.00			
Rose bowl whimsey	160.00	160.00	90.00			
CONCAVE COLUMNS						
Vase	100.00		75.00	100.00		
Vase whimsey	125.00		100.00	125.00		
CONCH & TWIG						
Wall pocket vase	250.00			250.00		
CONSOLIDATED CRISS-CROSS						
Bowl, master			125.00		200.00	
Bowl, sauce			50.00		75.00	
Butter			450.00		900.00	
Celery vase			150.00		175.00	
Creamer			250.00		375.00	
Cruet			275.00		800.00	
Finger bowl			100.00		125.00	
Ivy ball			300.00		700.00	
Mustard pot			150.00		275.00	
Pitcher			750.00		3,000.00	
Shakers, each			100.00		100.00	185.00 Rubina
Spooner			225.00		300.00	
Sugar			350.00		400.00	
Sugar shaker			325.00		600.00	600.00 Rubina
Syrup			325.00		825.00	725.00 Rubina
Toothpick holder			200.00		500.00	
Tumbler			100.00		125.00	

Pattern Name	Blue	Green	White	Vaseline/Canary	Cranberry	Other
CONSOLIDATED SHELL						
Rose bowl	175.00		125.00	250.00		265.00 Rubina
CONSTELLATION (SEAFOAM)						
Compote	225.00		150.00			
CONTESSA						
Basket, handled	60.00			75.00		250.00 Amber
Breakfast set, footed, two pieces	155.00					350.00 Amber
Pitcher	125.00					325.00 Amber
CONVEX RIB						
Vase	80.00	65.00	50.00			
CORAL						
Bowl	50.00	40.00	25.00	45.00		
CORAL & SHELL						
Bowl, 9½"	130.00					
CORAL REEF						
Bitters bottle	200.00		125.00		300.00	
Barber bottle	200.00		125.00		300.00	
Finger bowl	175.00		110.00		225.00	
Mini nightlamp	500.00		400.00		1,900.00	
Oil lamp, stemmed	450.00		335.00		1,800.00	
Finger lamp, footed	425.00		325.00		1,700.00	
Finger lamp, stemmed	500.00		400.00		2,100.00	
Rose bowl, rare	400.00			750.00		
CORINTH						
Vase, 8 – 13"	40.00		30.00			
CORNUCOPIA (NORTHWOOD)						
Handled vase	75.00		60.00			
CORNUCOPIA VASE						
Vase on stand				165.00		
CORN VASE *						
Fancy vase, scarce	235.00	280.00	125.00	230.00		
COROLLA						
Vase	225.00		175.00	200.00		
CORONATION						
Cake stand	100.00			70.00		
Creamer	45.00			40.00		
Sugar	45.00			40.00		
Pitcher	225.00			165.00		
Platter, oval	70.00			50.00		
Tumbler	40.00			40.00		
COUNTER SWIRL						
Vase	80.00			110.00		
COUNTRY KITCHEN & VARIANT						
Bowl, small, flared			200.00			
Bowl, small, square			250.00			
Bowl, large, 8" deep round,			275.00			
Bowl, medium, 7½" square			300.00			
Bowl, large, ruffled			300.00			
CRESTED WAVES						
Pitcher				400.00		
CRISS-CROSS & FILE						
Creamer, 3"	85.00					
CROCUS						
Vase, rare	325.00	300.00	225.00	375.00		
CROCUS DRAPE						
Vase				150.00		
CROWN JEWELS						
Creamer	80.00					
Pitcher	200.00					
Plate	100.00					
Platter	110.00					
Sugar	95.00					
Tumbler	60.00					
CURTAIN CALL						
Castor set, rare						550.00 Cobalt
CURTAIN OPTIC						
Guest set, two pieces	125.00	100.00	80.00	125.00		

Pattern Name	Blue	Green	White	Vaseline/ Canary	Cranberry	Other
Pitcher, various	225.00	210.00	150.00	200.00		
Tumbler, various	50.00	45.00	35.00	45.00		
CURTAIN TIE-BACKS						
Curtain ties, each			65.00			
CURVY						
Epergne				165.00		
CYCLONE						
Vase, very rare	1,000.00		650.00	900.00		
DAFFODILS						
Bowl whimsey	165.00		125.00	235.00		
Hand lamp	325.00	300.00	225.00	300.00	525.00	
Oil lamp	350.00	325.00	300.00	350.00	675.00	
Pitcher	900.00	950.00	600.00	4,000.00	7,500.00	
Tumbler, rare	400.00	350.00	300.00	400.00	550.00	
Vase	300.00			265.00		
Vase, with "thorn" feet				350.00		
Add 25% for goofus						
DAFFODILS SHADE (ENGLISH)						
Shade				325.00		
DAHLIA (DUGAN)						
Pitcher, gold trim	250.00					
Tumbler, gold trim	40.00					
DAHLIA TWIST						
Epergne, scarce	350.00	325.00	300.00			
Epergne, cherub with one lily	150.00		125.00	170.00		
Vase, scarce	90.00	70.00	55.00			
DAISIES LAMP						
Oil lamp				725.00		
DAISIES IN PENTAGON						
Oil lamp				875.00		
DAISY & BUTTON						
Bowl, novelty	65.00			65.00		
Bun tray	150.00			150.00		
Lifeboat	85.00			85.00		
DAISY & BUTTON WITH DIAMONDS						
Bowl, 4½"				85.00		
DAISY & DRAPE						
Vase, very rare				1,900.00		
DAISY & FERN (NORTHWOOD)						
(All moulds)						
Barber bottle					500.00	
Bowl, master	80.00	100.00	55.00		250.00	
Bowl, sauce	40.00	45.00	25.00		150.00	
Butter	225.00	250.00	175.00		300.00	
Creamer	75.00	90.00	60.00		425.00	
Cruet	200.00	175.00	150.00		525.00	
Finger bowl	200.00	150.00	175.00		450.00	
Mustard pot	100.00	125.00	75.00		150.00	
Night lamp	225.00	250.00	175.00		325.00	
Perfume	175.00	200.00	125.00		250.00	
Pitcher, three shapes	300.00	300.00	200.00		300.00-750.00	
Rose bowl					125.00	
Shakers, pair	300.00	275.00	175.00		300.00	
Spooner	75.00	100.00	55.00		425.00	
Sugar	100.00	125.00	75.00		250.00	
Sugar shaker	200.00	225.00	175.00		275.00	
Syrup, various	250.00	225.00	200.00		400.00	
Toothpick holder	160.00	175.00	125.00		225.00	
Tumbler	50.00	50.00	25.00		100.00	
Vase	150.00	150.00	100.00		200.00	
Prices for either mould used and also for Dugan pieces found.						
DAISY & GREEK KEY						
Sauce, footed	75.00	60.00	35.00			
DAISY & PLUME						
Basket, rare			150.00			
Bowl footed	50.00	45.00	30.00			
Rose bowl, footed	60.00	55.00	35.00			

Pattern Name	Blue	Green	White	Vaseline/Canary	Cranberry	Other
Whimsey, flared bowl	95.00					
DAISY BLOCK						
Row boat, 10", 12", and 15"		275.00	165.00	250.00		
DAISY DEAR						
Bowl, rare	65.00	55.00	35.00			
DAISY DRAPE						
Creamer				90.00		
DAISY IN CRISS-CROSS						
Barber bottle	1,700.00					
Pitcher	300.00				450.00	
Syrup	275.00				475.00	
Tumbler	60.00				100.00	
DAISY MAY (LEAF RAYS)						
Nappy or bonbon	55.00	45.00	35.00			
Whimsey on metal stand		95.00				
DAISY SWIRL						
Bowl	85.00			125.00		
Bowl whimsey	75.00	65.00	45.00			
Plate				165.00		
Whimsey on metal stand	80.00		60.00			
DAISY WITH PANELS						
Bowl, footed	95.00					
DAISY WREATH						
Bowl, rare	165.00					
DANDELION						
Mug, very rare	850.00			1,200.00		
DAVIDSON DRAPE						
Vase, squat	150.00			150.00		
DAVIDSON GERMANY SOUVENIR						
Plate, 5½				125.00		
DAVIDSON OPEN SALTS						
Salt dip, various shapes and sizes				50.00-90.00		
Add 25% with metal holder						
DAVIDSON PEARLINE						
Epergne, 14"	300.00			300.00		
DAVIDSON SHELL						
Spill vase	125.00			125.00		
Whimsey, ruffled	200.00					
DAVIDSON'S #269						
Marmalade set in metal holder				275.00		
DAVIDSON SWAN						
Swan novelty salt, two sizes	100.00-150.00			135.00 –180.00		
DECO LILY						
Vase, 7¾"		100.00				
DECORATED ENGLISH SWIRL						
Rose bowl					250.00	
DESERT GARDEN						
Bowl	45.00	40.00	25.00			
DIAGONAL SWIRL						
Vase in metal holder	125.00					
DIAGONAL WAVE						
Tumbler			25.00	65.00		
Vase	95.00			150.00		
DIAMOND						
Creamer			75.00			
DIAMOND & DAISY						
Basket, handled	100.00	110.00	55.00			
Bowl, novelty	60.00	70.00	35.00			
Rose bowl, whimsey		90.00				
DIAMOND & OVAL THUMBPRINT						
Vase	40.00	45.00	25.00			
DIAMOND BAND						
Vanity jar, with lid	70.00					
DIAMOND DOT						
Compote				100.00		
Shade				135.00		

Pattern Name	Blue	Green	White	Vaseline/Canary	Cranberry	Other
DIAMOND-IN-DIAMOND						
Vase	250.00		200.00			
DIAMOND MAPLE LEAF						
Bowl, handled	75.00	70.00	45.00			
Novelty, handled	40.00	50.00	25.00	50.00		
Add 10% for signed pieces						
DIAMOND OPTIC						
Compote	50.00		40.00			
Stemmed cardtray	60.00		50.00			
DIAMOND POINT						
Vase	40.00	50.00	30.00			
DIAMOND POINT & FLEUR DE LIS						
Bowl, novelty	50.00	55.00	40.00			
Nut bowl		65.00				
DIAMOND POINT COLUMNS						
Vase, scarce	200.00	175.00	75.00			
DIAMOND PYRAMID						
Bowl	250.00			200.00		
DIAMOND RINGS						
Bowl, rectangular				95.00		
DIAMONDS						
Bowl, various	65.00-100.00		50.00-75.00		90.00-165.00	80.00-155.00 Rubina
Bowl, handgrip	75.00		50.00		100.00	85.00 Rubina
Cruet	95.00		75.00		350.00	250.00 Rubina
Pitcher, two shapes	300.00		225.00		400.00	275.00 Rubina
Sugar shaker	130.00		100.00		165.00	145.00 Rubina
Tumbler	60.00		45.00		70.00	65.00 Rubina
DIAMONDS AND SWAGS						
Bowl				85.00		
DIAMONDS AND WEDGES						
Bowl			85.00			
DIAMOND SPEARHEAD						
Bowl, master	180.00	185.00	125.00	180.00		140.00
Bowl, sauce	55.00	60.00	35.00	45.00		40.00
Butter	500.00	575.00	400.00	500.00		475.00
Celery vase	250.00	250.00	150.00	250.00		250.00
Compote, tall	400.00	400.00	300.00	400.00		425.00
Creamer	200.00	225.00	150.00	200.00		200.00
Creamer, tall	200.00			200.00		275.00
Cup and saucer set				250.00		
Goblet	175.00	150.00	100.00	150.00		135.00
Jelly compote	200.00	150.00	125.00	175.00		200.00
Mini creamer	200.00	200.00	125.00	200.00		225.00 Sapphire
Mug	180.00	200.00	100.00	150.00		175.00
Oil bottle	125.00			100.00		100.00
Pitcher	725.00	625.00	400.00	500.00		625.00
Shakers, pair	150.00	175.00	130.00	175.00		175.00
Spittoon whimsey		55.00		500.00		
Spooner	175.00	200.00	150.00	175.00		175.00
Sugar	250.00	225.00	175.00	250.00		250.00
Syrup	650.00	700.00	550.00	625.00		750.00
Toothpick holder	150.00	125.00	100.00	125.00		145.00
Tumbler	125.00	100.00	60.00	90.00		100.00
Water carafe	200.00		175.00	225.00		
DIAMOND STEM						
Vase, three sizes, rare	150.00	175.00	80.00	150.00		125.00 Aqua
Vase, J.I.P whimsey	175.00	200.00	100.00	175.00		
DIAMOND TREE						
Bowl, scarce				140.00		
DIAMOND WAVE						
Demitasse cup and saucer, pair				110.00		
Pitcher with lid				350.00	175.00	250.00 Amethyst
Tumbler				65.00	50.00	
Vase, 5"				80.00	85.00	
DIAMOND WIDE STRIPE						
Finger bowl					175.00	
Pitcher					450.00	

Pattern Name	Blue	Green	White	Vaseline/Canary	Cranberry	Other
Rose bowl					200.00	
Tumbler					125.00	
DIMPLE						
Vase	140.00		110.00	185.00		
DOGWOOD DRAPE (PALM ROSETTE)						
Compote	150.00		120.00			
Plate, rare	125.00		90.00			
DOLLY MADISON						
Bowl, ruffled, 8"	50.00	40.00	35.00			
Bowl, master	60.00	70.00	50.00			
Bowl, novelty	60.00	70.00	45.00			
Bowl, sauce	30.00	35.00	20.00			
Butter	325.00	350.00	250.00			
Creamer	90.00	100.00	70.00			
Pitcher	400.00	425.00	300.00			
Plate, 6", scarce	110.00	110.00	65.00			
Spooner	80.00	90.00	50.00			
Sugar	150.00	160.00	100.00			
Tumbler	80.00	95.00	50.00			
DOLPHIN*						
Compote, scarce	85.00		50.00	75.00		
DOLPHIN & HERONS						
Compote, ftd, novelty	495.00		280.00	425.00		
Tray, ftd, novelty	490.00		275.00		800.00	
DOLPHIN & SHELL						
Spill vase			75.00			
DOLPHIN PETTICOAT						
Candlesticks, pair	175.00		125.00	165.00		
DORSET (ENGLISH)						
Bowls, various sizes	50.00-110.00			75.00-225.00		
Creamer	65.00			90.00		
Sugar	50.00			80.00		
DOT OPTIC						
Bowls, various	35.00-90.00	40.00-95.00	25.00 -70.00	45.00-100.00		
Pitchers, two styles	135.00-160.00	140.00-170.00	85.00-120.00	150.00-225.00		
Tumblers, two styles	30.00-45.00	35.00-45.00	25.00-40.00	40.00-55.00		
Vases, various	45.00-75.00	50.00-80.00	40.00-60.00	50.00-95.00		
DOTTED SPIRAL						
Bowl in metal holder				145.00		
Toothpick holder				100.00		
Vases, various				65.00-90.00		
DOUBLE DIAMONDS						
Bowl				90.00		
DOUBLE DOLPHIN (#1533)						
Compote, rare	150.00		100.00			
DOUBLE GREEK KEY						
Bowl, master	75.00		60.00			
Bowl, sauce	40.00		25.00			
Butter	325.00		250.00			
Celery vase	175.00		125.00			
Creamer	100.00		75.00			
Mustard pot	200.00		150.00			
Pickle tray	150.00		90.00			
Pitcher	400.00		325.00			
Shakers, pair	250.00		175.00			
Spooner	110.00		70.00			
Sugar	200.00		125.00			
Toothpick holder	250.00		200.00			
Tumbler	90.00		60.00			
DOUBLE MARMALADE						
Marmalades in metal holder						450.00 Lemonescent
DOUBLE PANEL (ENGLISH)						
Bowls, engraved				65.00-135.00		
DOUBLE RIB & BLOCK						
Bowl, 5½", with souvenir label				200.00		
Nappy				80.00		
Salt dip				70.00		

Pattern Name	Blue	Green	White	Vaseline/ Canary	Cranberry	Other
DOUBLE SALT WITH RING HANDLE						
Double salt			85.00			
DOUBLE STEMMED ROSE						
Bowl, very scarce			95.00			150.00 Light amethyst
DOVER DIAMOND						
Bowl	100.00			250.00		
Creamer	85.00			225.00		
Sugar, open, stemmed	75.00			200.00		
DRAGON & LOTUS						
Bowl, rare						325.00 Amethyst
DRAGONFLY LAMP						
Oil lamp with chimney			1,400.00			
DRAPERY (FENTON)						
Pitcher	450.00	425.00	275.00			
Tumbler	75.00	65.00	40.00			
DRAPERY (NORTHWOOD)						
Bowl, master	110.00		75.00			
Bowl, sauce	40.00		25.00			
Butter	200.00		175.00			
Creamer	10.00		80.00			
Pitcher	250.00		225.00			
Rose bowl	100.00		75.00			
Spooner	85.00		70.00			
Sugar	145.00		125.00			
Tumbler	75.00		50.00			
Vase	140.00	200.00	125.00	175.00		
DUCHESS						
Bowl, master	100.00		65.00	85.00		
Bowl, sauce	35.00		25.00	35.00		
Butter	200.00		150.00	175.00		
Creamer	65.00		45.00	65.00		
Cruet	225.00		175.00	200.00		
Lampshade	100.00		75.00			
Pitcher	200.00		165.00	185.00		
Spooner	70.00		50.00	70.00		
Sugar	110.00		75.00	110.00		
Toothpick holder	165.00		125.00	150.00		
Tumbler	40.00		25.00	35.00		
DUGAN'S #1013 (WIDE RIB)						
Vase	65.00	75.00	50.00			
Bowl, whimsey	50.00	55.00	40.00			
Plate	70.00	80.00	60.00			
DUGAN'S DIAMOND COMPASS (DRAGON LADY)						
Novelty bowl	140.00	130.00	90.00			
Rose bowl	160.00	150.00	90.00			
Vase	100.00	100.00	60.00			
DUGAN'S HEXAGON BASE						
Vase, two sizes		25.00-45.00	20.00-40.00			
DUGAN'S HONEYCOMB						
Bowl, various shapes, rare	150.00	175.00	150.00	200.00		
DUGAN'S INTAGLIO ACORN						
Bowl, 10"	115.00					
DUGAN'S INTAGLIO CHERRY						
Bowl			80.00			
DUGAN'S INTAGLIO DAISY						
Basket	130.00	150.00	100.00			
Bowl	90.00	100.00	75.00			
Plate	110.00	125.00	90.00			
DUGAN'S INTAGLIO GRAPE						
Plate, 12½", rare			250.00			
Bowl			125.00			
Compote			85.00			
DUGAN'S INTAGLIO HOLLY						
Bowl			75.00			
Compote			85.00			
Plate			95.00			

Pattern Name	Blue	Green	White	Vaseline/Canary	Cranberry	Other
DUGAN'S INTAGLIO MORNING GLORY						
Bowls, two sizes			40.00-85.00			
Compote			110.00			
DUGAN'S INTAGLIO PEACH						
Bowl			90.00			
Compote			100.00			
Plate, 13"			175.00			
DUGAN'S INTAGLIO PEAR & PLUM						
Bowl, 10"			135.00			
DUGAN'S INTAGLIO ROSE						
Bowl, small			35.00			
Bowl, large			80.00			
Plate, 10"			145.00			
DUGAN'S INTAGLIO STRAWBERRY						
Bowl, 9"			65.00			
Fruit bowl, stemmed			85.00			
DUGAN'S JUNIOR						
Vase, 4½"	50.00	50.00	35.00			
Vase, with silver filigree	70.00	75.00	55.00			
Floral etched add 15%						
DUGAN'S OLIVE NAPPY						
One shape	45.00	40.00	25.00			
DUGAN'S PLAIN PANEL						
Vase	55.00	55.00	35.00			
EGYPTIAN FAN						
Shade				95.00		
EIGHT RAYED NAPPY						
Nappy with handle						150.00 Purple opalescent
ELLIPSES						
Butter			125.00			
Creamer			65.00			
Spooner			60.00			
Sugar			75.00			
ELSON DEWDROP						
Berry bowl, small			15.00			
Berry bowl, large			45.00			
Breakfast set, two pieces			95.00			
Butter, covered			115.00			
Celery vase			65.00			
Creamer or spooner			35.00			
Mug			65.00			
Sugar with lid			60.00			
ELSON DEWDROP #2						
Bowl, sauce			15.00			
Cruet			90.00			
Punch cup			35.00			
Shakers, pair			110.00			
Spooner			35.00			
EMBOSSED SPANISH LACE						
Vase, 4¼"				100.00		
ENAMELED SWIRL						
Vase, fan shape						150.00 Lavender
ENGLISH BARS						
Vase, 12"				100.00		
ENGLISH BEADED PANELS						
Creamer	65.00					
ENGLISH CENTIPEDE						
Bowl	150.00		170.00			
ENGLISH DRAPE						
Vase				135.00		
ENGLISH DUCK						
Novelty dish				150.00		150.00 Blue
ENGLISH FERN						
Vase		70.00				
ENGLISH LILY						
Pitcher			200.00			
Vase				175.00	165.00	

Pattern Name	Blue	Green	White	Vaseline/Canary	Cranberry	Other
ENGLISH MYSTERY SHADE						
Shade, either shape					250.00	
ENGLISH OAK LEAF						
Boat shape	100.00			75.00		
Bowl	150.00			200.00		
Rectangular posy	125.00			165.00		
ENGLISH OPTIC EPERGNE						
Epergne						500.00 Rubina verde
ENGLISH RIPPLE						
Tumbler	80.00			80.00		
ENGLISH SALT DIP						
One shape				75.00		
ENGLISH SHELL						
Shell, 2½" x 3"				175.00		
ENGLISH SPOOL						
Vase	75.00			70.00		
ENGLISH SWAN						
Novelty dish, two sizes				150.00-200.00	175.00-225.00	
ENGLISH SWIRL						
Pitcher						200.00 White/cran-cased
Tumbler						50.00 White/cran-cased
ENGLISH WIDE STRIPE						
Pitcher					350.00	
ENTANGLED BRANCHES						
Oil lamp				350.00		
ESTATE						
Vase, scarce	95.00	85.00	65.00			
EUROPEAN LILY EPERGNES						
Single lily epergne, two sizes	145.00		125.00	175.00		
EVERGLADES						
Bowl, oval, master	200.00		125.00	200.00		
Bowl, oval, sauce	45.00		25.00	50.00		
Butter	325.00		250.00	375.00		
Creamer	150.00		95.00	150.00		
Cruet	425.00		325.00	475.00		
Jelly compote	125.00		95.00	150.00		
Pitcher	475.00		375.00	500.00		
Shakers, pair	275.00		225.00	300.00		
Spooner	125.00		95.00	150.00		
Sugar	185.00		120.00	225.00		
Tumbler	85.00		60.00	100.00		
EVERGLADES (CAMBRIDGE)						
Compote			75.00			
EXTERIOR THUMBPRINT						
Vase				275.00		
FAN						
Bowl, master	75.00	70.00	65.00			
Bowl, sauce	30.00	30.00	20.00			
Butter	400.00	400.00	200.00			
Card tray whimsey	125.00	110.00	90.00			
Creamer	125.00	120.00	75.00			
Gravy boat	65.00	65.00	35.00			
Novelty bowls	40.00	40.00	25.00			
Pitcher	300.00	300.00	200.00			
Spooner	125.00	110.00	85.00			
Sugar	200.00	200.00	150.00			
Tumbler	40.00	35.00	20.00			
Whimsey bowls	55.00	55.00	35.00			
FAN & SHELL (ENGLISH)						
Vase, stemmed				250.00		
FANCY FANTAILS						
Bowl	40.00	45.00	25.00	40.00		
Rose bowl	45.00	50.00	30.00	45.00		
FEATHERED HEARTS						
Shade					150.00	
FEATHERS						
Vase	35.00	30.00	25.00			

Pattern Name	Blue	Green	White	Vaseline/Canary	Cranberry	Other
Whimsey bowl, rare			125.00			
Whimsey nut bowl, rare	150.00	150.00				
FENTON #100						
Bowl				50.00		65.00 Amethyst
FENTON #220 (STRIPE)						
Creamer or sugar	75.00	80.00	65.00	95.00		
Pitcher with lid	250.00	250.00	175.00	225.00		
Tumbler, handled	45.00	50.00	35.00	60.00		
Tumble-up, complete	150.00	150.00	100.00	145.00		
Vase whimsey, 8", from pitcher	125.00	125.00	75.00	120.00		
FENTON'S #260						
Compote, tall	50.00		35.00	50.00		
FENTON #370						
Bonbon						50.00 Amber
Bowl						45.00 Amber
Nappy						55.00 Amber
Vase						50.00 Amber
Whimsey, ruffled, from candy jar						95.00 Cameo opal
FENTON #950						
Cornucopia candlestick, each						100.00 Amethyst
FENTON'S PLAIN JANE						
Hat whimsey			30.00			65.00 Amethyst
Pitcher			110.00			190.00 Amethyst
Tumbler			25.00			55.00 Amethyst
FERN						
Barber bottle	150.00		100.00		300.00	
Bowl, master	100.00		80.00		125.00	
Bowl, sauce	50.00		40.00		55.00	
Butter	275.00		225.00		400.00	
Celery vase	125.00		100.00	600.00	150.00	
Creamer	125.00		100.00		150.00	
Cruet	225.00		175.00		500.00	
Finger bowl	75.00		50.00		100.00	
Mustard pot	150.00		125.00		175.00	
Pitcher, various	275.00		200.00		750.00	
Shakers, pair	175.00		100.00		165.00	
Spooner	125.00		100.00		150.00	
Sugar	200.00		175.00		250.00	
Sugar shaker, various	125.00		100.00		550.00	
Syrup	275.00		220.00		600.00	
Toothpick holder, rare	350.00		200.00		475.00	
Tumbler	50.00		50.00		110.00	
FERN PANELS						
Hat						150.00 Amethyst
FESTIVE FLOWERS						
Vase, decorated			100.00			
FIELD FLOWERS						
Bowl, 7¾"	110.00		90.00			
Compote, two sizes	200.00		150.00	250.00		
FIELD OF FLOWERS						
Compote	125.00					
FILE & FAN						
Bowl	95.00					
FINECUT & ROSES						
Novelty bowls	45.00	50.00	40.00			
Rose bowl, rare	65.00	75.00	50.00			
FINE RIB (FENTON)						
Vase, very rare				500.00		
FINE RIB (NORTHWOOD)						
Vase, 9 – 13"	70.00	65.00	50.00	65.00		
FINE RIB EPERGNE						
Epergne				250.00		
FISH-IN-THE-SEA						
Vase, scarce	375.00	425.00	275.00	550.00		
Vase whimsey, scarce	295.00	390.00	270.00			
FISHNET						
Epergne (one shape, two pieces)						

Pattern Name	Blue	Green	White	Vaseline/Canary	Cranberry	Other
FISHSCALE & BEADS						
Bowl	50.00		30.00			
FLEUR-DE-LIS						
Pitcher			150.00			
FLEUR-DE-LIS IN PANELS						
Marmalade dish				150.00		
FLORA						
Banana bowl whimsey	120.00		100.00	150.00		
Bowl, master	100.00		80.00	100.00		
Bowl, sauce	50.00		30.00	40.00		
Butter	300.00		200.00	265.00		
Celery vase	130.00		100.00	110.00		
Creamer	100.00		80.00	100.00		
Cruet	750.00		450.00	600.00		
Jelly compote	150.00		110.00	150.00		
Novelty bowl	70.00		45.00	60.00		
Pitcher	500.00		410.00	480.00		
Shakers, pair	400.00		300.00	400.00		
Spooner	110.00		300.00	375.00		
Sugar	145.00		100.00	125.00		
Syrup	410.00		300.00	400.00		
Toothpick holder	480.00		300.00	400.00		
Tumbler	90.00		65.00	85.00		
FLORADINE						
Bowl, 8"						350.00-750.00
Butter						1,100.00
Creamer						400.00-800.00
Cruet						600.00-1,200.00
Pitcher						1,100.00-1,400.00
Sauce, 4"						250.00-350.00
Shakers, each						450.00-700.00
Spooner						350.00-600.00
Sugar						450.00-850.00
Sugar shaker						550.00
Syrup						1,600.00
Toothpick holder						700.00
Tumbler						450.00-1,400.00
FLORAL AND VINES						
Shade				110.00		
FLORAL EYELET						
Pitcher	525.00		400.00		850.00	
Tumbler	100.00		100.00		250.00	
FLORAL FREEZE						
Creamer	85.00					
Sugar, open	70.00					
FLOWER AND LEAF						
Basket				250.00		
FLOWER FORM						
Bulbous single lily epergne				165.00		
Toothpick				90.00		
FLOWERING VINE						
Butter	240.00					
Creamer	100.00					
Spooner	90.00					
Sugar	100.00					
FLOWER STARBURST						
Oil lamp				475.00		
FLUTED & BOX PLEATED EPERGNE						
Epergne, multi lilies and baskets				950.00		
FLUTED BARS & BEADS						
Novelty bowl	60.00	55.00	50.00	70.00		
Rose bowl	70.00	65.00	60.00	75.00		
Vase whimsey	65.00	60.00	55.00	75.00		
FLUTED SCROLLS						
Bowl, master	85.00	90.00	60.00	95.00		
Bowl, sauce	35.00	45.00	30.00	45.00		
Butter	165.00		125.00	185.00		

Pattern Name	Blue	Green	White	Vaseline/Canary	Cranberry	Other
Creamer	80.00		55.00	70.00		
Cruet	200.00		175.00	185.00		
Epergne, small	125.00	165.00	100.00	175.00		
Novelty bowl or whimsey	55.00		40.00	55.00		
Puff box (aka: baby butter dish)	80.00	90.00	60.00	95.00		
Pitcher	250.00		175.00	200.00		
Rose bowl	150.00		100.00	125.00		
Shakers, pair	100.00		75.00	85.00		
Spooner	80.00		55.00	60.00		
Sugar	140.00		100.00	110.00		
Tumbler	100.00		50.00	75.00		

Fluted scroll with flower band is priced the same as above.

FLUTED SCROLL WITH VINE

Pattern Name	Blue	Green	White	Vaseline/Canary	Cranberry	Other
Vase, footed	100.00		50.00	110.00		

FOOTED STRIPE

Pattern Name	Blue	Green	White	Vaseline/Canary	Cranberry	Other
Bowl, footed				95.00		

FORKED STRIPE

Pattern Name	Blue	Green	White	Vaseline/Canary	Cranberry	Other
Barber bottle			275.00			

FOUNTAIN

Pattern Name	Blue	Green	White	Vaseline/Canary	Cranberry	Other
Vase					250.00	

FOUNTAIN WITH BOWS

Pattern Name	Blue	Green	White	Vaseline/Canary	Cranberry	Other
Shade				200.00	250.00	
Vase, various shapes				125.00	150.00	

FOUR-FOOTED HOBNAIL

Pattern Name	Blue	Green	White	Vaseline/Canary	Cranberry	Other
Butter			155.00	175.00		225.00 Cobalt
Creamer			70.00	90.00		100.00 Cobalt
Spooner			70.00	85.00		100.00 Cobalt
Sugar			80.00	125.00		150.00 Cobalt

FOUR PILLARS

Pattern Name	Blue	Green	White	Vaseline/Canary	Cranberry	Other
Vase	75.00	70.00	40.00	75.00		

FROSTED LEAF & BASKETWEAVE

Pattern Name	Blue	Green	White	Vaseline/Canary	Cranberry	Other
Butter	275.00		200.00	250.00		
Creamer	150.00		130.00	135.00		
Spooner	150.00		125.00	135.00		
Sugar	175.00		150.00	165.00		
Vase whimsey	150.00		125.00	140.00		

FRUIT TREE

Pattern Name	Blue	Green	White	Vaseline/Canary	Cranberry	Other
Vase, ruffled				125.00		

GARLAND OF ROSES

Pattern Name	Blue	Green	White	Vaseline/Canary	Cranberry	Other
Stemmed tray, rare	175.00		100.00			

GIANT CLAM SHELL

Pattern Name	Blue	Green	White	Vaseline/Canary	Cranberry	Other
Clam shell bowl, 8"				250.00		

GONTERMAN (ADONIS) HOB

Pattern Name	Blue	Green	White	Vaseline/Canary	Cranberry	Other
Cruet						425.00 Amber

GONTERMAN (ADONIS) SWIRL

Pattern Name	Blue	Green	White	Vaseline/Canary	Cranberry	Other
Berry bowl, small						70.00 Amber top
Berry bowl, large						100.00 Amber top
Butter						350.00 Amber top
Celery vase						150.00 Amber top
Cologne						275.00 Amber top
Creamer						200.00 Amber top
Cruet						325.00 Amber top
Finger bowl						90.00 Amber top
Lamp shade						250.00 Amber top
Pitcher						500.00 Amber top
Spooner						150.00 Amber top
Sugar						225.00 Amber top
Syrup						400.00 Amber top
Toothpick holder						275.00 Amber top
Tumbler						100.00 Amber top

Blue top 5% less than .00 Amber top

GRACE DARLING

Pattern Name	Blue	Green	White	Vaseline/Canary	Cranberry	Other
Boat, 11¼" and 13"				400.00-450.00		

GRAPE & CABLE (NORTHWOOD & FENTON)

Pattern Name	Blue	Green	White	Vaseline/Canary	Cranberry	Other
Bonbon				450.00		
Centerpiece bowl	300.00	300.00	225.00	325.00		
Fruit bowl, large	325.00	300.00	245.00	325.00		

Pattern Name	Blue	Green	White	Vaseline/ Canary	Cranberry	Other
GRAPE & CABLE WITH THUMBPRINT						
Bowl, scarce	160.00	175.00				
GRAPE & CHERRY						
Bowl	90.00	80.00	65.00	100.00		
GRAPE CLUSTER						
Bowl, 5⅜", square						100.00 Light blue opal
GRAPEVINE CLUSTER						
Vase, footed	175.00		125.00	165.00		200.00 Aqua
GRECIAN URN						
Vase, 4½"	65.00					
GREEK KEY & RIBS						
Bowl	65.00	55.00	35.00			
GREEK KEY & SCALES						
Novelty bowl	90.00	80.00	50.00			
GREELEY (HOBBS)						
Cruet	750.00					
Cup	265.00					
Finger bowl	225.00					
Pitcher	1,200.00					
GREENER BOAT						
Boat shape, 5"	95.00					
Boat shape, 7"	125.00					
GREENER DEW DROP						
Bowl, 5"						95.00 Amber
Platter, stemmed						175.00 Amber
GREENER DIAMOND COLUMN						
Epergne, 13"						350.00 Amber
HALF LATTICE						
Rose or ivy bowl				125.00		
HARLEQUIN						
Rose bowl	200.00			275.00		325.00 Cran/vas
Shade				300.00		325.00 Cran/vas
Vase whimsey				350.00		350.00 Cran/vas
HARLEQUIN DECORATED						
Ewer, decorated				450.00		475.00 Cran/vas
Vase, decorated, various shapes and sizes				275.00-400.00	300.00-425.00	350.00-425.00 Cran/vase
HARLEQUIN STRIPED						
Shade				250.00		
HARLEQUIN VARIANT						
Rose bowl	225.00					
Vase, various shapes	265.00			350.00		
HARROW						
Cordial, stemmed	35.00					
Creamer	75.00					
Sugar, open	70.00					
Wine, stemmed	40.00					
HEART HANDLE OPEN O'S						
Ring tray	85.00	75.00	60.00			
HEART IN DIAMOND LAMP						
Oil lamp				375.00		
HEART POSEY						
Heart-shaped posey			125.00			
HEARTS & CLUBS						
Bowl, footed	60.00	55.00	35.00			
HEARTS & FLOWERS						
Bowl	185.00		150.00			
Compote	300.00		265.00			
HEATHERBLOOM						
Vase	40.00	30.00	20.00			
HEAVENLY STARS						
Bowl	185.00		125.00	250.00		
HELEN LOUISE						
Creamer	65.00			90.00		
Open sugar	60.00			80.00		
HERON & PEACOCK						
Mug	75.00		65.00			

Pattern Name	Blue	Green	White	Vaseline/Canary	Cranberry	Other
HERRINGBONE (PLAIN OR RIBBED)						
Bowl whimsey	250.00		200.00	300.00	400.00	
Cruet	350.00		225.00	450.00	850.00	
Pitcher	700.00		475.00	1,000.00	2,000.00	
Syrup	400.00		325.00	525.00	675.00	
Tumbler	90.00		65.00	125.00	150.00	
HERRINGBONE AND CROCUS						
Vase		85.00				
HIDDEN HEARTS						
Hat shape, in metal holder					135.00	
Vase				100.00		
HILLTOP VINES						
Novelty chalice	65.00	60.00	40.00			
HILLTOP VINES VARIANT						
Compote			65.00			
HOBBS POLKA DOT						
Bar bottle						175.00 Green/sapphire
Bowl						125.00 Green/sapphire
Celery						100.00 Green/sapphire
Cheese dish, covered						235.00 Green/sapphire
Creamer						125.00 Green/sapphire
Cruet						225.00 Green/sapphire
Custard cup						100.00 Green/sapphire
Finger bowl						125.00 Green/sapphire
Lemonade mug						150.00 Green/sapphire
Pitcher						475.00 Green/sapphire
Shakers, each						145.00 Green/sapphire
Sugar						135.00 Green/sapphire
Sugar shaker						250.00 Green/sapphire
Syrup						225.00 Green/sapphire
Tumbler						100.00 Green/sapphire
HOBBS SWIRL						
Barber bottle	165.00	175.00	110.00	225.00	200.00	
Berry bowl, small	65.00	80.00	50.00	90.00	85.00	
Berry bowl, large	85.00	95.00	70.00	110.00	100.00	
Bitters bottle	150.00	165.00	125.00	200.00	175.00	
Butter	175.00	185.00	145.00	250.00	195.00	
Celery	75.00	85.00	65.00	95.00	95.00	
Cheese dish	180.00	200.00	150.00	275.00	225.00	
Creamer	85.00	90.00	70.00	95.00	100.00	
Cruet, four shapes	95.00-175.00	100.00-190.00	75.00-135.00	125.00-225.00	125.00-175.00	
Custard cup	60.00	70.00	50.00	85.00	80.00	
Finger bowl	55.00	65.00	45.00	75.00	70.00	
Finger lamp	165.00	175.00	135.00	245.00	200.00	
Juice glass	60.00	70.00	50.00	80.00	75.00	
Lamp shade	100.00	115.00	85.00	130.00	125.00	
Pitcher, various styles	250.00-400.00	275.00-350.00	225.00-300.00	325.00-450.00	300.00-350.00	
Straw holder	375.00	400.00	325.00	550.00	425.00	
Sugar	50.00	60.00	40.00	70.00	70.00	
Sugar shaker	125.00	135.00	100.00	175.00	150.00	
Tumbler	60.00	70.00	50.00	80.00	80.00	
Water bottle	135.00	140.00	120.00	175.00	150.00	
HOBNAIL (HOBBS)						
Barber bottle	150.00		125.00	145.00		
Bowl, master, square	100.00		80.00	100.00		
Bowl, sauce, square	40.00		30.00	50.00		
Bride's basket	450.00			425.00	525.00	500.00 Rubina
Butter	300.00		200.00	225.00		
Celery vase	175.00		125.00	145.00		225.00 Rubina
Creamer	100.00		100.00	125.00		
Cruet	200.00		200.00	190.00		
Finger bowl	65.00		50.00	55.00		
Lemonade set, complete	600.00				700.00	
Pitcher, five sizes	200.00-400.00		150.00-250.00	175.00-325.00	300.00-600.00	250.00-450.00 Rubina
Shakers, each			200.00		400.00	
Spooner	10.00		100.00	125.00		
Sugar	200.00		135.00	175.00		

Pattern Name	Blue	Green	White	Vaseline/Canary	Cranberry	Other
Syrup	225.00		200.00	200.00		
Tumbler	75.00		50.00	75.00		125.00 Rubina
HOBNAIL & PANELLED THUMBPRINT						
Bowl, master	75.00		60.00	65.00		
Bowl, sauce	35.00		25.00	30.00		
Butter	200.00		145.00	175.00		
Cordial, stemmed	35.00			35.00		
Creamer	85.00		60.00	75.00		
Pitcher	300.00		150.00	300.00		
Spooner	85.00		65.00	75.00		
Sugar	125.00		100.00	90.00		
Sugar, open	70.00			65.00		
Tumbler	75.00		45.00	75.00		
Wine, stemmed	40.00			40.00		
HOBNAIL-IN-SQUARE (VESTA)						
Barber bottle			120.00			
Bowl, master			75.00			
Bowl, sauce			25.00			
Bowl with stand	150.00					
Butter			200.00			
Celery vase			145.00			
Compote, various			100.00			
Creamer			100.00			
Pitcher			245.00			
Shakers, pair			100.00			
Spooner			100.00			
Sugar			150.00			
Tumbler			50.00			
HOBNAIL SMOKE BELL						
Smoke bell			85.00			
HOBNAIL TOY MUG						
Mug, 2"				90.00		
HOBNAIL TWIST						
Vase or lily in metal holder						400.00 Rubina verde
HOBNAIL WITH BARS						
Berry bowl, small			35.00			
Berry bowl, large			75.00			
Butter			165.00			
Creamer			65.00			
Cruet			90.00			
Spooner			55.00			
Sugar			70.00			
HOLLY (FENTON)						
Bowl, rare			150.00			
HOLLY & BERRY						
Nappy, very scarce			95.00			
HOLLY BERRY LAMP						
Oil lamp, rare			1400.00			
HONEYCOMB						
Vase	75.00	100.00	45.00			
HONEYCOMB (BLOWN)						
Barber bottle	175.00		125.00		175.00	200.00 Amber
Bowl	95.00	70.00	55.00			
Cracker jar	325.00		250.00		400.00	425.00 Amber
Pitcher	325.00		225.00		500.00	450.00 Amber
Syrup	300.00		275.00		425.00	450.00 Amber
Tumbler	80.00		50.00		100.00	75.00 Amber
HONEYCOMB & CLOVER						
Bowl, master	100.00	75.00	50.00			
Bowl, sauce	50.00	35.00	25.00			
Bowl, novelty	75.00	75.00	50.00			
Butter	400.00	350.00	250.00			
Creamer	150.00	140.00	125.00			
Pitcher	400.00	350.00	285.00			
Spooner	150.00	150.00	100.00			
Sugar	300.00	275.00	150.00			
Tumbler	100.00	80.00	55.00			

Pattern Name	Blue	Green	White	Vaseline/Canary	Cranberry	Other
HONEYCOMB OPEN EDGE						
Bowl, 9¼"	125.00					
HORSE CHESTNUT						
Blown vase				100.00		
Compote				250.00		
ICE CASTLES						
Lamp shade			200.00			
IDYLL						
Bowl, master	60.00	60.00	45.00			
Bowl, sauce	30.00	30.00	25.00			
Bowl, 6 – 7"	40.00	45.00	30.00			
Butter	350.00	375.00	300.00			
Creamer	150.00	125.00	75.00			
Cruet	225.00	200.00	175.00			
Pitcher	375.00	375.00	300.00			
Shakers, pair	125.00	115.00	100.00			
Spooner	150.00	125.00	75.00			
Sugar	175.00	200.00	150.00			
Toothpick holder	400.00	325.00	275.00			
Tray	125.00	110.00	100.00			
Tumbler	100.00	90.00	70.00			
IMITATION CUT #1						
Basket	130.00					
IMITATION CUT #2						
Basket			100.00			
INFINITY						
Bowl, oval	80.00					
INSIDE RIBBING						
Bowl, master	70.00		40.00	75.00		
Bowl, sauce	30.00		20.00	35.00		
Butter	225.00		150.00	250.00		
Celery vase	60.00		35.00	60.00		
Creamer	75.00		55.00	80.00		
Cruet	150.00		100.00	150.00		
Jelly compote	75.00		30.00	65.00		
Pitcher	300.00		160.00	300.00		
Rose bowl	80.00					
Shakers, pair	125.00		75.00	100.00		
Spooner	75.00		60.00	80.00		
Sugar	125.00		100.00	125.00		
Syrup	155.00		100.00	150.00		
Toothpick holder	200.00		175.00	200.00		
Tray	55.00		30.00	50.00		
Tumbler	65.00		30.00	70.00		
INTAGLIO						
Bowl, master, footed	225.00		100.00	250.00		
Bowl, sauce, standard	35.00		25.00	50.00		
Butter	500.00		275.00			
Creamer	100.00		50.00			
Cruet	200.00		150.00	300.00		
Jelly compote	60.00		45.00	80.00		
Novelty bowl	50.00		30.00	65.00		
Pitcher	250.00		150.00			
Shakers, pair	100.00		75.00			
Spooner	100.00		60.00			
Sugar	175.00		100.00			
Tumbler	110.00		65.00			
INTAGLIO HOLLY (DUGAN'S)						
Bowl, small			30.00			
Bowl, large			75.00			
INTAGLIO LATTICE						
Bowl			100.00			
INTAGLIO MORNING GLORY						
Bowl, small			30.00			
Bowl, large			75.00			
INTAGLIO PANELS						
Bowl, 4¾"			45.00			

Pattern Name	Blue	Green	White	Vaseline/Canary	Cranberry	Other
Celery vase			55.00			
INTERIOR FLUTE						
Vase	40.00	35.00	25.00			50.00 Lavender
INTERIOR PANEL						
Fan vase	55.00	50.00	30.00	55.00		100.00 Amethyst
Rolled rim whimsey						125.00 Cameo opal
Ruffled vase whimsey						100.00 Cameo opal
Trumpet vase whimsey						115.00 Cameo opal
INTERIOR POINSETTIA						
Tumbler	50.00	65.00	40.00			
INTERIOR SWIRL						
Rose bowl	100.00		60.00	100.00		
INTERIOR WIDE STRIPE						
Pitcher			140.00		200.00	
Tumbler			45.00		65.00	
INVERTED CHEVRON						
Vase	75.00	65.00	45.00			
INVERTED COINDOT						
Rose bowl			55.00	100.00		
Tumbler		60.00	35.00			
INVERTED FAN & FEATHER*						
Bowl, master	300.00		375.00		200.00	
Bowl, sauce	100.00	100.00		40.00		
Butter	450.00		365.00			
Card tray whimsey	225.00	250.00	175.00	250.00		
Creamer	225.00		175.00			
Cruet, rare	500.00					
Jelly compote, rare	250.00		175.00			
Novelty bowl, very rare		250.00		300.00		
Pitcher	725.00		475.00			
Plate, very rare				500.00		
Punch bowl, rare	900.00					
Punch cup, rare	50.00					
Rose bowl	225.00	250.00		250.00		
Rose bowl whimsey	225.00	250.00	190.00	265.00		
Shakers, pair	350.00					
Spittoon whimsey	325.00		225.00	325.00		
Spooner	200.00		150.00			
Sugar	275.00		225.00			
Toothpick, rare	450.00	550.00				
Tumbler	100.00		75.00			
Vase whimsey, rare	200.00	175.00	150.00			
IRIS (ENGLISH)						
Hand lamp	225.00	250.00	145.00	325.00		
Pitcher	165.00	175.00	145.00	285.00		
Tumbler	50.00	60.00	40.00	75.00		
Vase	75.00	90.00	70.00	100.00		
IRIS (NORTHWOOD)						
Lamp	250.00	225.00	165.00	325.00		
Pitcher	275.00	225.00	175.00	275.00		
Tumbler	70.00	65.00	55.00	85.00		
Vase	75.00	70.00	60.00	95.00		
IRIS WITH MEANDER						
Bowl, master	200.00	150.00	75.00	155.00		
Bowl, sauce, two sizes	50.00	35.00	20.00	40.00		
Butter	300.00	275.00	225.00	275.00		
Creamer	100.00	80.00	60.00	75.00		
Cruet	500.00	400.00	275.00	400.00		
Jelly compote	55.00	50.00	35.00	45.00		
Pitcher	400.00	375.00	275.00	325.00		
Relish/pickle dish	85.00	75.00	55.00			
Plate	100.00	85.00	60.00	80.00		
Shakers, each	225.00	200.00	125.00	350.00		
Spooner	100.00	80.00	55.00	75.00		
Sugar	175.00	150.00	100.00	175.00		
Toothpick holder	150.00	125.00	75.00	125.00		
Tumbler	80.00	75.00	55.00	75.00		

Pattern Name	Blue	Green	White	Vaseline/Canary	Cranberry	Other
Vase, tall	60.00	55.00	35.00	60.00		
IVY BALL						
Swirled ball in metal holder			50.00			
JAZZ						
Vase	50.00	55.00	30.00			
JEFFERSON #270						
Master bowl	100.00	85.00	55.00			
Sauce	45.00	45.00	25.00			
JEFFERSON SHIELD						
Bowl, rare	180.00	200.00	150.00			
JEFFERSON SPATTER						
Vase				75.00		
JEFFERSON SPOOL						
Vase	75.00	60.00	45.00	85.00		
Vase, variant	95.00	80.00	55.00	100.00		
Vase whimsey	85.00	70.00	60.00			
JEFFERSON STRIPE						
Bowl whimsey	85.00	90.00	65.00		125.00	
Vase, J.I.P.	60.00	65.00	40.00			
JEFFERSON WHEEL						
Bowl	50.00	45.00	35.00			
JEWEL & FAN						
Banana bowl	125.00	145.00	100.00	140.00		135.00 Emerald
Bowl	60.00	55.00	40.00	75.00		
JEWEL & FLOWER						
Bowl, master	75.00		50.00	75.00		
Bowl, sauce	35.00		25.00	40.00		
Butter	400.00		225.00	325.00		
Creamer	125.00		100.00	150.00		
Cruet	700.00		325.00	645.00		
Novelty bowl	55.00		30.00	55.00		
Pitcher	650.00		325.00	475.00		
Shakers, pair	175.00		125.00	165.00		
Spooner	125.00		100.00	125.00		
Sugar	200.00		125.00	200.00		
Tumbler	100.00		65.00	80.00		
JEWELED HEART						
Bowl, master	65.00	60.00	50.00			
Bowl, sauce	30.00	25.00	20.00			
Butter	325.00	300.00	225.00			
Condiment set (four pieces, complete)	1,000.00	1,000.00	750.00			
Compote	150.00	150.00	100.00			
Creamer	175.00	150.00	100.00			
Cruet	400.00	400.00	310.00			
Novelty bowl	50.00	40.00	30.00			
Pitcher	400.00	300.00	200.00			
Plate, small	75.00	70.00	55.00			
Shakers, pair	350.00	350.00	275.00			
Spooner	175.00	150.00	100.00			
Sugar	200.00	195.00	125.00			
Sugar shaker	350.00	350.00	275.00			
Syrup	500.00	475.00	400.00			
Toothpick holder	250.00	250.00	200.00			
Tray	250.00	225.00	200.00			
Tumbler	100.00	65.00	40.00			
JEWELS & DRAPERY & VARIANT						
Novelty bowl	75.00	65.00	35.00	125.00		70.00 Aqua
Vase	85.00	75.00	45.00			75.00 Aqua
JOLLY BEAR						
Bowl, rare	225.00	175.00	125.00			
JUBILEE						
Bowl	100.00					
KEYHOLE						
Bowl	55.00	60.00	40.00			
Bowl, tricorner J.I.P. whimsey	70.00	75.00	60.00			
Rose bowl whimsey	150.00	150.00	125.00			

Pattern Name	Blue	Green	White	Vaseline/ Canary	Cranberry	Other
KING MELON						
Oil lamp	265.00					
KING RICHARD						
Compote	200.00		150.00	225.00		
KING'S PANEL						
Creamer	35.00			50.00		
Novelty bowl in holder	85.00			95.00		
Sugar, open	30.00			40.00		
KING'S X						
Spill, rare	145.00					
KITTEN'S (FENTON)						
Cup, very rare						650.00 Amethyst
Saucer, very rare						550.00 Amethyst
KNOBBY SEAWEED						
Vase						225.00 Cran/vaseline
LABELLE						
Toothpick holder				80.00		
LADY CAROLINE						
Basket	60.00			60.00		
Creamer	60.00			60.00		
Spill	65.00			65.00		
Spill vase whimsey, no handles	75.00			75.00		
Sugar, two shapes	55.00			55.00		
Whimsey, three-handled	75.00			70.00		
LADY CHIPPENDALE						
Basket	80.00			115.00		80.00 Cobalt
Butter	165.00			195.00		125.00 Cobalt
Compote, tall	140.00			160.00		100.00 Cobalt
Creamer or spooner	60.00			65.00		50.00 Cobalt
Novelty bowls, various	40.00-70.00			50.00-80.00		35.00-55.00 Cobalt
Sugar	75.00			90.00		65.00 Cobalt
LADY FINGER (DAVIDSON)						
Spill vase	150.00			150.00		
LADY SLIPPER						
Novelty vase	185.00		125.00	250.00		
LATE COINSPOT						
Pitcher	150.00	150.00	110.00			
Tumbler	45.00	35.00	25.00			
LATTICE (ENGLISH)						
Vase				95.00		
LATTICE & DAISY						
Tumbler, very scarce	90.00		60.00	125.00		
LATTICE & POINTS						
Bowl, novelty			55.00			
Hat shape			60.00			
Vase			75.00			
LATTICE MEDALLIONS						
Bowl	55.00	50.00	40.00			
Nut bowl whimsey	75.00	65.00	50.00			
Rose bowl	75.00	65.00	50.00			
LAURA (SINGLE FLOWER FRAMED)						
Bowl, scarce	55.00	50.00	35.00			
Nappy, scarce	60.00	55.00	35.00			
Plate, ruffled, rare	150.00	150.00	125.00			
LAUREL SWAG & BOWS						
Shade, gas						125.00 Amethyst
LEAF & BEADS						
Bowl, footed or dome	60.00	55.00	35.00			
Bowl, whimsey, pulled points	75.00	65.00	45.00			
Rose bowl	85.00	75.00	55.00			
LEAF & DIAMONDS						
Bowl	50.00	65.00	30.00			
LEAF & LEAFLETS (LONG LEAF)						
Bowl	60.00		45.00			
LEAF CHALICE						
Novelty compote (several shapes from same mould)	80.00	85.00	65.00	110.00		175.00 Cobalt
Whimsey, four cornered	85.00	90.00	70.00	135.00		

Pattern Name	Blue	Green	White	Vaseline/ Canary	Cranberry	Other
LEAF GARLAND						
Bowl, small				75.00		
Compote	100.00					
LEAF GARLAND & RIBS						
Creamer, 3"				110.00		
Sugar				85.00		
LEAF ROSETTE & BEADS						
Bowl, low, very scarce	200.00	200.00	125.00			
LEAFY STRIPE						
Basket whimsey				250.00	375.00	
Bride's bowl, 9"					350.00	250.00 Honey amber
LILY PAD						
Epergne, with bowl and lily				250.00		
LILY POOL EPERGNE						
Epergne	275.00		225.00	300.00		
LILY VASE						
Vase, with applied base						135.00 Cranberry/green
LINED HEART						
Vase	40.00	40.00	30.00			
LINKING RINGS						
Bowl	125.00			160.00		
Compote	185.00			250.00		
Juice glass	70.00			95.00		
Milk pitcher	145.00			225.00		
Pitcher	375.00			500.00		
Tray	110.00			130.00		
LITTLE NELL						
Vase	40.00	35.00	20.00			
LITTLE SWAN (DUGAN OR NORTHWOOD)						
Novelty, two sizes	100.00	100.00	50.00	90.00		
LOOPED MAZE						
Milk pitcher, or banquet creamer			100.00			
LOOPS WITH RING TOP						
Handled vase						100.00 White/pink
LORDS & LADIES						
Butter	100.00			125.00		
Celery boat (in wire basket)	200.00			225.00		
Creamer	70.00			85.00		
Open sugar	75.00			90.00		
Plate, 7½"	100.00			125.00		
LORNA						
Vase	40.00		30.00	45.00		
Add 50% for whimsey vase shape						
LOTUS						
Bowl with underplate	160.00		140.00	160.00		
LOVE FLOWER						
Loving cup, handled	200.00					
LUSTRE FLUTE						
Bowl, master	200.00	275.00	175.00			
Bowl, sauce	45.00	60.00	30.00			
Butter	475.00		275.00			
Creamer	150.00		90.00			
Custard cup	50.00		30.00			
Pitcher	400.00		325.00			
Spooner	150.00		95.00			
Sugar	235.00		150.00			
Tumbler	100.00		65.00			
Vase	85.00		65.00			
MANY DIAMONDS						
Bowl on metal stand						110.00 White w/blue crest
MANY LOOPS						
Bowl, ruffled	50.00	45.00	35.00			
Bowl, deep round or tricorner	60.00	55.00	40.00			
Rose bowl, scarce	75.00	70.00	45.00			
MANY RAYS						
Bowl, 8½ – 9"				125.00		

Pattern Name	Blue	Green	White	Vaseline/ Canary	Cranberry	Other
MANY RIBS (MODEL FLINT)						
Vase	95.00		55.00	100.00		
MAPLE LEAF						
Jelly compote	100.00	100.00	70.00	250.00		
MAPLE LEAF CHALICE						
One shape	75.00	85.00	50.00	65.00		
MARKHAM SWIRL BAND WITH OPAL COBWEB						
Oil lamp	300.00		250.00	325.00	550.00	
MARY ANN						
Vase, rare	300.00		250.00			
Reproduced in white opal						
MARY GREGORY						
Small pitcher with lid			325.00			
MAVIS SWIRL						
Barber bottle	100.00		85.00	145.00		
Pitcher	185.00		125.00	250.00	400.00	
Rose bowl	70.00		60.00	85.00		
Shakers, pair	125.00		100.00	145.00		
Toothpick holder	90.00		75.00	90.00		
Trinket dish	40.00		30.00	45.00		
Tumbler	65.00		50.00	75.00		
MAY BASKET						
Basket shape, three sizes	70.00-95.00	65.00-90.00	55.00-75.00	95.00-135.00		
MEANDER						
Bowl	60.00	55.00	35.00			
Nut bowl whimsey	70.00	65.00	45.00			
MEDIEVAL ARCHES						
Bowl, square				70.00		
MEISENTHAL SWAN						
Swan novelty			125.00			
MELON OPTIC SWIRL						
Bowl, rare	80.00	90.00	60.00	85.00		
MELON SWIRL						
Pitcher	450.00					
Tumbler	75.00					
MELON WITH BARS						
Pitcher						300.00 Amber
MELON WITH SPRIG						
Cruet			125.00			
Pitcher, rare	300.00		175.00			
Shakers, each			70.00			
Toothpick holder			80.00			
MERMAIDS & SHELLS						
Novelty bowl			200.00	425.00		400.00 Rose opalescent
MICA SPATTER						
Vase, J.I.P. shape						250.00 Cranberry spatter
MINIATURE EPERGNE						
Epergne, one-lily	150.00			150.00		
MIRROR FRAME						
Mirror, round				100.00		
MONKEY (UNDER A TREE)						
Mug, very rare			600.00			
Pitcher, rare			1,200.00			
Tumbler, rare			500.00			
MORNING GLORY						
Basket, or open sugar, tab handles		85.00				
MURANO FLORAL						
Vase, decorated, speckled			390.00			
MYSTIC MAZE						
Vase, blown				200.00		
NAILSEA						
Creamer, 3⅝"			80.00			
NATIONAL'S # 17						
Bouquet vase, 8"	150.00	150.00		150.00		
NATIONAL SWIRL						
Pitcher	275.00	275.00				
Tumbler	50.00	50.00				

Pattern Name	Blue	Green	White	Vaseline/ Canary	Cranberry	Other
Bouquet vase, 10½"				175.00		
NESTING ROBINS						
Bowl			300.00			
NETTED CHERRIES						
Bowl, various shapes	55.00		45.00			
Plate	75.00		65.00			
NETTED ROSES						
Bowl	70.00	90.00	50.00			
Plate	120.00	130.00	100.00			
NORTHERN STAR						
Banana bowl	75.00	70.00	50.00			
Bowl	65.00	60.00	40.00			
Plate	100.00	100.00	50.00			
NORTHWOOD'S MIKADO						
Nappy, with poppy interior, very rare				500.00		
NORTHWOOD'S POPPY						
Pickle dish, very rare	400.00					
NORTHWOOD SWIRL						
Tumbler	50.00			65.00		
OAK LEAF						
Novelty bowl	150.00			150.00		
OCEAN SHELL						
Novelty, footed, three variations	75.00	90.00	55.00			
OCEAN WAVE						
Advertising bowl, rare				275.00		
OHIO STATE SEAL						
Cup plate			75.00			
OKTOBERFEST						
Ale glass				250.00		
OLD MAN WINTER						
Basket, small	75.00	85.00	60.00			
Basket, large, footed	150.00	165.00	100.00	275.00		
ONYX ("FINDLEY")						
Bowl						400.00-1,600.00
Butter, covered						1,300.00
Celery vase						900.00-1,800.00
Creamer						500.00-1,000.00
Cruet						700.00-1,500.00
Lamp						5,500.00
Pickle castor						700.00-1,200.00
Pitcher						1200.00-1,500.00
Sauce						800.00
Shakers						600.00-900.00
Spooner						600.00-1,300.00
Sugar						550.00-1,100.00
Sugar shaker						600.00
Syrup						1,800.00
Toothpick holder						600.00
Tumbler						500.00-1,800.00

All pieces are lustre ware with various accents; gold, silver, bronze, ruby, etc. Prices vary greatly pending such.

Pattern Name	Blue	Green	White	Vaseline/ Canary	Cranberry	Other
OPAL BLOSSOM						
Vase, 6"		275.00				
OPAL BULL'S EYE						
Mustard, with lid and spoon				140.00		
Open salt in metal holder, 1½"				85.00		
OPAL DAISY						
Slanted box, two sizes				125.00-175.00		
OPAL DOT						
Water tray				125.00		
OPALESCENT SWIRL						
Shade, various shapes				100.00		
OPAL FLOWER						
Cylinder shade					165.00	
OPALINE BROCADE (ENGLISH)						
Compote, with twisted stem				350.00		
Shade, various shapes and sizes				600.00-750.00		

Pattern Name	Blue	Green	White	Vaseline/Canary	Cranberry	Other
OPAL LOOPS						
Decanter			160.00			
Flask			195.00			
Glass pipe			180.00			
Vase			110.00			
OPAL OPEN (BEADED PANELS)						
Bowl, novelty	50.00	55.00	30.00	50.00		
Compote	75.00	70.00	65.00	85.00		
Ring bowl, handled	100.00	90.00	55.00	85.00		
Rose bowl, novelty	50.00	60.00	30.00	50.00		
Vase, novelty	40.00	40.00	25.00	40.00		
OPAL SPIRAL						
Sugar	90.00					
Tumbler	325.00					
OPAL STRIPE						
Vase, with applied flowers				135.00		
OPAL URN						
Vase	80.00		50.00	80.00		
OPEN BLOSSOM						
Vase, 6"	150.00	150.00	125.00	200.00		
OPEN EDGE BASKET (FENTON)						
Bowl, various	40.00	35.00	25.00	40.00		
Console set, three pieces	250.00	275.00	200.00	250.00		
Nappy	50.00	40.00	35.00	40.00		
Plate	60.00	80.00	45.00	100.00		
OPEN O'S						
Bowl, novelty	55.00	50.00	25.00	45.00		
Rose bowl whimsey	100.00	90.00	55.00	85.00		
Spittoon whimsey	125.00	100.00	75.00	100.00		
Vase, squat	85.00	75.00	65.00	95.00		
OPTIC BASKET						
One shape				150.00		
OPTIC PANEL						
Vase J.I.P.				100.00		
ORANGE TREE						
Mug, rare						250.00 Custard opal
OSCAR'S LEGACY						
Iris window insert				125.00		
OVAL WINDOWS						
Flower holder with metal frog/lid				150.00		
Vase, 7"				65.00		
OVER-ALL HOB						
Bowl, master	75.00		40.00	70.00		
Bowl, sauce	30.00		20.00	25.00		
Butter	250.00		175.00	225.00		
Celery vase	75.00		50.00	75.00		
Creamer	100.00		50.00	90.00		
Finger bowl	60.00		30.00	60.00		
Mug	75.00		55.00	75.00		
Pitcher	225.00		165.00	200.00		
Spooner	100.00		50.00	90.00		
Sugar	175.00		100.00	150.00		
Toothpick holder	200.00		135.00	200.00		
Tumbler	65.00		25.00	50.00		
OVERLAPPING LEAVES (LEAF TIERS)						
Bowl, footed	175.00	175.00	150.00			
Plate, footed	250.00	275.00	195.00			
Rose bowl, footed	175.00	185.00	150.00			
PALISADES (LINED LATTICE)						
Bowl, novelty	45.00	50.00	35.00	55.00		
Rose bowl whimsey	45.00	50.00	40.00	50.00		
Vase, novelty	50.00	45.00	35.00	50.00		
PALM & SCROLL						
Bowl, footed	65.00	60.00	40.00	60.00		
Rose bowl, footed	75.00	70.00	50.00	70.00		
PALM BEACH						
Bowl, master	85.00			85.00		

Pattern Name	Blue	Green	White	Vaseline/Canary	Cranberry	Other
Bowl, sauce, two sizes	40.00			50.00		
Butter	300.00			300.00		
Card tray whimsey, rare				500.00		
Creamer	150.00			140.00		
Jelly compote	175.00		150.00	200.00		
Nappy, hndl, rare				425.00		
Pitcher	450.00			475.00		
Plate, 8", rare	550.00			600.00		
Spooner	150.00			150.00		
Stemmed card tray, rare	500.00			500.00		
Sugar	225.00			225.00		
Tumbler	100.00			100.00		
Wine, very rare				425.00		
PAN AMERICAN						
Vase, with embossed lettering	250.00		225.00	400.00		
PANELED ACORN						
Vase				150.00		
PANELED ACORN VASE						
Vase, rare				650.00		
PANELED CORNFLOWER						
Bowl, handled, pinched			75.00+			
Vase			135.00			
PANELED FLOWERS						
Nut cup, footed	85.00		50.00			
Rose bowl, footed	75.00		45.00			
PANELED FRONDS						
Basket	135.00					
PANELED HOLLY						
Bowl, master	200.00		150.00			
Bowl, sauce	75.00		35.00			
Butter	400.00		325.00			
Creamer	175.00		125.00			
Novelty bowl	90.00		65.00			
Pitcher	700.00		425.00			
Shakers, pair	250.00		150.00			
Spooner	175.00		125.00			
Sugar	250.00		175.00			
Tumbler	110.00		85.00			
PANELED LATTICE BAND						
Tumbler, rare				150.00		
PANELED SPRIG						
Cruet			150.00			
Shakers, pair			125.00			
Toothpick holder			100.00			
PANELS WITH DRAPED CRIMP						
Bowl, 8½ – 9"	80.00					
PANELS WITH SPIRAL BAND						
Vase				95.00		
PEACOCK BASKET						
Basket, handled			150.00			
PEACOCK FEATHERS						
Bowl on metal stand						125.00 Rose pink
PEACOCKS (ON THE FENCE)						
Bowl, scarce	300.00		210.00			375.00 Cobalt
PEACOCK TAIL						
Tumbler, rare	100.00	95.00	75.00			
PEARL FLOWERS						
Novelty bowl, footed	60.00	50.00	30.00			
Nut bowl, footed	50.00	45.00	35.00			
Rose bowl, footed	70.00	80.00	40.00			
PEARLINE RIB						
Novelty bowl in holder	150.00			175.00		
PEARLS & SCALES						
Compote	65.00	60.00	40.00	75.00		80.00 Emerald
Rose bowl, rare	100.00	100.00	60.00	95.00		110.00 Emerald
PEDESTAL SALT						
Salt dip			75.00			

Pattern Name	Blue	Green	White	Vaseline/Canary	Cranberry	Other
PEPPERMINT STRIPE EPERGNE						
Epergne, single lily					750.00	
PETALS WITH CUPPED PEARL						
Vase				100.00		
PHOENIX COINSPOT						
Pitcher, rare				450.00		
PHOENIX DRAPE						
Butter	175.00				235.00	
Celery vase	80.00				100.00	
Juice glass	60.00				70.00	
Pitcher	225.00				325.00	
Punch cup	30.00				45.00	
Tumbler	65.00				80.00	
PHOENIX HONEYCOMB						
Pitcher, rare	375.00					
PIASA BIRD						
Bowl	55.00		45.00			
Plate, footed	125.00		100.00			
Rose bowl	90.00		75.00			
Spittoon whimsey	95.00		85.00			
Vase	75.00		65.00			
PICCADILLY						
Basket, small	100.00	90.00	70.00			
PICKET						
Planter, two sizes	75.00		60.00	75.00		
PIG NOVELTY						
Novelty pig, various sizes				175.00-250.00		
PILGRIM						
Candlestick, each			95.00			
PILLARED VASE						
Vase, 12"				85.00		
PINEAPPLE						
Compote or open sugar	65.00					
PINEAPPLE & FAN (HEISEY)						
Creamer				600.00		
Sugar				650.00		
Vase, extremely rare				4,000.00		
PINWHEEL						
Cake plate, 12", stemmed	125.00			135.00		
PISTACHIO						
Pitcher				235.00		
Tumbler				70.00		
PLAID						
Bowl			300.00			
PLAIN JANE						
Nappy, footed	50.00	60.00	30.00	85.00		
PLAIN OPAL						
Creamer, footed			55.00			
PLAIN PANELS (NORTHWOOD)						
Vase	45.00	40.00	30.00			
PLUME AND ACORN						
Bowl, 5"			75.00			
PLUMES AND SCROLLS						
Bowl	65.00					
POINSETTIA						
Bowl whimsey	150.00	125.00	100.00		200.00	
Fruit bowl, two sizes	125.00	110.00	85.00		175.00	
Pitcher, either shape	350.00-500.00	375.00-550.00	250.00-400.00		1,000.00-2,200.00	
Sugar shaker	300.00	300.00	200.00		450.00	
Syrup, various	300.00-700.00	350.00-750.00	200.00-450.00		450.00-900.00	
Tumbler	75.00		45.00		125.00	
POINSETTIA LATTICE						
Bowl, scarce	300.00		125.00	475.00		
POLAR MEDALLIONS						
Milk pitcher				135.00		
POLKA DOT*						
Bowl, large	75.00		50.00		125.00	

Pattern Name	Blue	Green	White	Vaseline/Canary	Cranberry	Other
Cruet	400.00		250.00		750.00	
Pitcher, rare	250.00		150.00		850.00	
Shakers, pair	100.00		60.00		300.00	
Sugar shaker	200.00		150.00		300.00	
Syrup	250.00		125.00		725.00	
Toothpick holder	425.00		300.00		525.00	
Tumbler	70.00		30.00		125.00	
POLKA DOT WITH THORN HANDLE						
One shape	75.00					
POMPEIAN (DUGAN)						
J.I.P. whimsey			75.00			
POPSICLE STICKS						
Bowl, footed	55.00	50.00	35.00			
Nut bowl whimsey	65.00	60.00	45.00			
Shade	60.00		35.00		200.00	
Toothpick holder					325.00	
POSEIDON						
Bowls, various			45.00-75.00	55.00-90.00		
Butter with lid				165.00		
Plate				80.00		
POSEIDON SHELL						
Footed bowl, 8½"x4¾"	85.00					
PRAM						
Novelty bowl, 6½" x 3" wide	225.00					
PRAYER RUG (FENTON)						
Bonbon, gilded, rare	150.00			225.00		
Vase, J.I.P. shape, very scarce				165.00		
PREAKNESS						
Single lily epergne in metal holder			145.00			
PRESSED COINSPOT (#617)						
Card tray	75.00	100.00	50.00	100.00		
Compote	65.00	75.00	45.00	75.00		
Rose bowl whimsey			75.00			
PRESSED DIAMOND						
Bowl, boat shaped, 13"			125.00			
PRIMROSE (DAFFODILS VARIANT)						
Pitcher			900.00			
PRIMROSE SCROLL						
Bowl, 6"				100.00		
PRIMROSE SHADE						
Shade						250.00 Rubina verde
PRINCE CHARLES						
Bowl, 4"	65.00		50.00			75.00 Amber
PRINCESS DIANA						
Biscuit set (jar and plate, complete)	100.00			110.00		
Butter	125.00			110.00		
Compote, metal base	150.00			135.00		
Compote, large	90.00			110.00		
Creamer	55.00			50.00		
Novelty bowl	50.00			45.00		
Open sugar	70.00			65.00		
Pitcher	150.00			120.00		
Plate, crimped	65.00			60.00		
Salad bowl	55.00			50.00		
Tumbler	50.00			40.00		
Water tray	55.00			50.00		
PRINCE WILLIAM						
Basket, handled, 6½" long	300.00			300.00		
Creamer	65.00			60.00		
Open sugar	65.00			60.00		
Oval plate	65.00			70.00		
Pitcher	225.00			250.00		
Toothpick holder	65.00					
Tumbler	45.00			35.00		
PRISM HOBNAIL						
Creamer				80.00		

Pattern Name	Blue	Green	White	Vaseline/ Canary	Cranberry	Other
PULLED COINSPOT						
Mug					150.00	
PULLED LOOP						
Vase, two sizes, scarce	40.00-80.00	55.00-90.00	25.00-55.00			
PUMP & TROUGH*						
Pump	130.00		100.00	130.00		
Trough	75.00		50.00	75.00		
PUSSY WILLOW						
Vase, 4½"				85.00		
QUEEN'S CANDLESTICKS						
Candlesticks, pair				200.00		
QUEEN'S CROWN						
Bowl, small	40.00			85.00		
Bowl, large	55.00			150.00		
Compote, low	60.00			125.00		
Epergne, complete, very rare				3,500.00		
QUEEN'S SPILL						
Candlesticks	325.00			350.00		
Spill vase, 4"	90.00			90.00		
QUEEN VICTORIA						
Plate	150.00			150.00		
QUESTION MARKS						
Card tray	75.00					
Compote	70.00	85.00	45.00	150.00		
QUILT						
Bowl, 5½"			140.00			
QUILTED DAISY						
Fairy lamp	500.00		375.00	450.00		
QUILTED DIAMONDS						
Bowl on metal stand						400.00 White/cranberry
QUILTED PHLOX LATTICE (NORTHWOOD)						
Salt shaker			90.00		135.00	
Sugar shaker			125.00		200.00	
Syrup			165.00		240.00	
Toothpick			100.00		145.00	
QUILTED PILLOW SHAM						
Creamer	75.00			70.00		
Open sugar	75.00			65.00		
Oval butter	100.00			100.00		
QUILTED ROSE						
Pitcher			100.00			
Tumbler			25.00			
QUILTED WIDE STRIPE						
Finger bowl	55.00		40.00		70.00	
Pitcher	200.00		165.00		250.00	
Tumbler	65.00		45.00		80.00	
RAINBOW STRIPE						
Compote						250.00 Vas/cranberry
RAISED RIB (FENTON)						
Bowl, two shapes						125.00 Cameo opal
RASPBERRY PRUNTS						
Creamer				90.00		
RAY						
Vase	55.00	50.00	30.00			
RAYED HEART						
Compote	75.00	60.00	45.00			
RAYED JANE						
Nappy	50.00		25.00	65.00		
REEDS & BLOSSOMS						
Bowl		145.00				
REFLECTING DIAMONDS						
Bowl	60.00	65.00	40.00			
Bowl, ice cream shape	65.00	70.00	50.00			
Plate whimsey	85.00	80.00	65.00			
REFLECTIONS						
Footed novelty bowls	30.00-50.00	30.00-50.00	20.00-40.00			

Pattern Name	Blue	Green	White	Vaseline/ Canary	Cranberry	Other
REGAL (NORTHWOOD'S)						
Bowl, master	125.00	150.00	100.00			
Bowl, sauce	35.00	45.00	20.00			
Butter	225.00	175.00	125.00			
Celery vase	150.00	175.00	100.00			
Creamer	100.00	65.00	50.00			
Cruet	750.00	750.00	600.00			
Plate, rare	165.00	150.00	100.00			
Pitcher	325.00	300.00	200.00			
Shakers, pair	375.00	375.00	300.00			
Spooner	100.00	65.00	50.00			
Sugar	150.00	100.00	70.00			
Tumbler	100.00	85.00	45.00			
REGALIA						
Shade			125.00			
REVERSE DRAPERY						
Bowl	45.00	45.00	25.00			
Plate	90.00	85.00	50.00			
Vase whimsey	100.00	100.00	75.00			145.00 Amethyst
REVERSE SWIRL						
Bowl, master	70.00		40.00	55.00	85.00	
Bowl, sauce	25.00		20.00	25.00	40.00	
Butter	200.00		165.00	175.00	250.00	
Celery vase	175.00		100.00	150.00	200.00	
Creamer	125.00		100.00	125.00	195.00	
Cruet	275.00		110.00	175.00	475.00	
Cruet set and holder, four pieces	300.00		200.00		375.00	
Custard cup	50.00		35.00		150.00	
Finger bowl	70.00		45.00		100.00	
Hanging lamp, rare					1700.00	
Mini-lamp	375.00		200.00		325.00	
Mustard pot	80.00		45.00	75.00	125.00	
Oil lamp	350.00		300.00	345.00		
Pitcher	250.00		175.00	225.00	800.00	
Rose bowl				75.00	95.00	
Shakers, pair	100.00		60.00	100.00	175.00	
Spooner	125.00		80.00	100.00	150.00	
Sugar	175.00		100.00	150.00	225.00	
Sugar shaker	175.00		125.00	150.00	275.00	
Syrup	175.00		100.00	150.00	425.00	
Toothpick holder	155.00		100.00	125.00	275.00	
Tumbler	60.00		35.00	60.00	100.00	
Water bottle	150.00		100.00	150.00	200.00	

Prices are for Reverse Swirl and Reverse Swirl Spatter, but not all pieces are found in the same colors in the spatter pattern as with the regular one.

Pattern Name	Blue	Green	White	Vaseline/ Canary	Cranberry	Other
RIB & BIG THUMBPRINTS						
Vase	45.00	40.00	25.00			
RIBBED BEADED CABLE						
See Beaded Cable						
RIBBED COINSPOT						
Butter	325.00		295.00		425.00	
Celery vase	225.00		210.00		250.00	
Creamer	400.00		350.00		450.00	
Pitcher	1,000.00		800.00		1,300.00	
Spooner	300.00		225.00		375.00	
Sugar	395.00		300.00		500.00	
Sugar shaker	465.00		385.00		550.00	
Syrup	950.00		725.00		1,150.00	
Tumbler	150.00		120.00		200.00	
All pieces, very scarce to rare						
RIBBED ENAMELED EPERGNE						
Epergne, single lily on stand, 22½"				650.00		
RIBBED EPERGNE						
Five-lily epergne in metal holder				350.00		
RIBBED (OPAL) LATTICE						
Bowl, master	70.00		45.00		150.00	
Bowl, sauce	30.00		20.00		40.00	
Butter	225.00		175.00		800.00	

Pattern Name	Blue	Green	White	Vaseline/Canary	Cranberry	Other
Creamer	75.00		65.00		400.00	
Cruet	225.00		175.00		500.00	
Pitcher	275.00		225.00	850.00	1,000.00	
Shakers, pair	145.00		100.00		300.00	
Spooner	75.00		65.00		400.00	
Sugar	125.00		100.00		650.00	
Sugar shaker, two sizes	140.00		100.00		425.00	
Syrup	175.00		150.00		600.00	
Toothpick holder	300.00		175.00		350.00	
Tumbler	50.00		40.00		150.00	
RIBBED OPAL RINGS						
Pitcher, rare	675.00		525.00		975.00	
Sugar	185.00		155.00		375.00	
Tumbler	100.00		85.00		300.00	
RIBBED OPTIC						
Tumble-up	70.00	80.00	50.00	75.00	100.00	
RIBBED PILLAR						
Berry bowl, small					40.00	
Berry bowl, large					95.00	
Butter					200.00	
Celery vase					85.00	
Creamer or spooner					65.00	
Cruet					165.00	
Pitcher					300.00	
Shakers, pair					135.00	
Sugar					65.00	
Sugar shaker					125.00	
Syrup					155.00	
Tumbler					60.00	
RIBBED SPIRAL						
Bowl, master	75.00		45.00	65.00		
Bowl, sauce	30.00		20.00	25.00		
Bowl, ruffled	55.00		40.00	50.00		
Bowl whimsey	100.00		85.00	115.00		
Butter	375.00		300.00	350.00		
Creamer	100.00		45.00	65.00		
Cup and saucer	110.00		60.00	100.00		
Jelly compote	70.00		50.00	65.00		
Pitcher	525.00		385.00	475.00		
Plate	75.00		45.00	60.00		
Shakers, pair	225.00		125.00	225.00		
Spooner	110.00		50.00	75.00		
Sugar	200.00		150.00	175.00		
Toothpick holder	175.00		125.00	175.00		
Tumbler	115.00		60.00	100.00		
Vase, squat, 4 – 7"	60.00		35.00	75.00		
Vase, standard, 8 – 14"	45.00		25.00	55.00		
Vase, funeral, 15 – 22"	145.00		90.00	200.00		
Whimsey, three-handled				125.00		
RIBBED TRIANGLE AND FANS						
Bowl, 9½" x 7½"	95.00					
RIBBON SWIRL						
Bowl	125.00	110.00	100.00			
Rose bowl	140.00	125.00	120.00			
Spittoon	200.00	175.00	165.00			
Vase	175.00	165.00	150.00			
RIBBON WAVE						
Salt dip, in metal holder						125.00 Rubina verde
RICHELIEU						
Basket, handled	100.00		60.00	80.00		
Bowl	70.00		50.00	65.00		
Cracker jar with lid	200.00		150.00	185.00		
Creamer	65.00		45.00	60.00		
Divided dish, rare	100.00		75.00	100.00		
Jelly compote	75.00		50.00	75.00		
Nappy, handled	90.00		70.00	95.00		
Open sugar	65.00		40.00	60.00		

Pattern Name	Blue	Green	White	Vaseline/Canary	Cranberry	Other
Basket, open	100.00		70.00	100.00		
Pitcher	160.00		130.00	150.00		
Tray	65.00		40.00	55.00		
Triple sweet dish	75.00		60.00	75.00		
Tumbler	30.00		20.00	30.00		
RIC-RAC						
Vase				100.00		
RIGOREE						
Sauce						200.00 Rubina verde
RIGOREE SPILL						
Spill vase						150.00 Rubina verde
RINGED BARREL						
Toothpick holder	150.00			150.00		
RINGED FLUTE WITH BEADED MEDALLIONS						
Basket	90.00					
RING HANDLE						
Basket	145.00	150.00	120.00	160.00		
Ring tray	100.00	80.00	75.00	95.00		
Shakers, pair	100.00		75.00			
RINGS AND ARCHES						
Bowl	70.00					
RINGS WITH WAVE BAND						
Vase				145.00		
RIPPLE						
Vase	250.00	175.00	150.00	300.00		
RIPPLED RIB						
Vase			40.00			
ROARING LION						
Cordial				100.00		
Glass, pilsner shape				150.00		
Goblet				165.00		
ROCOCCO						
Bowl, bride's basket	300.00		250.00	300.00	400.00	
Plate, 6", rare			200.00			
Plate, 10", rare	400.00		350.00	400.00	600.00	
ROLLED WIDE STRIPE (ENGLISH)						
Spill with holder, 2½" without holder	90.00		70.00	150.00		
ROSE ("ROSE & RUFFLES")						
Bowl, small	100.00			100.00		
Candlesticks, pair	250.00			250.00		
Cologne	250.00			250.00		
Compote, tall	100.00			100.00		
Console bowl	80.00			80.00		
Covered bowl, large	150.00			150.00		
Pin tray or soap dish	75.00			75.00		
Pomade	100.00			100.00		
Powder jar, two sizes	125.00			125.00		
Tray, center handled	90.00			90.00		
Tray, dresser	100.00			100.00		
Vase, 6"	100.00			100.00		
ROSE BUSH						
Wall pocket, very scarce			150.00			
ROSE SHOW						
Bowl, rare	325.00		250.00			
ROSE SPATTER						
Celery						190.00 Tortoise shell
Pitcher, rare						400.00 Tortoise shell
ROSE SPRAY						
Compote, round	45.00	60.00	30.00			85.00 Amethyst
Compote, J.I.P.			75.00			
ROULETTE						
Bowls, various shapes	50.00	45.00	30.00			
Nut bowl whimsey	90.00	65.00	55.00			
Plate, square, scarce	100.00	100.00	60.00			
ROYAL DAISY						
Compote	225.00					

Pattern Name	Blue	Green	White	Vaseline/Canary	Cranberry	Other
ROYAL FAN						
Posy vase				85.00		
ROYAL JUBILEE						
Basket, handled	110.00			110.00		125.00 Amber
ROYAL SCANDAL						
Wall vase	250.00		200.00	250.00		
ROYAL SUNBURST						
Bowl				85.00		
RUBINA DIAMONDS						
J.I.P. vase						225.00 Rubina verde
RUBINA VERDE						
J.I.P. vase						250.00 Rubina verde
RUFFLES & RINGS						
Novelty bowl	55.00	50.00	30.00			
Nut bowl	60.00	55.00	40.00			
Rose bowl	65.00	60.00	45.00			
RUFFLES & RINGS WITH DAISY BAND						
Bowl, footed	95.00	85.00	60.00			
SALMON						
Bowl, fish shape			325.00	450.00		
SCHEHEREZADE						
Novelty bowl	50.00	45.00	30.00			
SCOTTISH MOOR						
Celery vase	150.00		100.00			
Cracker jar	350.00		225.00			
Cruet	400.00		225.00			
Pitcher	350.00		275.00		475.00	1,500.00 Orange
Tumbler	80.00		65.00		90.00	275.00 Orange
Vase	90.00		60.00			
SCROLL						
Bowl				80.00		
SCROLL FLUTED (IMPERIAL)						
Celery tray	25.00	25.00	20.00	30.00		
Creamer	25.00	25.00	20.00	30.00		
Rose bowl	30.00	30.00	25.00	35.00		
Sugar	25.00	25.00	20.00	30.00		
SCROLL WITH ACANTHUS						
Bowl, master	55.00		40.00	50.00		
Bowl, sauce	25.00		20.00	25.00		
Butter	375.00		325.00	350.00		
Creamer	100.00		65.00	75.00		
Cruet	225.00		200.00	375.00		
Jelly compote	65.00		60.00	65.00		
Pitcher	400.00		325.00	350.00		
Shakers, pair	225.00		195.00	200.00		
Spooner	85.00		70.00	75.00		
Sugar	175.00		150.00	165.00		
Toothpick holder	300.00		275.00	325.00		
Tumbler	100.00		65.00	75.00		
SCROLL WITH BUTTONS						
Creamer			95.00			
SCROLL WITH CANE BAND						
Bowl, rare		150.00				
SEA SCROLL						
Compote	125.00	135.00	95.00			
SEA SHORE						
Bowl	100.00					
SEA SPRAY						
Nappy, round, tricorner, or square	60.00	60.00	45.00			
Whimsey	50.00	50.00	40.00			
SEAWEED						
Bowl, master	60.00		40.00		125.00	
Bowl, sauce	30.00		20.00		70.00	
Butter	475.00		225.00		650.00	
Celery vase	100.00		80.00		175.00	
Creamer	125.00		100.00		225.00	
Cruet, two shapes	425.00		200.00		725.00	

Pattern Name	Blue	Green	White	Vaseline/Canary	Cranberry	Other
Finger bowl	250.00		200.00		500.00	
Pickle caster, complete					650.00	
Pitcher	1,100.00		475.00		1,400.00	
Rose bowl			500.00			
Shakers, pair	150.00		125.00		350.00	
Spooner	125.00		100.00		175.00	
Sugar	175.00		145.00		225.00	
Sugar shaker	275.00		200.00		450.00	
Syrup	850.00		325.00		1,150.00	
Toothpick holder	325.00		225.00		500.00	
Tumbler	70.00		45.00		125.00	
SEAWEED VARIANT						
Vase						135.00 White w/rubina top
SERPENT THREADS						
Epergne, 23"				425.00		
SHAMROCK						
Oil lamp				375.00		
SHARKS TOOTH						
Oil lamp, rare				800.00		
Spooner, rare				325.00		
Smoke shade, rare						500.00 Rubina
SHELDON SWIRL						
Lamp, either size	575.00		475.00	675.00	725.00	
SHELL						
Novelty shell, two sizes, rare	175.00			200.00		
SHELL & DOTS						
Novelty bowl	50.00		40.00	100.00		
Nut bowl	45.00	55.00	40.00			
Rose bowl	45.00		35.00			
SHELL & SEAWEED						
Rose bowl						450.00 Rubina verde
SHELL & WILD ROSE						
Novelty bowl, open edge	60.00	55.00	45.00	100.00		
Nut bowl whimsey	80.00	70.00	55.00	175.00		
SHELL INK WELL						
Double ink well			150.00			
SHOE						
Novelty shoe	85.00		65.00			
SILVER OVERLAY						
Vase		95.00	75.00			
SIMPLE SIMON						
Compote	65.00	60.00	40.00			
SINGING BIRDS						
Mug, rare	600.00		450.00	800.00		
SINGLE POINSETTIA (FENTON)						
Bowl			275.00			350.00 Amethyst opal
SIR LANCELOT						
Bowl, footed	65.00	60.00	40.00			
SIX PETALS						
Bowl			75.00			
SKIRTED DOTS						
Salt, open sugar or marmalade				95.00		
SMOOTH RIB						
Bowl	25.00	20.00	15.00	50.00		
Bowl on metal stand			65.00			
SNAIL LOOP AND BALL						
Creamer			65.00			
SNOWBALL ROYALE						
Christmas ornament, rare				500.00		
SNOWFLAKE						
Hand lamp	400.00		275.00		600.00	
Night lamp	1,300.00		800.00		1,800.00	
Oil lamp	325.00		225.00		550.00	
SNOWFLAKES & ICICLES						
Pitcher, enameled	235.00					
SNOWFLAKE SPATTER						
Vase	150.00	125.00	75.00			

Pattern Name	Blue	Green	White	Vaseline/Canary	Cranberry	Other
SOLAR FLARE						
Plate				135.00		
SOMERSET						
Bowl, large	100.00			400.00		
Bowls, five sizes, stackable	60.00-125.00			85.00-375.00		
Cake plate	125.00			200.00		
Compotes, various sizes	150.00-250.00			225.00-350.00		
Creamer, footed, two sizes	100.00			145.00		
Creamer, without feet, two sizes	70.00-85.00			90.00-125.00		
Nappy, two shapes	65.00-80.00			90.00-110.00		
Oval dish, 5½ – 9½"	50.00-85.00			80.00-150.00		
Pickle jar with lid	95.00			175.00		
Pitcher, two sizes	100.00-200.00			300.00-450.00		
Sugar, footed, two sizes	75.00-95.00			120.00-140.00		
Sugar, without feet, two sizes	65.00-80.00			90.00-120.00		
Sugar bowl	90.00			175.00		
Tumbler, two sizes	65.00-80.00			115.00-135.00		
Underplate, two sizes	85.00-125.00			140.00-165.00		
SOWERBY BASKET						
Basket, handled, 3½" x 2"			125.00			
SOWERBY SALT						
Salt dish	65.00	70.00	55.00			
SPANISH LACE						
Bowl, master	100.00		65.00	80.00	150.00	
Bowl, sauce	30.00		25.00	30.00	40.00	
Bride's basket, two sizes	125.00		90.00	150.00	200.00	
Butter	425.00		225.00	400.00	500.00	
Celery vase	125.00		85.00	150.00	175.00	
Cracker jar	700.00				900.00	
Creamer	150.00		100.00	125.00	175.00	
Cruet	275.00		200.00	300.00	750.00	
Finger bowl	75.00		50.00	85.00	150.00	
Jam jar	300.00		200.00	325.00	500.00	
Liqueur jug					850.00	
Mini-lamp	200.00		125.00	225.00	350.00	
Perfume bottle	300.00		100.00	225.00	275.00	
Pitcher	250.00-500.00	275.00-400.00	100.00-300.00	350.00-450.00	6,50.00-1,000.00	
Rose bowl, many shapes	75.00		50.00	75.00	150.00	
Shakers, pair	125.00		75.00	125.00	225.00	
Spooner	150.00		100.00	145.00	175.00	
Sugar	275.00		200.00	250.00	325.00	
Sugar shaker	150.00		100.00	150.00	225.00	
Syrup	250.00		175.00	350.00	650.00	
Tumbler	60.00	50.00	40.00	55.00	125.00	
Vase, many sizes	100.00		50.00	125.00	225.00	
Water bottle	300.00		200.00	325.00	425.00	
SPATTER						
Bowl	55.00	50.00	30.00	55.00	125.00	
Pitcher	250.00	250.00	175.00	265.00	450.00	
Tumbler	35.00	35.00	20.00	30.00	95.00	
Vase, 9"	95.00	90.00	55.00	100.00		100.00 Orange
SPATTERED COINSPOT						
Pitcher					450.00	
Tumbler					100.00	
SPECKLED CELERY VASE						
Celery vase	140.00	140.00	100.00		185.00	
SPECKLED CHRYSANTHEMUM BASE						
Berry, small					65.00	
Berry, large					125.00	
Butter					385.00	
Celery vase					165.00	
Creamer or spooner					100.00	
Cruet					250.00	
Finger bowl					125.00	
Mustard					150.00	
Pitcher					550.00	
Shaker					275.00	

Pattern Name	Blue	Green	White	Vaseline/Canary	Cranberry	Other
Straw holder with lid					375.00	
Sugar					150.00	
Syrup					300.00	
Toothpick holder					225.00	
Tumbler					90.00	
SPECKLED STRIPE						
Barber bottle	290.00		265.00	290.00		
Covered jar	390.00		350.00	390.00		
Finger bowl and underplate	250.00		200.00	300.00		
Shakers, pair	240.00		190.00	240.00		
Sugar				50.00		
Vase, three sizes	110.00-200.00	100.00-190.00	75.00-150.00	100.00-185.00		
SPINEY CACTUS						
Vase, 3⅛" and 5"	50.00-75.00					
SPIRALEX						
Vase	55.00	60.00	40.00	90.00		
SPIRAL OPTIC						
Pitcher						250.00 Amethyst opal
Tumbler						50.00 Amethyst opal
SPIRAL WEB						
Marmalade in metal holder						475.00 Cran/vaseline
SPOKES & WHEELS & VARIANTS						
Bowl	55.00	50.00	35.00			
Plate, rare	85.00	80.00				75.00 Aqua
SPOOL						
Compote, either shape	50.00	50.00	35.00			65.00 Emerald
SPOOL OF THREADS						
Card tray whimsey	100.00					
Compote	60.00		40.00	55.00		
SQUARE						
Match holder or spill vase	80.00		60.00			
SQUARE HORN EPERGNE						
Epergne, multi-horn						1,000.00 Rubina verde
SQUARE WINDOWS						
Shade			80.00			
SQUIRREL & ACORN						
Bowl	185.00	175.00	170.00			
Compote	190.00	180.00	175.00	200.00		
Vase	190.00	180.00	175.00			
Whimsey	190.00	185.00	175.00			
S-REPEAT						
Bowl, master	85.00	100.00	65.00	200.00		
Pitcher	475.00		350.00			
Tumbler	65.00		45.00			
STAG & HOLLY						
Bowl, footed, rare			1,400.00			1,850.00 Amethyst
STAR BASE						
Bowl, small, square	40.00					
Bowl, large, square	70.00					
Cup and saucer	80.00					
Nappy	55.00					
Plate	45.00					
Shakers, each	65.00					
STARFLOWER						
Vase				225.00		
STAR IN DIAMOND						
Bowl, oval, 5⅜" x 3½"	55.00					
STARRY NIGHT						
Bowl, various shapes			55.00			
STARS & BARS						
Pull knob, each			20.00			
STARS & STRIPES						
Barber bottle			100.00		300.00	
Compote (age ?)					375.00	
Lamp shade			65.00			
Pitcher			250.00		1,100.00	
Tumbler	100.00		75.00			

Pattern Name	Blue	Green	White	Vaseline/Canary	Cranberry	Other
STIPPLED IVY						
Basket, very scarce	150.00					
STIPPLED SCROLL & PRISM						
Covered stemmed piece, two sizes	40.00-80.00	30.00-70.00	20.00-55.00			
Goblet, 5"	40.00	30.00	25.00			
Goblet, 7½"	55.00	35.00	30.00			
Goblet, 9"	75.00	40.00	35.00			
STORK & RUSHES						
Mug	150.00		175.00			
Tumbler			95.00			
STORK & SWAN						
Syrup			150.00			
STOURBRIDGE						
Creamer				85.00		
Sugar				70.00		
STRAWBERRY						
Bonbon			125.00			
STRAWBERRY & DAHLIA TWIST						
Epergne with lily	450.00	400.00	325.00			
STRETCHED DIAMONDS						
Vase, enameled	175.00					
STRIPE						
Barber bottle	160.00				300.00	
Bowl			60.00		100.00	
Condiment set	400.00				750.00	
Cruet					500.00-750.00	
Oil lamp					625.00	
Pitcher	275.00			350.00	575.00	
Rose bowl	100.00				225.00	
Shakers, pair	100.00				250.00	
Spittoon	150.00				300.00	
Syrup	275.00				450.00	
Toothpick holder	250.00				400.00	
Vase			600.00		125.00	
Tumbler	55.00			70.00	100.00	
STRIPE BRACKET LAMP						
Lamp in wall mounted holder	145.00		125.00	245.00	225.00	
STRIPE CONDIMENT SET						
Four piece set, complete with holder						450.00 mix of 3 colors
STRIPED LEMONESCENT						
Creamer				265.00		
Sugar				250.00		
Vase				225.00		
STRIPE WITH FAN						
Bowl shape, enameled decoration					125.00	
STRIPE WITH FLY						
Creamer in silverplated holder				250.00		
Creamer, polka dot pattern					225.00	
SUNBURST-ON-SHIELD (DIADEM)						
Bowl, master	150.00			200.00		
Bowl, sauce	40.00			40.00		
Breakfast set, two pieces	200.00			250.00		
Butter	375.00		275.00	400.00		
Creamer	100.00		80.00	135.00		
Cruet, rare	325.00		350.00	750.00		
Nappy, rare	225.00			350.00		
Novelty bowl, 7½"	100.00		75.00	100.00		
Pitcher	600.00			950.00		
Spooner	125.00		90.00	145.00		
Sugar	225.00		175.00	250.00		
Tumbler	125.00			200.00		
SUNDERLAND						
Basket	110.00					
Compote				150.00		
Nappy, handled	80.00					
Tumbler	60.00					

Pattern Name	Blue	Green	White	Vaseline/Canary	Cranberry	Other
SUNK HOLLYHOCK						
Bowl, scarce				125.00		
SUNK HONEYCOMB						
Bowl, very rare				225.00		
SUNSET						
Bowl, 9"	75.00					65.00 Pink
SURF SPRAY						
Pickle dish, very scarce	75.00	70.00	45.00			
SUSSEX						
Creamer	150.00			150.00		
Sugar, open	150.00			150.00		
SWAG WITH BRACKETS						
Bowl	45.00	45.00	30.00	45.00		
Bowl, master	85.00	65.00	45.00	65.00		
Bowl, sauce	35.00	35.00	25.00	30.00		
Butter	275.00	250.00	200.00	250.00		
Creamer	100.00	85.00	55.00	80.00		
Cruet	500.00	325.00	175.00	250.00		
Jelly compote	60.00	55.00	30.00	50.00		
Pitcher	300.00	300.00	200.00	290.00		
Shakers, pair	200.00	175.00	125.00	200.00		
Spooner	100.00	110.00	55.00	100.00		
Sugar	150.00	140.00	75.00	125.00		
Toothpick holder	350.00	300.00	250.00	300.00		
Tumbler	85.00	75.00	40.00	75.00		
Whimsey sugar	100.00	125.00		175.00		
SWAN NOVELTY						
Novelty swan				225.00		
SWASTIKA						
Pitcher	1,800.00	3,000.00	1,100.00		3,300.00	
Syrup	1,550.00	2,000.00	900.00		3,800.00	
Tumbler	175.00	225.00	100.00		425.00	
SWIRL						
Bowl, master	50.00	55.00	40.00		75.00	
Bowl, sauce	20.00	25.00	15.00		35.00	
Butter	125.00	125.00	65.00		175.00	
Cheese dish			250.00		400.00	
Celery vase	75.00	85.00	50.00		150.00	
Creamer	75.00	85.00	40.00		100.00	
Cruet, two sizes	175.00	200.00	100.00		300.00	
Cruet set, complete					475.00	
Custard cup	40.00	50.00	30.00		75.00	
Finger bowl	65.00	60.00	35.00		100.00	
Finger lamp			350.00		600.00	
Handled novelty whimsey			75.00			
Lampshade	100.00	100.00	40.00		175.00	
Mustard jar	100.00	110.00	60.00		150.00	
Pitcher, various shapes and tops	175.00-275.00	175.00-275.00	90.00-150.00	300.00-500.00	350.00-600.00	2,000.00 Amethyst
Rose bowl	60.00	70.00	40.00		90.00	
Shakers, pair	175.00	150.00	100.00		250.00	
Shot glass	80.00		65.00			
Spittoon	90.00	85.00	70.00		150.00	
Spooner	75.00	80.00	40.00		125.00	
Strawholder, rare	800.00		575.00		1,200.00	
Sugar	100.00	110.00	50.00		175.00	
Sugar shaker	150.00	100.00	75.00		175.00	
Syrup	125.00	115.00	75.00		160.00	
Tankard pitcher		800.00*				
Toothpick holder	125.00	140.00	70.00		150.00	
Tumbler	30.00	25.00	15.00	45.00	95.00	
Vase	60.00	65.00	35.00		150.00	
Water bottles, bitters and barber	100.00-250.00	90.00-200.00	65.00-100.00		350.00-450.00	
SWIRLED INTERIOR FLUTE						
Vase	70.00					
SWIRLING MAZE						
Bowl, salad	100.00	90.00	60.00	90.00	150.00	
Pitcher, any (average)	500.00	450.00	300.00		800.00	

Pattern Name	Blue	Green	White	Vaseline/ Canary	Cranberry	Other
Tumbler	65.00	55.00	25.00		100.00	
SWIRL LAMP						
Oil lamp				400.00		
SWIRL WITH ENAMELED BIRD						
Vase, applied frit decoration			200.00			
TARGET						
Vase	75.00	70.00	45.00			
TARGET SWIRL						
Bottle whimsey	125.00		100.00		275.00	
Salt in metal holder, rare				175.00		
Tumbler	80.00		65.00		95.00	
Vase, two sizes	300.00		225.00		500.00	
Vase, squat, various shapes	300.00		200.00		500.00	400.00 Amethyst
TAZZA						
Compote, plain				275.00		
THIN & WIDE RIB						
Vase	60.00	60.00	45.00	75.00		
THISTLE & WREATH						
Cup plate, 3½"			125.00			
THISTLE LILY						
Vase						250.00 Rubina verde
THISTLE PATCH (INTAGLIO POPPY)						
Novelty, footed	90.00		40.00	75.00		
Add 10% for goofus						
THISTLES						
Shade						200.00 Rubina verde
THOMAS WEBB CROCODILE						
Novely piece				425.00		
THORN LILY						
Epergne, three-lily with base				375.00		
Epergne, one-lily, various metal holers				150.00		
THORN VASE (THOMAS WEBB)						
Vase			325.00	400.00		350.00 Pink
THOUSAND EYE						
Bottles, various			25.00-55.00			
Bowls, various			25.00-50.00			
Butter			125.00			
Celery vase			100.00			
Compotes, various			45.00-85.00			
Creamer			75.00			
Cruet			150.00			
Pitcher			110.00			
Shakers, pair			75.00			
Spooner			75.00			
Sugar			100.00			
Toothpick holder			125.00			
Tumbler			30.00			
THREAD & RIB						
Epergne	800.00	900.00	600.00	800.00		
THREADED GRAPE						
Banana boat	225.00					
Compote, 8", large	200.00	175.00	100.00			
Tri-corner whimsey			185.00			
THREADED MELON						
Basket	250.00					
THREADED OPTIC (BAND & RIB)						
Bowl, 7 – 9"	60.00		45.00			
Rose bowl	40.00		30.00			
THREADED STRIPE						
Bowl						100.00 Amber
THREE FINGERS & PANEL						
Bowl, master, rare	100.00		75.00	100.00		
Bowl, sauce, rare	40.00		25.00	40.00		
THREE FRUITS						
Bowl, scarce	225.00		145.00			
THREE FRUITS WITH MEANDER						
Bowl, footed	165.00		110.00			

Pattern Name	Blue	Green	White	Vaseline/ Canary	Cranberry	Other
THREE LILY WATERFALL						
Epergne	275.00		250.00	375.00		
TINES						
Vase		75.00				
TINY RIB						
Bowl, footed, 6"	100.00					
TINY TEARS						
Vase	50.00	45.00	35.00			
TOKYO						
Bowl, master	45.00	40.00	25.00			
Bowl, sauce	30.00	30.00	15.00			
Butter	200.00	175.00	100.00			
Creamer	100.00	80.00	40.00			
Cruet	200.00	200.00	100.00			
Jelly compote	55.00	55.00	30.00			
Pitcher	350.00	300.00	175.00			
Plate	70.00	70.00	35.00			
Shakers, pair	100.00	85.00	45.00			
Spooner	100.00	85.00	45.00			
Sugar	150.00	135.00	60.00			
Syrup	150.00	145.00	70.00			
Toothpick holder	250.00	200.00	125.00			
Tumbler	75.00	70.00	45.00			
Vase	55.00	50.00	35.00			
TRAFALGER FOUNTAIN						
Epergne	325.00		275.00	350.00		350.00 Amber
TRAILING VINES						
Novelty bowl	120.00		85.00	135.00		
TREE FORM						
Posy vase	250.00			375.00		
TREE OF LIFE						
Handled whimsey	125.00					
Shakers, each	100.00		50.00			
Vase	100.00		60.00			
Vase whimsey, two shapes	125.00		75.00			
TREE OF LOVE						
Basket, rare				325.00		
Butter, covered, rare			350.00			
Compote			55.00			
Handled whimsey, center handled			255.00			
Novelty bowl			45.00			
Plate, rare, two sizes			135.00			
TREE STUMP						
Mug	85.00	95.00	60.00			
TREE TRUNK						
Vase	45.00	50.00	35.00			
TRELLIS						
Tumbler				65.00		
TRIANGLE						
Match holder	75.00		55.00			
TRIDENT						
Pitcher						425.00 Amber opal
Tumbler						75.00 Amber opal
TRI-FOLD EPERGNE						
Epergne, with lilies and baskets						900.00 Vaseline/cran
TRI-FOOTED SPILL						
Footed spill						250.00 Vaseline/cran
TROUT						
Bowl			150.00			
TRUMPET VASE						
Vase, 37 – 42", rare				1,000.00	1,500.00	
TULIP						
Cylinder shade						145.00 Rubina verde
TULIP COMPOTE						
Compote whimsey						300.00 White/amethyst
TULIP VASE (RICHARDSON GLASS)						
Vase, 6"				375.00		

229

Pattern Name	Blue	Green	White	Vaseline/ Canary	Cranberry	Other
TUT						
Whimsey vase	125.00	125.00	100.00	165.00		
TWIGS						
Vase, small, 5½"	65.00	75.00	50.00	75.00		
Vase, panelled, 7"	85.00	100.00	65.00	85.00		
Vase whimsey, various top shapes	100.00	110.00	80.00	75.00		
TWIGS & LEAVES						
Basket, twig handle	250.00			300.00		
TWIST (MINIATURES)						
Butter	275.00		175.00	275.00		
Creamer	85.00		45.00	85.00		
Spooner	85.00		50.00	85.00		
Sugar	150.00		80.00	150.00		
TWISTED RIBS						
Vase	45.00	40.00	25.00			
TWISTED ROOTS						
Vase				325.00		
TWISTED ROPE						
Vase, very rare	275.00	325.00	200.00	325.00		
TWISTED TRUMPET						
Epergne		195.00				
TWISTER						
Bowl	50.00	45.00	35.00			
Plate	100.00					
Vase whimsey	75.00	75.00	45.00			
UNIVERSAL EPERGNE						
Epergne, various patterns & bases	125.00	135.00	95.00	165.00		
UNIVERSAL NORTHWOOD TUMBLER						
Tumbler	80.00		65.00	85.00		
VENETIAN (DUGAN)						
Rose bowl, various shapes and sizes	75.00-100.00	55.00-85.00	35.00-50.00	60.00-95.00	75.00-100.00	
Vase, various shapes and sizes	85.00-135.00	65.00-95.00	55.00-125.00	70.00-130.00	90.00-150.00	
VENETIAN BEAUTY						
Lamp (mini night lamp)	125.00		100.00		300.00	
VENETIAN (SPIDER WEB)						
Vase	85.00					
VENETIAN DRAPE						
Bowl with underplate, decorated			175.00			
VENICE						
Oil lamp	400.00		350.00			
VERTICAL STRIPE						
Vase with enameling	175.00					
VESTA VENETIAN (ENGLISH)						
Compote, very scarce				300.00		
Shade, very scarce				275.00		
V-HATCH						
Vase, ruffled						80.00 White/cran
VICTORIA & ALBERT						
Biscuit jar	165.00		110.00	150.00		
Covered butter	155.00		110.00	150.00		
Creamer	80.00		50.00	75.00		
Sugar	90.00		60.00	85.00		
VICTORIAN						
Vase, applied flowers and vines	165.00	175.00	110.00	165.00		175.00 Amber opal
VICTORIAN HAMPER						
Handled basket	75.00			75.00		
VICTORIAN STRIPE WITH FLOWERS						
Vase				300.00		
VICTORIAN SWIRL WITH FLOWERS						
Vase, decorated			200.00	275.00		
VIKING						
Bowl, boat shaped, 8½"	200.00					250.00 Amber opal
VINTAGE (FENTON)						
Bowl, rare	100.00		75.00			150.00 Amethyst opal
Add 10% for gold decoration						
VINTAGE (JEFFERSON/NORTHWOOD)						
Bowl, dome base	55.00	55.00	30.00			

Pattern Name	Blue	Green	White	Vaseline/Canary	Cranberry	Other
WAFFLE						
Epergne						700.00 Olive opal
WAR OF THE ROSES						
Bowl	75.00			70.00		
Boat shape, large	125.00			125.00		
Boat shape, small	100.00			100.00		
Compote, metal stand	150.00			150.00		
WATERLILY & CATTAILS (FENTON)						
Bonbon	60.00	65.00	45.00			85.00 Amethyst
Bowl, master	75.00	70.00	50.00			85.00 Amethyst
Bowl, sauce	35.00	30.00	25.00			40.00 Amethyst
Bowl whimsey	85.00	75.00	65.00			100.00 Amethyst
Breakfast set, two pieces	150.00	135.00	100.00			175.00 Amethyst
Butter	400.00	350.00	250.00			425.00 Amethyst
Creamer	100.00	75.00	60.00			125.00 Amethyst
Gravy boat, handled	60.00	55.00	45.00			80.00 Amethyst
Novelty bowl	45.00	40.00	30.00			55.00 Amethyst
Pitcher	425.00	400.00	250.00			425.00 Amethyst
Plate	100.00	85.00	55.00			125.00 Amethyst
Relish, handled	100.00	90.00	70.00			125.00 Amethyst
Rose bowl	85.00	125.00	50.00			135.00 Amethyst
Spittoon from bowl, rare	250.00					
Spooner	100.00	75.00	60.00			150.00 Amethyst
Sugar	200.00	150.00	100.00			225.00 Amethyst
Tumbler	75.00	65.00	30.00			85.00 Amethyst
Vase whimsey			150.00			
WATERLILY & CATTAILS (NORTHWOOD)						
Pitcher, rare	375.00					
Tumbler, rare	85.00					
WAVES						
Decanter	165.00			195.00		
Demitasse cup & saucer, set			100.00			
Guest set	200.00			265.00		
Light shade	80.00			125.00		
Pitcher, various shapes	450.00			575.00	525.00	
Plate, whimsey, very scarce		100.00				
Tumbler	70.00			85.00		
WEBB CENTERPIECE						
Fancy centerpiece epergne, very rare			850.00			
WEBB DRAPES						
Vase, 10½"				500.00		
WEDDING BELL						
Bell, with ringed top				325.00		
WEST VIRGINIA STRIPE						
Pitcher	225.00		165.00		400.00	
Tumbler	65.00		45.00		90.00	
WHEAT						
Oil lamp				475.00		
WHEEL & BLOCK						
Novelty bowl	45.00	40.00	30.00			
Novelty plate	135.00	100.00	65.00			
Vase whimsey	55.00	45.00	35.00			
WIDE PANEL						
Epergne, four-lily, scarce	800.00	850.00	600.00	925.00		
WIDE RIB						
Vase	125.00		100.00	145.00		
WIDE STRIPE						
Cruet	200.00	500.00	175.00		550.00	
Pitcher	250.00		175.00		450.00	
Shakers, pair			150.00		250.00	
Sugar shaker	175.00		150.00		275.00	
Syrup	225.00		200.00		325.00	
Toothpick holder	275.00	400.00	225.00		350.00	
Tumbler	60.00		40.00		100.00	
WILD BOUQUET						
Bowl, master	200.00	175.00	100.00			
Bowl, sauce	65.00	50.00	40.00			

Pattern Name	Blue	Green	White	Vaseline/ Canary	Cranberry	Other
Butter	500.00	450.00	325.00			
Creamer	200.00	150.00	100.00			
Cruet	400.00	425.00	250.00			
Cruet set with tray	475.00	425.00	300.00			
Jelly compote	175.00	135.00	100.00			
Pitcher	275.00	250.00	200.00			
Shakers, pair	200.00	175.00	125.00			
Spooner	200.00	150.00	100.00			
Sugar	300.00	275.00	195.00			
Toothpick holder	425.00	375.00	225.00			
Tumbler	95.00	90.00	50.00			150.00 Persian blue
WILD DAFFODILS						
Mug	85.00		65.00			100.00 Amethyst
WILD GRAPE						
Bowl			40.00			
Compote			40.00			
WILD ROSE (FENTON)						
Banana bowl	70.00		50.00			80.00 Amethyst
Bowl	60.00		40.00			75.00 Amethyst
Shade			75.00			
WILLIAM & MARY						
Bowl	95.00			165.00		
Butter, covered	175.00			250.00		
Cake plate, stemmed	140.00			160.00		
Celery vase	90.00			110.00		
Compote	100.00			90.00		
Creamer	65.00			60.00		
Master salt	50.00					
Open sugar, stemmed	70.00			65.00		
Plate	100.00			95.00		
WILLOW REED						
Basket	175.00					
WILTED FLOWERS						
Bowl	50.00	60.00	40.00			
Handled basket	95.00	110.00	65.00			
Rose bowl, very scarce			85.00			
WINDFLOWER						
Bowl, rare	175.00		125.00			
Nappy, rare			285.00			
WINDOWS ON STRIPE						
Oil lamp				450.00		
WINDOWS (PLAIN)*						
Barber bottle					325.00	
Finger bowl	50.00		45.00		75.00	
Mini lamp	175.00				1850.00	
Oil lamp					625.00	
Pitcher, various	150.00-200.00		90.00-150.00		350.00-550.00	
Shade	60.00		35.00		200.00	
Toothpick holder					325.00	
Tumbler	55.00		35.00		125.00	
WINDOWS (SWIRLED)						
Barber bottle	225.00		175.00		375.00	
Bowl, master	55.00		40.00		100.00	
Bowl, sauce	40.00		30.00		55.00	
Butter	400.00		300.00		550.00	
Celery vase	100.00		50.00		175.00	
Creamer	100.00		75.00		225.00	
Cruet	325.00		225.00		475.00	
Cruet set, complete	275.00		200.00		625.00	
Mustard jar	75.00		55.00		150.00	
Pitcher, various	300.00-425.00		200.00-300.00		600.00-800.00	
Plate, two sizes	125.00		65.00		250.00	
Shakers, pair	175.00		125.00		300.00	
Spooner	10.00		75.00		225.00	
Sugar	250.00		175.00		350.00	
Sugar shaker	150.00		125.00		325.00	
Syrup, two shapes	300.00		200.00		500.00	

Pattern Name	Blue	Green	White	Vaseline/Canary	Cranberry	Other
Toothpick holder	300.00		175.00		375.00	
Tumbler	85.00		65.00		125.00	
WINDSOR STRIPE						
Vase					125.00	
WINGED SCROLL						
Nappy, rare				425.00		
Sauce, rare				700.00		
WINTER CABBAGE						
Bowl, footed	50.00	45.00	35.00			
WINTERLILY						
Vase, scarce	225.00	250.00	175.00			
WISHBONE & DRAPERY						
Bowl	50.00	45.00	35.00			
Plate	60.00	60.00	50.00			
WOOD VINE LAMP (GAIETY BASE)						
Oil lamp			450.00			
WOVEN WONDER						
Novelty bowl	55.00		40.00			
Rose bowl	60.00		45.00			
WREATH & SCROLL						
Oil lamp				525.00		
WREATH & SHELL						
Bank whimsey, rare				235.00		
Bowl, master	100.00		70.00	125.00		
Bowl, sauce	40.00		25.00	35.00		
Butter	250.00		150.00	225.00		
Celery vase	200.00		100.00	175.00		
Cracker jar	600.00		475.00	550.00		
Creamer	175.00		85.00	150.00		
Ivy ball, rare	175.00		125.00	165.00		
Ladies spittoon	100.00		65.00	125.00		
Novelty bowl	75.00	150.00	55.00	65.00		500.00 Pink
Pitcher	600.00		200.00	375.00		
Rose bowl	100.00		65.00	85.00		
Salt dip	140.00		85.00	100.00		
Spooner	175.00		80.00	125.00		
Sugar	200.00		100.00	150.00		
Toothpick holder	300.00		200.00	275.00		
Tumbler, flat or footed	125.00		50.00	75.00		
Add 10% for decorated items						
WREATHED GRAPE & CABLE						
Centerpiece whimsey			300.00			
Orange bowl, footed, very rare			350.00			
X-HATCH						
Bowl, ruffled						175.00 Rubina verde
ZINFANDEL						
Pitcher, decorated						350.00 Rose opal
Tumbler, decorated						75.00 Rose opal
ZIPPER & LOOPS						
Vase, footed	65.00	70.00	45.00			
ZIPPERED FLUTE						
Vase		125.00				

Price Guide
to Opalescent Glass 1930 – 1970

After much deliberation, I've decided to add a price guide for items made after 1930 that are shown in the book. To have taken on the pricing of all items made in the last 73 years would have been a massive task and since this book is geared to only old glass (I only include these after 1930 patterns to illustrate what to be aware of in buying old glass), it was something I wouldn't consider, now or in the future.

Here then are prices for the items I show in this book in the colors shown. I hope it will give readers some idea of what newer glass is selling for and is meant to be only a ballpark reference and not a price setter.

Pattern Name	Blue	Green	White	Vaseline/ Canary	Cranberry	Other
ADAM'S RIB						
Candlesticks, pair	80.00					
APPLE TREE WHIMSEY VASE						
Vase, from pitcher, rare				225.00*		
BUTTERFLY						
Atomizer, complete	75.00					
CACTUS						
Vase, 9"	60.00		50.00	70.00		
CANTERBURY						
Baskets, various	40.00-80.00		25.00-60.00			30.00-70.00 Pink opal
Bowls, various	25.00-55.00		20.00-45.00			25.00-50.00 Pink opal
Vases, various	30.00-65.00		25.00-55.00			30.00-50.00 Pink opal
CHECKERBOARD						
Celery tray				45.00		
COIN DOT (FENTON)						
Barber bottle					75.00	
Vase					55.00	
CORNUCOPIA CANDLESTICK (FENTON)						
Candle holder			70.00			
CORN VASE REPRODUCTION						
Vase	55.00			70.00		60.00 Amber
COSMOS FLOWER ATOMIZER						
Atomizer	70.00	70.00	55.00			
CRANES						
Bowl			90.00			
CUBIST ROSE						
Bowl			225.00			
DAISY & BUTTON						
Compote, covered	45.00			60.00		
Fan vase	25.00			30.00		
Rose bowl on stand	65.00					
DAISY & BUTTON WITH THUMBPRINT						
Goblet	45.00			65.00		
DANCING LADIES						
Vase, footed			285.00			
DECO DAISY						
Plate			55.00			
DEVILBISS WIDE SWIRL						
Atomizer			135.00			
DIAMOND OPTIC WATER CARAFE						
Water bottle					75.00	
DOGWOOD						
Bowl			225.00			
DOT & MITRE						
Oil lamp					150.00	
DOT OPTIC (FENTON)						
Lamp, electric, using vase shape			125.00			
Shade			55.00			
Vase			65.00			
DUNCAN & MILLER						
Ashtray				30.00		
Vase	30.00					

Pattern Name	Blue	Green	White	Vaseline/Canary	Cranberry	Other
EASTER CHICK						
Plate, 7½"	25.00					
ELLEN						
Vase, 5"		30.00	20.00			25.00 Pink
EMPRESS						
Vase			80.00			
EYE DOT						
Oil lamp			90.00			
FENTON COIN DOT						
Basket with handle	40.00				50.00	
Pitcher	80.00				95.00	
FENTON HAND VASE						
Vase, 3½"	25.00		15.00			
FENTON HOBNAIL						
Atomizer	60.00	60.00	45.00	75.00	90.00	
Compote, covered	35.00	35.00		60.00	75.00	80.00 Plum
Fan vase	60.00	50.00	40.00	70.00	85.00	
Hat shapes, various sizes	35.00-80.00	35.00-80.00	30.00-60.00	45.00-90.00	65.00-135.00	
Lamp, two sizes and shapes	125.00		85.00		165.00	
Pitcher	75.00					
Tumbler	15.00					
Vase, made from pitcher mold	90.00					
Condensed list. Many shapes and colors were made, too numerous to list.						
FENTON RIB						
Ashtray	25.00					
FENTON'S #37 MINIATURES						
Creamer	20.00		15.00	25.00		
Vase	15.00		10.00	20.00		
FENTON'S #894						
Vase, various shapes				125.00		
FENTON'S BEATTY HONEYCOMB						
Vase	30.00	35.00				
FENTON SPANISH LACE						
Pitcher	70.00				95.00	
FENTON SWIRL						
Bowl, with separate base standard	70.00					
Hat shape	65.00	70.00	50.00	80.00	90.00	
Vase, various shapes & sizes	55.00	60.00	40.00	80.00	85.00	
Condensed list. Many shapes and colors were made, too numerous to list.						
FLYING BIRDS						
Dresser box			125.00			
FOSTORIA HEIRLOOM						
Bowl	30.00		20.00	40.00		
Epergne/candle holder				225.00		
Novelty bowl	40.00		30.00	50.00		
Plate	35.00		25.00	45.00		
Vase, various sizes	15.00-40.00	15.00-40.00	15.00-45.00	15.00-50.00		
FRISCO						
Rose bowl		25.00				
GIBSON SPITTOON						
Spittoon whimsey		25.00				
GRAPE & VINE						
Vase, J.I.P. shape	45.00					
HOBNAIL (CZECHOSLOVAKIAN)						
Puff box	35.00	40.00		50.00	60.00	
Tumbler	15.00	15.00		25.00	25.00	
HOBNAIL VARIANT						
Vase	25.00		15.00			
HOBNAIL (WESTMORELAND)						
Creamer	45.00					
Goblet	35.00					
Sugar	40.00					
HONEYCOMB WITH FLOWER RIM						
Vase	25.00					
JERSEY SWIRL						
Compote, low covered				45.00		
Compote, high covered				65.00		

Pattern Name	Blue	Green	White	Vaseline/Canary	Cranberry	Other
Footed sauce				20.00		
Goblet				35.00		
Master salt				25.00		
Plate, 6"				25.00		
Plate, 10"				35.00		
Salt dip				20.00		
Wine				25.00		
LACE-EDGED BASKETWEAVE						
Vase, footed	30.00	35.00	25.00			
LACE-EDGED BUTTONS						
Bowl	25.00	25.00	20.00			
LACE-EDGED DIAMONDS						
One shape, with handles	25.00	25.00	20.00			
MOON & STARS						
Goblet	20.00			30.00		
NAUTILUS						
Compote, very rare				400.00		
NEEDLEPOINT						
Tumbler, three sizes	15.00-25.00	15.00-25.00				20.00-30.00 Orange
OPALBERRY						
Plate			225.00			
OPEN-EDGE BASKETWEAVE						
Bowl, various shapes	25.00	25.00	20.00	30.00		
PANACHE						
Atomizer	80.00					
PEACOCK GARDEN VASE						
Vase, 4", 6", 8", and 10"			300.00-600.00			
PETTICOATS ATOMIZER						
Atomizer	60.00		40.00	75.00		
PINECONE & LEAVES						
Bowl			65.00			
PINECONE SPRAY						
Plate			55.00			
PLUME TWIST ATOMIZER						
Atomizer, 4"			75.00	115.00		
PLYMOUTH						
Pilsner			35.00			
QUEEN'S PETTICOAT						
See Fostoria's Heirloom						
QUILTED PINECONE						
Atomizer	70.00					
RING						
Pitcher			70.00			
RING & PETALS						
Butter with lid	75.00					
ROSETTE						
Oil lamp					200.00	
SEAWEED & SHELL						
Bowl, 5¾"	75.00					
SPIRAL OPTIC (FENTON)						
Candy with lid					80.00	
Hat	60.00	65.00	55.00	80.00	90.00	
Vase	50.00			45.00	70.00	
Vase, #894, 10½", either top	70.00	75.00	65.00	100.00	125.00	
Condensed list. Many shapes and colors known.						
SPIRAL WAVES						
Plate, 15"			65.00			
STAMM HOUSE DEWDROP						
Bowl, large			65.00			
Bowl, small			25.00			
STARS & STRIPES						
Basket with handle	45.00				60.00	
Bottle	50.00				75.00	
Creamer	25.00				40.00	
Cruet	55.00				60.00	
Finger bowl	25.00				25.00	
Syrup	60.00				60.00	

Pattern Name	Blue	Green	White	Vaseline/ Canary	Cranberry	Other
Tumbler	20.00				25.00	
SWAN BOWL						
Bowl with swan neck handles	135.00	140.00				160.00 Rose opalescent
SWIRL						
Pitcher	90.00					
SWIRLED FEATHER						
Candy dish	30.00	30.00	25.00		35.00	
Cruet	45.00	45.00	35.00		55.00	
Fairy lamp	30.00	30.00	25.00		40.00	
Hurricane lamp	60.00	60.00	50.00		65.00	
Tumbler	20.00	20.00	15.00		25.00	
Vanity set	95.00	95.00	75.00		115.00	
Vase	25.00	25.00	20.00		35.00	
SYLVAN						
Bowls, various	35.00-90.00		25.00-60.00			35.00-80.00 Pink opalescent
Relish trays, various	25.00-80.00		20.00-65.00			30.00-90.00 Pink opalescent
Vases, various	45.00-100.00		35.00-70.00			50.00-110.00 Pink opalescent
TOKYO {REPRODUCTION)						
Compote	25.00					
TROUT (FENTON)						
Bowl			75.00			
TWIGS (REPRODUCTION)						
Vase	30.00	30.00	25.00	35.00		
WATER BALLET						
Plate, or low bowl			100.00			
WILDFLOWER						
Goblet	25.00			30.00		
WINDOWS (L.G. WRIGHT)						
Creamer	20.00				35.00	
Cruet	45.00				60.00	
Epergne	75.00				100.00	
Fairy lamp	30.00				40.00	
Finger bowl	20.00				25.00	
Lamps, various	50.00-95.00				65.00-125.00	
Syrup	40.00				50.00	
Tumbler	15.00				25.00	
Vase	30.00				40.00	
WREATHED CHERRY						
Creamer	20.00			30.00		
WRIGHT'S THREAD & RIB EPERGNE						
Epergne	175.00			195.00		

Other Titles *by Mike Carwile*

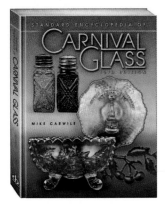

Standard Encyclopedia of Carnival Glass, 12th Edition

Mike Carwile

The twelfth edition introduces nearly 100 new patterns and 300 replacement photographs, bringing this edition's total to over 2,000 colorful patterns. The bound-in price guide includes virtually every piece of carnival glass ever made with prices given for various colors in each pattern. A multitude of both American and foreign companies are represented, with brief histories included. 2010 values.

Item #8047 · ISBN: 978-1-57432-635-2 · 8½ x 11 · 400 Pgs. · HB · $29.95

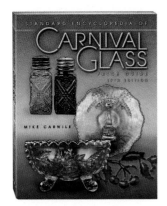

Standard Ency. of Carnival Glass Price Guide, 17th Edition

Mike Carwile

Listed alphabetically by pattern name are over 25,000 price listings for this ever-poplar carnival glass, featuring updated values, company names, sizes, and prices given for ten different colors. Prices listed are based on research of major carnival glass auctions, shop taggings, internet sales, and private sales when available. 2010 values.

Item #8048 · ISBN: 978-1-57432-636-9 · 8½ x 11 · 96 Pgs. · PB · $9.95

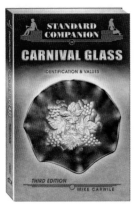

Standard Companion to Carnival Glass, 3rd Edition

Mike Carwile

This easy-to-use, small format book highlights the approximately 250 carnival glass patterns available. Each pattern shines with all necessary facts and a detailed photograph to illustrate the pattern. Data about each piece includes name of pattern, manufacturer, year of production, colors and shapes available, and information on reproductions. 2007 values.

Item #7347 · ISBN: 978-1-57432-531-7 · 5½ x 8½ · 288 Pgs. · PB · $17.95

Standard Encyclopedia of Pressed Glass, 6th Edition

Mike Carwile

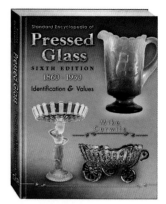

American pressed glass, which was at its zenith in the 1870s, entails hundreds of patterns and dozens of shapes with elaborate geometric, animal, fruit, and floral designs. Available in crystal and sparkling colors, this collectible glassware flourished until the end of the 1920s. This all-new encyclopedia features more than 1,700 photos showcasing the exquisite patterns and beautiful colors of the quality pressed glass produced for 60 years in America. 2010 values.

Item #7941 · ISBN: 978-1-57432-621-5 · 8½ x 11 · 320 Pgs. · HB · $34.95

Standard Companion to Non-American Carnival Glass

Bill Edwards & Mike Carwile

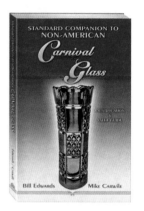

Focusing on non-American carnival glass, this handy pocket guide showcases over 350 of the best collectible patterns from Australia, England, Germany, Czechoslovakia, Finland, Sweden, and India. A brief section on foreign marks adds interest. Data given for each pattern includes maker, date of manufacture, shapes, colors, and values. 2006 values.

Item #6927 · ISBN: 978-1-57432-488-4 · 5½ x 8½ · 336 Pgs. · PB · $16.95

Standard Encyclopedia of Millersburg Crystal

Bill Edwards & Mike Carwile

This book is filled with almost 200 photos, including opalescent, frosted, gilded, ruby and lime stained, and maiden blush stained glass. An extensive history of the factory, old advertisements, and factory and employee photos are highlights. Also featured are Butler Brothers catalogs and Jefferson's Canadian Glass Factory catalogs from Ontario. 2001 values.

Item #5832 · ISBN: 978-1-57432-225-5 · 8½ x 11 · 144 Pgs. · HB · $24.95